NEWSPAPER ROW

★★★★

Other Books by Herbert A. Kenny

Literary Dublin: A History
Cape Ann/Cape America
A Catholic Quiz Book
(with G. P. Keane)
The Secret of the Rocks
A Boston Picture Book
(with Barbara Westman)

Poetry
Twelve Birds
Suburban Man
Sonnets to the Virgin Mary

For Younger Readers
Dear Dolphin
Alistare Owl

NEWSPAPER ROW
Journalism in the Pre-Television Era

☆☆☆☆

by Herbert A. Kenny

The Globe Pequot Press

Chester, Connecticut 06412

Photographs and illustrations appear courtesy of the *Boston Globe*.

Library of Congress Cataloging-in-Publication Data

Kenny, Herbert A.
  Newspaper row.

  Bibliography: p.
  Includes index.
    1. American newspapers—Massachusetts—Boston—
History—20th century. 2. Journalism—Massachusetts—
Boston—History—20th century. I. Title.
  PN4899.B63K4 1987   071'.4461   87-23672
  ISBN 0-87106-772-2

Manufactured in the United States of America
First Edition/First Printing

ACKNOWLEDGMENTS

Innumerable people deserve my thanks for the assistance they gave me in the compilation of this book. At the beginning were the late Philip S. Weld, who was a great journalist and a great friend, and Joseph Garland, who kept insisting that I do it. Special thanks go to the beneficiaries of the estate of Kenneth Roberts for permission to quote liberally from that most attractive autobiography *I Wanted to Write*. Material from *Flowing Stream: The Story of Fifty-Six Years in American Newspaper Life* by Florence Finch Kelly, copyright 1938 by E. P. Dutton, renewed 1967 by Sherwin F. Kelly, is reprinted by permission of the publisher, E. P. Dutton, a division of NAL Penguin, Inc. When the doing began, dozens of persons helped with advice and information: Thanks to the late John I. Taylor of the *Boston Globe* for insisting on the title; and to William Davis Taylor for encouragement and help with the research; thanks to John Cronin of the *Herald-American* library and to Betty McKeown in the *Boston Globe* library. Thanks also to Gerald V. Hern, Elliot Norton, the late Rose Walsh, all of them former *Boston Post* staffers; Robert Taylor, Leo Shapiro, and the late Nat Kline, all of the *Boston Globe*; John Deedy, who remembered Boston and Worcester and other places; Jerrold R. Hickey of Boston University; James Ford, Sinclair Hitchings, and Henry Scannell of the Boston Public Library and Harry Katz and others at the Boston Atheneum; the Manchester Public Library and the Sawyer Free Library in Gloucester.

I owe special thanks to John T. Galvin, who took time out from his own historical studies to review crucial chapters in the manuscript and correct errors; and to Anne Ford for her happy recollections and comical recounting. I also thank Howard Simons, head of the Nieman Fellows at Harvard University, for reinforcing my conviction that yesterday's news can become fresh history thanks to the short memory of man. In no one of my books did my wife, Teresa, do as much work as she did on this, having descended from the lofty role of Muse to the chores of ink-stained editing and proofreading.

Charles Everitt as publisher made this a better book than it would otherwise have been, and Eric Newman and Bruce Markot, my editors, made it more accurate than I had it. I thank them all. Some thanks are due to my grandchildren, who managed to distinguish, I don't know how, the manuscript from scrap paper—especially to Matthew Carroll for tending the computer, and to the Sullivan sisters (they'll understand this) for hospitality when I was able to leave my word processor for the Old Bailey, and to John and Jean Van Dell for more of the same.

CONTENTS

*This book is dedicated
to the memory of
my father, Herbert A. Kenny,
who wrote editorials
in Newspaper Row
years before I did.*

NEWSPAPER ROW
★★★★

The reporter will probably be required to cultivate some special subject, in addition to his wide, varied knowledge—to become a literary authority on commerce, or industry, or science, or social reform, or sport, and he may also be expected to develop into an artist-journalist. But whatever is required of him will not be required in vain. He has, notwithstanding some errors, done his work well in the past, and with his capacity for toil, his undoubted talent, and imperturbable good humor, he will no doubt be always able to hold his own in the battle of life. Indeed, his confidence is not bounded by the limits of this world—he views his prospects in the next with tolerable complacency; for, not long ago, a pressman, asked solemnly amid the fervid excitement of a revival gathering, the momentous question, "Are you saved?" replied in a calm, confident tone, "Oh, no, I'm a reporter."

—*John Pendleton*

Everybody must allow that our newspapers (and the other collections of intelligence periodically published), by the materials they afford for discourse and speculation, contribute very much to the emolument of society; their cheapness brings them into universal use; their variety adapts them to every one's taste: the scholar instructs himself with advice from the literary world; the soldier makes a campaign in safety, and censures the conduct of generals without fear of being punished for mutiny; the politician, inspired by the fumes of the coffee-pot, unravels the knotty intrigues of ministers; the industrious merchant observes the course of trade and navigation; and the honest shopkeeper nods over the account of a robbery and the price of goods till his pipe is out. One may easily imagine that the use and amusement of these diurnal histories render it a custom not likely to be confined to one part of the globe or one period of time. The Relations of China mentions a gazette published there by authority, and the Roman historians sometimes quote the Acta Diurna, or Daily Advertiser, of that Empire.

—Dr. Samuel Johnson

Newspaper Row in its heyday, "the busiest street in Christendom."

PROLOGUE

The largest crowd that ever gathered in Newspaper Row in Boston was not for a president of the United States, nor a motion picture star, nor a war hero, nor an astronaut, nor a foreign dignitary, nor a beautiful woman, although most of these had been welcomed there at one time or another. This crowd, its size estimated variously to be from 50,000 to 250,000, gathered to see a commercial artist from the state of Maine, dressed in a noisome bear skin and sporting a two-months' growth of beard.

He was Joe Knowles, the lone figure in the most successful and wildest promotion stunt-news story the *Boston Post* or any other newspaper ever undertook, and it may well stand as a symbol of the madcap journalism that pervaded the newspaper business in Boston in the first half of the twentieth century. (For the complete story on Knowles, see chapter 6.) It was during this time that the *Post*, by the genius of its publisher, Edwin A. Grozier, built the paper's circulation from 20,000 to 600,000 to make it for a decade or two the largest standard-size (as opposed to tabloid) newspaper in the United States.

For Oswald Garrison Villard, journalist, pacifist, and reformer, the *Boston Post* was the "particularly low but successful scarlet woman of journalism." Villard was at heart a social engineer, and his strictures upon the newspapers of the day were severe. His idealism could not accept the conditions that existed in the arena of commercial competition. Emphasis on crime and sordid events outraged him, and he denied entertainment any place in a newspaper, a view not even held by the newspaper he admired the most, the *Christian Science Monitor*. Few editors then or now would find themselves in 100 percent agreement with Villard.

When I walked into the *Boston Post* offices in 1933 to start work as a college correspondent and begin a half-century of involvement with Boston journalism, I walked into history and a theater of a vigorous but declining lunacy. The history was enacted on so small a stage that scholars may never bother with it, nor can I begin to give it any satisfactory chronological order. I can only put together a collage of vignettes and connecting narrative that may capture the sense and spirit of the madcap heroics and sometimes villainous subheroics—and let us not forget public service—that marked the newspaper business in Boston in the first half of the century.

Villard, in his popular book *The Disappearing Daily*, called Boston a "journalistic poor farm." Someone else is known to have called it the "graveyard of American journalism." They had a point to make but chose the wrong metaphors. For the *Post*, Villard's "scarlet woman" comes closer. Boston was far from a graveyard; the city was bursting with journalistic life, competition, comic rivalries, brilliant reportage (too often applied to unworthy subject matter), and a good deal of pioneer work in the history of journalism.

Matthew Arnold, the famous English critic, wrote, "Do not tell me only of the magnitude of your industry and commerce, of the beneficence of your institutions, your freedom, your equality, of the great and growing number of your churches and schools, libraries and newspapers; tell me if your civilization . . . tell me if your civilization is interesting." The story of Newspaper Row demonstrates that it certainly was.

At the same time that the *Post* was unable to slip its own parochial heritage, it was bucking an economic drift that would drive more than 1,000 major city dailies out of existence, the result being that, today, it is a rare city that has more than one daily newspaper. In its heyday, in 1928, the *Post* reached its all-time high in circulation (628,000) and must have seemed as indestructible as the passenger pigeon had once seemed. Besides the changes in mores and economics that were working against the *Post*, it suffered poor management. Its second publisher died in a lunatic asylum, and its third and last publisher behaved as if he had escaped from one and, stripped of his millions, died a drunken bum.

Boston's Newspaper Row embraced more newspapers than the *Post*, eleven in all at one time. But the story of Newspaper Row is best told in terms of the *Boston Post*, against the background of the *Globe*, which survived it, for the *Post* was born in Newspaper Row and died there after dominating the local newspaper scene for twenty years. The *Transcript*, which also lived and died in the Row, stands in interesting contrast to the *Post.* The *Herald* helped establish Newspaper Row by building a plant there; but early on, it moved away, then absorbed the *Traveller,* moved farther away, and later bought the *Journal* and took it out of the Row, only to be absorbed itself by the *Record-American-Advertiser,* owned by the Hearst Corporation. The *Herald* in turn would become the property of Rupert Murdoch, the Australian-born tycoon, and it survives today.

The *Christian Science Monitor,* a church organ that publishes daily, much beloved by Villard but a lesser organ today than the one he knew, had no real connection with Newspaper Row, but it did serve peripherally to take circulation from the *Transcript.* Because of the intense emphasis on local news among the major dailies, the *Monitor,* for a while, found a fairly wide audience in Greater Boston. For a five-year period, from 1921 to 1926, Frederick Enwright published the *Boston Telegram* to intensify the local competition and enliven the political scene, but his plant and offices were far from Newspaper Row.

The *Boston Globe* was the last paper to leave Newspaper Row; it moved to Dorchester, which is eight miles away but still within the city proper. While there, it marked its one hundredth anniversary under one-family ownership, surpassing the record that was once the proud boast of the *Boston Transcript.* When the *Globe* left Washington Street in 1958, Newspaper Row was dead.

Man is a gregarious animal, the philosophers say, and journalists, despite their professional detachment, remain so. But it was not a gregarious spirit that brought newspapers in the early nineteenth century to cluster in one location. It was commercial practicality. Like spiders, newspaper editors sat in their offices and waited for business. News was brought to them, and advertising was brought to them. Henry Ingraham Blake became the father of American reporting because, rather than wait, he hustled down to the Boston waterfront and gathered news from the returning ship captains. When he left his paper, it died without his diligence, yet rival papers were still slow to adopt his methods. By the time editors thought of chasing news and advertising, they were thus already, for the most part, locked into their location. Someone who wanted to advertise in more than one newspaper, particularly before the day of the telephone, did not have to go too far to find half a dozen newspaper offices. Thus Fleet Street

was born in London and Park Row in New York City—but neither
ever held in their cities the unique position that Newspaper Row
commanded in Boston. That 200 yards of narrow Washington
Street, right in the middle of the city, offered more than a sense of
place. It was, as we shall see, the heart of a community.

CHAPTER ONE

The Beginnings

Boston has very properly been called "the cradle of American journalism." On September 25, 1690, *Publick Occurrences: Both Foreign and Domestic* appeared in the city. Generally regarded as the first newspaper published in the colonies, it was promptly suppressed by the authorities because it contained "reflections of a very high nature"—actually, references to some brutalities of British rule. No second edition ever appeared. The publisher was Benjamin Harris, and although the address of his shop is uncertain, it could not have been far from the section that came to be called Newspaper Row. In 1704, the postmaster in Boston, John Campbell, published the *Boston Newsletter* in the same area and has been called the father of American journalism. Before the century had closed, Henry Ingraham Blake published *The Massachusetts Mercury* and won from historians his title, the father of American reporting. The area would remain the center of newspaper publishing in Boston from Campbell's day until 1958—250 years.

Newspaper Row extended along Washington Street from the corner of Milk Street, where Benjamin Franklin was born, to the Old State House at the corner of State Street, where one could say the United States of America was born. After all, the Boston Massacre took place beside this building, the Declaration of Independence was read from its balcony, and a stone's throw away stands Faneuil Hall, The Cradle of Liberty.

The word *agora* was used by the ancient Greeks for their public meeting place, and classical writers regarded the *agora* as the most typical feature of Greek daily life. The area was the scene of their religious, political, judicial, social, and commercial activities. It was an open space, either in the center of the city or

5

near the harbor, and was surrounded by public buildings. Sometimes it was enclosed by colonnades with statues, altars, trees,
and fountains to adorn it. *Mutatis mutandis,* Newspaper Row was
Boston's *agora.* The description, despite the passage of the centuries, could hardly be more precise. The *Boston Post,* the *Globe,*
the *Herald,* and other newspapers made Newspaper Row what it
was, and when they left, the *agora* was elsewhere. Today it is not
easily distinguised, if it exists at all.

We are dealing with a period of almost three-quarters of a
century lodged between 1891, when Edwin A. Grozier quit working for Joseph Pulitzer in New York and returned to Boston, and
1956, when the *Post* closed its doors. Grozier had been an editor
as well as a secretary for Pulitzer and had helped make the *World*
the leading newspaper in New York City. On the eve of Grozier's
return to Boston, the city boasted nine daily papers, four semi-
weeklies, six Sunday papers, five fortnightly publications,
seventy-five monthly periodicals, five quarterlies, and a number
of annuals. While some of these were published in the side streets
off Washington Street, the designation of the latter as the very
heart of Newspaper Row came with the construction of three
publishing plants, those of the *Herald* in 1878, the *Daily Advertiser* in 1883, and the *Globe* in 1887.

In later years the *Globe* would expand into the *Advertiser*
building, and the *Post* would take over the *Herald* plant. The *Post*
in 1891 was in Milk Street, in the building on the site of Benjamin
Franklin's birthplace, close by the *Transcript.* The *Journal* was on
the same side of Washington Street as was the Globe, and the
Herald was on the opposite side, right at the corner of Pi Alley.
The *Boston Evening Record* was published out of the *Advertiser*
building. The *Boston Courier,* the *Sunday Budget,* and the *Saturday Evening Gazette* were weekend papers that would soon disappear as the Sunday editions of the *Herald, Globe,* and *Post* and
the large Saturday-evening edition of the *Transcript* overwhelmed
them. (By the way, no one knows who first gave the Row its
name. The term, however, seems to have come from the days
when people had to walk there to buy their newspapers.)

These papers, at least those that remained, became surrounded by a host of satellites. Newspaper Row would also receive the offices of the Associated Press, the Acme News Photo
Service, World Wide Photos, the United Press, and companies
performing similar or complementary services.

NEW DAILY PAPER

IN BOSTON.

Will be published Monday, March 4, a new and independent morning commercial and business journal of the first class, and of the largest news paper size. Its model and arrangement will be original, and the purpose will be to produce a journal equal in enterprise, ability and intrinsic value, to any newspaper issued at home or abroad. Its editorial corps will embrace the ablest writers of the times, and its various departments will be in charge of competent and experienced persons. The newspaper will be known as

THE BOSTON DAILY GLOBE,

and will commence with every mechanical appliance complete, including the most perfect and rapid steam presses, and with all the necessary means in its business department for securing accuracy and despatch. In the interest of neither sect nor party, nothing will interfere with its plain and outspoken independence, while its endeavor will be, by consistency and fairness, to challenge the respect of an intelligent public.

TERMS—$12 per annum. Single copies four cents.

GLOBE PUBLISHING CO.,
No. 92 Washington st., Boston.

Persons desiring to receive the paper at their residence or places of business, will please leave their names and address at our counting-room.

Office now open for the accommodation of Advertisers, and the transaction of other business.

The *Boston Globe* enters the competition on Newspaper Row, announcing its arrival in 1887.

The concentration of newspapers, news services, and the like was unrivaled. Although Washington Street was called the Fleet Street of America, it had more journalists per square foot than its British counterpart. The street teemed with traffic. When Grozier moved to Newspaper Row, horsecars were plodding past and had been doing so since 1872. Trolleys replaced them in the Row in 1897, although horse-drawn cars continued elsewhere for years. Karl Baedeker, in *The United States with an Excursion into Mexico: A Handbook for Travellers*, published in 1883, called Washington Street "the most crowded thoroughfare in Christendom." The construction of the subway in 1908 relieved some of the pressure.

That stretch of Washington Street, moreover, had seen more early history than any like strip of dirt, stone, or macadam in the United States. In this regard it had a head start, as it began with the Puritans.

Those doughty pioneers had their town house, their *agora*, and their pillory and stocks at the north end of Newspaper Row. Nearby, in what is Spring Lane, John Winthrop, the governor of the colony, had his home, gave his orders, wrote his famous journal, and, on one occasion, horsewhipped his niece. Honored today with a statue on the lawn of the State House (two stone throws from Newspaper Row if you have a good arm), Ann Hutchinson moved around the area, more or less agitating the women of the city, and faced her cruel trial in the town house.

Spring Lane is a crooked forty yards of cement walkway running from Washington Street to Devonshire Street and roughly parallel to Water Street. The Puritans came to Boston from Charlestown looking for water (although they also drank a good deal of rum), and they deemed the object of their search deserved a street in its name. (Boston in the early seventeenth century was known as Shawmut, which in one Indian tongue means "sweet water.") As schoolboys used to learn, William Blackstone, the first European settler in Boston, invited the Puritans (who had found no good water of their own) to come and share his spring, couldn't stand them when they came, and fled south, riding, some say, on a snow-white bull.

In any event, Boston's first streets were cowpaths. That explains why they are so crooked and why Washington Street at Newspaper Row has a bend in it, although it was the city's main street. It's a condition no modern city planner would allow.

At the southern end of Newspaper Row stands the Old South Meeting House, where the colonists planned the revolt against the colonial governor, whose Province House was close by. At the north end stands the Old State House, very like the Old South Meeting House in its red-brick architectural style. Both today are museums, although the Meeting House still houses meetings, lectures, and the like. The Old State House, built in 1713, is cited as the oldest public building in the United States excluding churches. It also houses the most resplendent subway kiosk in America, for trains run in its bowels as they do in the bowels of the Old South Meeting House. Both thus enjoy a good deal of foot traffic in their basements. The former also boasts a bookstall that sells pamphlets and souvenirs, while the latter houses one of the finest secondhand bookstores in the city, an annex of Goodspeed's on Beacon Hill, the city's foremost antiquarian bookstore.

The Old Corner Bookstore, the most famous bookstore in the history of Boston, stood at the heart of Newspaper Row on the corner of School and Washington streets and is again a bookstore today. It was made famous by James T. Fields, who, with William D. Ticknor, published the *North American Review*, the *Atlantic Monthly*, and the works of Henry Wadsworth Longfellow, Ralph Waldo Emerson, Henry David Thoreau, Nathaniel Hawthorne, Harriet Beecher Stowe, John Greenleaf Whittier, and many others but missed Whitman, Melville, and Poe. The shop, in one of the oldest brick buildings in Boston, now harbors The Globe Corner Bookstore, run by the *Boston Globe* and The Globe Pequot Press, subsidiaries of Affiliated Publications. During its halcyon days, the store was known informally as Parnassus Corner because of the Olympians who went in and out. Later, both it and the Old State House were sullied by the lascivious hands of commercialism but were rescued from deterioration and destruction by ad hoc committees of high-minded citizens.

The Old Corner Bookstore housed the publishing firm of Ticknor and Fields (revived in recent years as a subsidiary of Houghton Mifflin Co.) until shortly before Edwin A. Grozier arrived to take over the *Post*. Parnassus Corner in its heyday was at the heart of what Van Wyck Brooks called one of his books: *The Flowering of New England*. Earlier, angry Puritans marched Governor Andrus by it to get him out of the Massachusetts Bay Colony. Later on, the broadcloth mob dragged William Lloyd Garrison past it with a halter around his neck, not because, as newspapermen might surmise, he edited the *National Philanthropist*, the first total-abstinence (from alcoholic beverages) journal in America, but because of his abolitionist views. On another occasion a crowd stormed up Newspaper Row to deliver from jail an apprehended runaway slave. Garrison launched *The Liberator* in 1831, the same year that the *Boston Post* was born and sixty years before Grozier took hold.

What added to the intellectual and gossipy intensity of Newspaper Row was the city's most popular luncheon restaurant, Thompson's Spa. It opened in 1882 to serve soft drinks only but grew into a restaurant, ultimately the most popular one in the city. The day of the two-martini lunch had not yet arrived. The man with a real thirst tanked up somewhere else. Within the Spa's confines all sorts of hijinks, commercial blather, journalistic extravagances, and political and legal monkey business were conjured and could be observed or overheard daily. Its physical setup as well as location and clientele made it unique.

First of all, its quarters ran all the way from Newspaper Row to City Hall Avenue, which flanked the seat of city government and was not 200 yards from the State House with its golden dome (Massachusetts is a commonwealth, not a state; it has a state house rather than a capitol) that dominates Beacon Hill. Between City Hall and the State House lay the county courthouse and the offices of the Supreme Judicial Court of Massachusetts. On the other side of Newspaper Row lay the city's great financial district and the offices and courtrooms of a U.S. federal district. The Spa drew customers from all those seats of power.

In the preferred section of the Spa, there were no tables but curious squares of counters and stools. Matching files of these ran on either side of its interior. Each square or rectangle was ringed on three sides by about fifteen stools, five to a side, with the fourth side up against the wall. Each was managed by a woman who served from within the square, taking orders and relaying them to the kitchen below, which in time rattled up the orders on a dumbwaiter. The women—some young, some old—were, without exception, charming. They became confidantes, much as bartenders can be, and many of them married customers. Some men might eat at a different counter each day; but generally each counter was a sort of club, where the regulars gathered faithfully, day after day, year after year. In the center on the Washington Street end was a soda fountain, three-sided and marble-topped, which was manned by three or more ancient retainers. They knew the customers so well that they would start the mayor's soda or a judge's frappe or some other concoction for some other dignitary before he crossed the threshold.

The alert journalist knew at which counter every man of reputation lunched each day or if, by chance, he was to be found instead at Locke Ober's, Jakie Wirth's, or other restaurants of distinction some distance away. Nearby was Young's Hotel, for many years an elegant dining spot and the site of many ceremonial dinners and bachelor parties. Only a little farther away was the Parker House, favored by Charles Dickens, among other celebrities. With the advent of the automobile, Young's Hotel was turned into courtrooms and ultimately demolished. Fortunately the Parker House has survived. The Row also boasted a barroom or two and restaurants of lesser celebrity, including the Laboratory Kitchen, situated on the second floor of one of the *Post* buildings and run by a public-spirited women's organization. It became a favorite with *Globe* and *Transcript* writers and temperance advocates. For persons of modest means, there were also a hash house or two and saloons that offered sandwiches; the latter were required by law but ignored by all except the ravenous and impoverished, which often meant newspapermen.

The concentration of politicians, judges and lawyers, prosecutors, federal marshals, journalists, editors, bankers, brokers, authors, artists, and men of questionable character made Newspaper Row surely the site of the most significant daily assemblage in the East. One distinction of Boston that contributed to this concentration of movers and shakers cannot be claimed by any other U.S. metropolis: It is the capital as well as the largest city of its commonwealth. In New York, the capital is Albany; in California, Sacramento; in Illinois, Springfield. The major cities are somewhere else. In Boston, however, one can walk from the waterfront to the State House. From Newspaper Row to the State House, moreover, was only a two-minute stroll, and the walk took one past the front door of City Hall. The result was that representatives, senators, commissioners, attorneys general, and other state officials mingled daily with the throng in Newspaper Row.

One can readily imagine the interchange of information, lies, nonsense, sage advice, high humor and exquisite dialogue that went on among its denizens—to say nothing of the animadversions of the hangers-on and eccentrics drawn into their wakes. In the saloons, of course, the loftiest and most mystical thoughts were exchanged, and the patrons of the two types of hostelry—

those that served alcoholic beverages and those that did not—
were not mutually exclusive. The only word for the intellectual,
informational, and emotional interchange that went on is a word
found in an obscure British journal: *interinanimation*, which cannot be found in even the *Oxford English Dictionary* but precisely
describes the interaction among the madding throng in Newspaper Row—they breathed life into one another. The whole became
magically far, far more than the sum of its parts.

Newspaper Row may have lacked the statues that the *agora*
of Athens honored, but it was otherwise the *agora* of the Athens
of America. Instead of trees, it had bulletin boards and blackboards, whereon office boys or artists, dusty from the chalk they
used for marking, posted the latest news, even after radios became commonplace. There was never a belt of electric lights to
flash the news. No matter; these boards were much easier to read.
The *Post* had blackboards; the *Globe* had smaller blackboards but
boasted the more elegant bulletin boards, with long sheets of
white paper brilliantly lettered by staff artists. The latter method
made it more difficult to change the bulletins quickly—and, in a
small way, that symbolized the difference between the *Globe* and
the *Post*, for the *Post* was intent on the latest news, while the
Globe remained more reflective.

After scanning the latest news, the hungry citizen moved into
one of the eating places, his agenda for conversation given him
by the bulletins. Just as these bulletin boards made do for trees,
so the soda bar at Thompson's Spa, the bars, and (during Prohibition) the speakeasys substituted for fountains. If there was no
church or altar as such—the Old South Meeting House had been
a church, although the Puritans didn't like the word—at least
each unit in a newspaper's printer's union was called a "chapel."

Seven streets ran into Newspaper Row and were considered
part of it, at least in those few yards closest to Washington Street.
State Street and Court Street came in at the north end, the first
from the east and the other from the west, fronting each other. At
the other end was Milk Street, coming up from the waterfront. In
between these streets were three others. Water Street entered
Newspaper Row from the east, as did Spring Lane, roughly parallel to it but a foot passage only. Running west from Newspaper
Row was Williams Court, familiarly known as Pi Alley. The origin
of the name was moot. Some said it was from pie served at a
restaurant whose doors opened on it, while others held that the

Office boys posted the latest news, headlines, sports results, and other essential information on blackboards, outlining the drama of the day for the passersby on the Row.

name came from the jumbled (or pied) type that drunken printers hurled from the windows of the *Boston Herald* to hide their derelictions before they were observed by a foreman. Pi Alley, as it ran through to City Hall Avenue, flanked Thompson's Spa. After hours, the kitchens of Thompson's Spa could be entered from Pi Alley, and impoverished newsmen could buy the day's leftovers at greatly reduced prices. Long before Thompson's Spa opened, the Bell in Hand Tavern helped the thirsty and was owned originally by the town crier.

Newspaper Row was most perceptibly Boston's *agora* on election nights in the days before radio. Everyone knew that the first returns and the final counts would be received by the newspapers and announced and posted before they were available elsewhere. If the count dragged on and the returns came slowly, the *Post* provided live entertainers, canned music, motion pictures, and political analyses over loudspeakers. All horse-drawn or motorized traffic would be shunted down Water Street for the night, and the only vehicles permitted on Washington Street were the *Post*

Bernard Goldfine, a prominent industrialist and philanthropist, presented two cows to the *Post* after reading of the newspaper's offer to send one cow to Israel for every two donated by readers.

trucks waiting to carry the papers to delivery centers. The *Globe* ran a rival but more modest show. *Globe* trucks did not use Newspaper Row because the *Globe* buildings went through to Devonshire Street, which ran along the rear of the plant and provided an easier egress from the city. Both plants, *Post* and *Globe*, however, were strangled by traffic in the narrow streets. The favorable conditions that made newspapers cluster in this section of the city had changed, and now this same clustering became a handicap to efficient production and delivery.

Live entertainment was not confined to election nights. Newspaper Row at noon was the ideal place to publicize any show in town or to present a musical-comedy star or an aspiring gubernatorial candidate. In those rousing 1920s, for example, the famed magician and escape artist Harry Houdini hung by his feet in a strait jacket and chains over Newspaper Row shortly after noon one day and freed himself in record time, to the gasps and cheers of the crowd below. Show people gathered to perform or sing to the crowd from the *Post's* upstairs windows, which could be removed, if the occasion warranted, to provide a sort of stage.

If such light entertainment was not available, organ grinders with their monkeys strolled the pavement, or a zealot who could prove that the world was flat extracted himself from his customary audience on the Boston Common and brought his arguments to the *agora*. On one occasion cows destined for Israel stood stolidly in the middle of Washington Street, oblivious to the part their ancestors had played in laying out the streets of the area.

On more than one occasion while he was governor, Calvin Coolidge (he was the last Massachusetts governor to walk to the train until Michael Dukakis, who, on occasion, takes the subway) walked down School Street from the State House to lunch with friends. The city's more colorful mayors were regular visitors to the Row. One other feature emphasized the journalistic essence of the area: It had the best newsstand in the city for purchasing out-of-town or foreign newspapers, a stand curled in the side of the Old South Meeting House.

All vice was determinedly kept out of Newspaper Row— except for bookies, who served the gambling fraternity, and (from 1920 to 1933) bootleggers, who served the thirsty. On paydays many a wife came to the Row to stand by while her husband collected his pay, some to make sure that too much of it didn't go to the local bartender or bootlegger.

Every day, too, young men lined up, newspaper employees among them, including pressmen with the square hats they folded out of newspapers. They came, of course, to ogle the women of spirit who sought out the Row to be ogled or the more attractive women who worked on the newspapers but who were understood to be career women or others of presumed high moral character.

The man who said that fewer papers can make for better papers had a point, and the Boston experience proves it, if proof is needed. For many of the years covered here, Boston was the most competitive arena in America. The scramble for circulation was intense. There was no television to provide fantasy for the masses, so newspapers provided fantasy along with the facts, often mixing the two together. Sometimes the fantasy got out of hand and became indistinguishable from lunacy, but that sold papers, and paper sales meant circulation, and circulation meant advertising, and advertising meant profits.

The results of yellow journalism were not all negative. In retrospect, the fantasy is fun to read, a bit campy and bordering at times on black humor. In its day, when the man on the street was not given the vicarious touches of violence such as he gets on television, the newspapers provided it. The circulation figures prove that the excitement the papers generated was compelling. Newspaper Row made the newspaper business much more fun and far more exciting than it is today.

The period from 1831, when the *Post* was founded, until the eve of the Civil War has been called the age of the penny press; but in the last decades of the nineteenth century, the fruits of the industrial revolution were ready to be picked, and the penny press leaped into mass production.

The physical proximity in Boston of all those journalistic enterprises and government offices—municipal, state, federal, and financial—gave the city its *agora*, and the *agora* for several decades gave the citizens—many of them immigrants or the children of immigrants finding their way—a sense of belonging, a sense of community, a sense of place, which in a way made for more civility than can be found in the city today.

Urbanization was underway, along with industrialization, and the impact of small towns, whose ethos had set society's tone for so long, was diminishing. In 1920 Sinclair Lewis, in his novel *Main Street*, told America that this change had happened. Five years earlier, with *The Birth of a Nation*, D. W. Griffith showed America that the motion picture was not just a toy but a powerful myth-making medium. Then in 1919, the Volstead Act became the law of the land. The act empowered the federal government to enforce the Eighteenth Amendment to the Constitution, which forbade the sale of alcoholic beverages. The result was that gangsterism, which had been disorganized, became big business. The newspaper business had become big, too. At the same time, the mass market was born, but the approach to it was uncharted. Grozier found one way.

CHAPTER TWO

★★★★

Grozier Buys the *Post*

The first issue of the *Daily Morning Post* in Boston was published November 9, 1831, at 19-21 Water Street, which can be considered part of Newspaper Row. The publisher was Colonel Charles G. Greene. The paper was Democratic in its politics, small in size, and small in circulation. It measured nine inches by fifteen inches and bore four columns of type. By 1833 it had five columns and a commensurate increase in size. It continued to grow until, in 1839, it became a standard-size, eight-column newspaper. By that time, Colonel Greene had made it the outstanding Democratic daily newspaper in New England. Throughout his life, even when the paper had passed from his hands, he remained a power in the Democratic party in Massachusetts.

The number of newspapers throughout the United States multiplied rapidly after the War of 1812. From that year until 1860, when the Civil War loomed, the nation experienced a period of expansion and growth. A journalist, John L. O'Sullivan, gave it a name when, in 1845, he wrote that it was "our *manifest destiny* [italics added] to overspread the continent allotted by Divine Providence for the free development of our yearly multiplying millions." Indeed, an efflorescence of newspapers spread throughout the entire continent. At the close of the War of 1812, seven newspapers flourished in New York, their names gone into the slipstream of history: the *National Advocate*, the *Mercantile Advertiser*, the *Gazette*, the *Columbian*, the *Courier*, the *National Advocate*, and the *Evening Post*. From 1830, when the *Boston Transcript* first appeared, until 1840, when Boston's population stood at 93,383, fifteen papers came and went. At one time during this decade, twelve newspapers were active.

Two years before Greene founded the *Post*, Godwin Brown Cotton founded the *Gazette* in San Felipe, Texas. From then on, newspapers began to go westward with the explorers; and by 1863, no territory was without one. The aim of the *Post* was, according to Greene himself, "the dissemination of all variety of information usually promulgated through the columns of a newspaper." There is a touch of tautology there. The editorials advocated the modification of the tariff laws, free bridges, the abolishment of laws authorizing imprisonment for debt, and, generally, the platforms of the various Democratic presidential candidates. The paper prospered. Indeed, it came unscathed through the upheaval attendant on the Civil War. In the Populist groundswell that followed, the *Post*, like other newspapers, began to grope for readers other than its own elite or claque.

The first newsboy in America to hawk papers was Bernard Flaherty, an Irish immigrant lad who responded to an advertisement in the *New York Sun* in the 1830s. The first newsboy in Boston did not start shouting his headlines until 1844. He worked for the *Traveller*, but the *Herald* soon adopted the practice and met with such success that it put a paperboy in its logo. After the Civil War the newsboy became more and more an important figure in the distribution of newspapers. Before his day, a reader subscribed to a paper by yearly payment and either received it through the mail or went to the office to buy it.

What put an end to Greene's ownership of the *Post* was the Great Boston Fire of November 9 and 10, 1872. It destroyed acres of buildings in downtown Boston, is vividly recounted in the novel *In Red Weather* by Robert Taylor, and was brilliantly represented in a special Sunday supplement (published in 1972 on the fire's one hundredth anniversary) by the *Globe*. The *Post*'s quarters, then at 19-21 Water Street, were not touched by the flames; but so much water was doused on them to save them and their neighbors that offices and equipment were ruined. The *Post* decided to move, went to 17 Milk Street, and was there when Grozier took over in 1891.

The city of Boston purchased the old Water Street site from the *Post* for $325,000, which enabled the *Post* to reestablish itself; but internal quarrels between Colonel Greene and his son Nathaniel H. Greene on how best to operate the paper during the depression that set in under President Ulysses S. Grant persuaded them to offer the paper for sale. The next few years make a sad chapter in the history of what had been a distinguished Democratic newspaper.

The man who bought the *Post* from the Greenes had an admirable façade. He was the Reverend E. D. Winslow, an ordained minister, a Republican leader, a member of the state senate, and a stern advocate of Prohibition. At the time he bought the *Post*, he was also the publisher of the *Boston Daily Mail*. He was reputed to have paid $160,000 for the *Post*. He immediately formed the Post Publishing Company, with himself as treasurer. Bent on selling stock, he left the management of the newspaper to others while he manipulated stock certificates in his office at the *Daily Mail*. He was both a man of vision and a crook. Newspaper Row would not see his like again for seventy years. Two years after he purchased the *Post*, he disappeared. An investigation revealed his affairs were in a hopeless tangle. His books disappeared with him. Only one thing was clear: He had sold twice as much stock as the papers of incorporation permitted.

Disorganization set in, and the *Post* would not recover until Grozier appeared. In 1876, William Gaston, a distinguished Democrat whose son and namesake would later be governor, and Leopold Morse, a leading merchant and also a Democrat, took over. They had as treasurer G. F. Emery, a man, even as they, with no publishing experience. An axiom in the newspaper business has it that as soon as any newspaper is left to the charge of auditors and accountants, it is doomed. Emery, to save money, brought in Albert Cohick, a notorious "ratter," as union busters were called. Cohick brought a team of nonunion printers with him, men better trained in violence than in setting type. The *Post* printers were locked out without notice; one or two of them, when they protested, were tumbled downstairs. The news spread quickly through the city, and what little circulation the *Post* had declined further.

Gaston and Morse quit. A new management threw in additional money, bought new equipment, and adjusted advertising rates; but by 1885, still another reorganization was needed. The nonunion printers were dismissed, and the union men brought back. Sensationalism, which was proving a circulation builder in New York, was tried and failed. Still another reorganization came about. Sensationalism was abandoned and stodginess embraced. The *Post*, it seemed, carried news about Harvard College only, plus some literary essays and articles on the fine arts. An editor from New Haven was hired and promptly fired the union printers and hired nonunion men. The *Post* languished. In 1891, the paper had 3,000 paid subscribers and about 20,000 street and counter sales. It was in that year that Grozier took over.

CHAPTER THREE

Pulitzer's Protegé

Like another famous New Englander, Robert Frost, Edwin A. Grozier is listed as having been born in San Francisco. The fact is more unusual than that: He was born aboard the clipper ship skippered by his father, Captain Joshua F. Grozier, as it sailed through the middle of the Golden Gate entering San Francisco. The date was September 12, 1859. He was brought back to Massachusetts and reared in Provincetown, where he attended local schools until he was fifteen. After preparatory studies at Chauncy Hall, a Back Bay prep school, he entered Brown University but transferred to Boston University, where he took his bachelor's degree. He was wise enough to make himself a master of shorthand, which was more highly regarded then than now. Even then, he thought of one day owning a newspaper. Before he was seventeen, while sailing with his father, he wrote a series of articles that were published in the *Post*, the paper he would later own. He worked as a reporter both on the *Boston Globe* and the *Boston Herald*, the latter then the city's leading daily, before becoming secretary to Governor George D. Robinson. From there he went to the employ of Joseph Pulitzer, first as a private secretary and then as an editor. The name of Pulitzer, a Hungarian Jew who never lost his accent and who was one of the journalistic geniuses of the nineteenth century, still adorns the country's major journalism and literary awards, the Pulitzer Prizes.

Pulitzer began as a reporter on a German-language newspaper in St. Louis, served in the Missouri legislature in 1870, and in 1878 bought the *St. Louis Dispatch* and merged it with the *St. Louis Post* to leave that city one of the nation's best newspapers. When he turned his attention to New York City, the *New York*

World was owned by Jay Gould, one of the robber barons, who used it more as a toy than anything else. Pulitzer bought it from him in 1883 and soon after transformed American journalism from the stuffy to the sensational, invented the banner headline, and put sparkle and enterprise into the business. In doing so, he pumped blood into its veins, marrow into its bones, and profits into its coffers.

Pulitzer made Grozier city editor of the *World* in 1887. Two years later he made him editor of the *Evening World* and, within a year after that, editor of the *Sunday World*. On one occasion, Pulitzer rewarded him with a bonus of $1,000 in gold coins. Grozier's progress enabled him to absorb some of the genius of Pulitzer, and later, in a way, he would outdo his master. In a city much smaller than New York City, he would build a larger circulation than the *World's*.

As private secretary to Pulitzer, he was able to observe genius first-hand and learn the master's methods. Because of his relentless energy and insatiable curiosity, however, the nerve-racked Hungarian was not an easy man to work with. Grozier must have been relieved, then, not to have been named editor of the *Morning World*, since that particular paper stood first in the publisher's heart. Pulitzer worried about every word that went into it and demanded similar concern and attention from his editors.

The *Evening World* was different. In the top job there, Grozier had a free hand to experiment with his own ideas, a freedom that he would not have had on the morning paper. So quickly did he boost circulation on the *Evening World* that Pulitzer soon moved him to the *Sunday World*, the least successful although the most flamboyant of the three. Grozier was able to refine that flamboyance to build circulation. Two years there in complete command were ideal training for the career of a publisher-to-be. When he finally became a publisher, if circulation is the test, he would beat his tutor and trainer at his own game and, for a while, surpass all the morning newspapers in the nation.

When Pulitzer bought the *World* from Gould, he put up $100,000 but owed twice as much. He knew in his heart he could make the additional money in a few years and did so. Grozier acquired the *Post* in much the same manner. While on vacation in Boston, he learned that the paper could be bought at a low price. Before he made the purchase, he went to General Charles H. Taylor, publisher of the *Boston Globe* and a man for whom he had worked. Grozier said that he intended to buy the *Post* but would not do so if General Taylor objected. Taylor gave him every encouragement.

When he assumed control of the paper, its circulation was small, advertising was negligible, the plant was inefficient, and there was a debt of $150,000. He might have gone into insolvency court and evaded the debts. Instead, he called in the creditors and told them that, given time, he would pay every dollar owed. They agreed and in time were paid. The first years were not easy. On pay day, the staff and the printers would gather around the cashier's window and wait for the advertising receipts to come in. Often the workers were paid off in nickels and dimes. One early boost in revenue came from liquor advertising, which some of the papers hesitated to accept. Grozier had no such compunction. Still, his lean months were many.

Besides Pulitzer's policy of sound news coverage and crisp writing, Grozier also adopted the Pulitzer plan of sensational promotion schemes, about which the latter had been mad. On one occasion, inspired by reports of canals on Mars, Pulitzer decided to put a message in a field with letters large enough to be read by creatures on Mars if they had telescopes to match ours. Only when his promotion manager asked what language the message was to be in did the genius backtrack. Much more successful was his idea of sending Nellie Bly around the world to challenge the eighty days of Phileas Fogg in Jules Verne's popular story. She made it in seventy-two days, six hours, eleven minutes, and fourteen seconds. The idea might well have been Grozier's; it has his touch.

Before Grozier could manage major promotions, however, he needed cash. He went after circulation by cutting the price of the *Post* from three cents to one cent and reducing the advertising rates. The *Post* had been Democratic, and he continued it so. He adopted the slogan "With a mission, without a muzzle." By the opening years of the twentieth century, he began calling the *Post* "New England's Great Breakfast Table paper." By that time, it was.

In the first quarter of the twentieth century, the *Boston Post* became the leading standard-size (as opposed to tabloid) morning newspaper in the United States, yet it went out of business in 1956. Grozier was in command for thirty-three years, but the paper lasted only thirty-two years after his death, having drained the legacy of his genius. He brought the paper from the corner of Milk Street to the heart of Newspaper Row and developed it in the most intensely competitive city in America. In doing so, he became the dominant presence on Newspaper Row for two decades.

CHAPTER FOUR

The Rabbit Warren

When the *Post* went out of business in 1956, I was its night city editor, a wheel-horse job that I had worked hard to get but that had paid little. My nearly twenty-five years with the paper, however, gave me an affection for it and a growing insight into its history and mystique. My rewards were power, knowledge (or information), and the euphoria that comes from doing work one enjoys while rendering service to a large number of persons. Plus excitement. The newspaper business may be maddeningly erratic, but it is never dull. One is frequently damned and denounced, rarely praised, and sometimes abused by one's colleagues and the public; but among newspaper people themselves, there is a camaraderie unparalleled elsewhere. An old wheeze has it that when someone says, "You newspaper writers must meet such interesting people," the answer is, "Yes, and they are all in the newspaper business." Robert Davis entitled his account of journalistic antics in Chicago *Such Interesting People.* They surrounded my desk.

The scene of my operations was the most elaborately contrived, dysfunctional, and incredible "rabbit warren" in the history of newspaperdom. Nothing on Fleet Street or elsewhere matched the curiosity of the headquarters of the *Boston Post.* Six buildings that had once been merely closely abutting neighbors were linked together over a period of years by Grozier in an artificial symbiosis, the implementation of which was deemed less costly than new construction. This was the only justification for bringing them together, for they were unmatched in size, style, structure, texture, or architectural intent. They were uniform in only one regard: the level at which they met the sidewalk.

They were joined together by breaking through walls and making connecting passageways and linking one with another by a web of ironworks, fire escapes, and aerial walkways. Anyone moving from one building to another found himself either shuffling up one, two, or three steps; striding up a ramp sloping from one floor to another; or, conversely, descending. These ingenious stairs, ramps, fire doors, and fire escapes were all part of the reconstruction of the houses (one of which had allegedly been a brothel) to make them—against their wills, one senses—serve the sublime enterprise of publishing a daily newspaper. It is amazing today to think that the *Post* produced more papers out of that hodgepodge each day than major dailies today manage only with massive plants, the most sophisticated equipment, and double the number of employees.

Half a dozen other businesses rented quarters from the *Post* in one or another of the six buildings. The city room was on the third floor, reached only by stairs unless one found the elevator three buildings over. Directly under the city room were the offices of two loan sharks with some such reassuring name as The Kindly Boston Home Financing Company. Mounting from the street to the city room, a visitor passed first the doors of this business establishment and then, at the top of the stairs, the men's room, from which someone was always emerging adjusting his clothing. It remains in the memory in grim contrast to the luxurious entrances to newspaper plants today.

The city room itself was entered from that stairway by a small vestibule in which were a table, two chairs, and a small bench, and it was here that a visitor waited before being conducted into an august presence. The city room itself was one hundred feet long and fewer than twenty feet wide. My desk was at the forward part of that long, crowded, untidy, ill-ventilated room. One desk stood behind me and one before me, the latter that of the city editor. These titles have little relation to the duties associated with them today. For peculiar reasons, the city editor and his underling, the night city editor, were in charge of the whole building. The managing editor might be in charge of what went into the newspaper (editorials, makeup, and news presentation), but the city editor was in charge of reporters, columnists, rewrite men, the art department, cartoonists, and the building itself. The two city editors were, by extension, definitely in charge of news gathering. There was no such breakdown as exists today of city

The author's desk (left) in the crowded city room of the *Post*. At right are the mailboxes in which the staff received assignments, private mail, bonuses, and so on. The windows looked down on Newspaper Row.

editor, metropolitan editor, science editor, business editor, and arts editor. Only the sports editor had semi-autonomy. Otherwise, the city editor was it. The music critic moved to his baton, the dance critic to his choreography.

If I turned from my desk, I saw to my immediate right two desks occupied at night by a rewrite man and a picture editor. Beside them was a door leading to various rooms, one of which harbored the copy desk, where headlines were written by a circle of editors. Another room held a noisy battery of remote-controlled black teletype machines of antique vintage. Emitting a constant cacophonous clatter, these machines brought to the *Post* the news gathered around the world by the Associated Press and the United Press. They were tended by various young men, tousled and tormented, who, whether they were discharged or disgusted with the conditions or the pay, came and went with distracting frequency.

Beyond the door that led to those rooms were four telephone booths that deserved the immortality of the Smithsonian Institution but instead have been consigned to oblivion. They were, in fact, telephone booths within telephone booths, each with double doors, broken locks, and a single electric bulb illuminating a dusty interior. In each were a heap of copy paper and a shelf to write on. Throughout the night, district men (assigned to daily coverage of the news in a given area), rewrite men, and staff writers entered and emerged from those suffocation chambers, seeking or receiving information from innumerable sources. On the wall opposite those booths were the typewriters of three reporters and a wooden cabinet that no one ever saw opened.

No staff writers, reporters, or district men had desks or lockers of their own, let alone offices. Offices were reserved for some columnists (but not all), some critics (but not all), the Washington correspondent who was never there, and one or two highly regarded cartoonists. The men and women who put out the Sunday paper, which was in fact a supplement to the daily, had a large room of their own several buildings away, the one with the elevator. Most of the writers there had desks of their own, and one of them, as an aid to contemplation, had a rowing machine.

The journalists in the city room had humbler emplacements. For them there were benches running almost the length of the room. These benches were marked by numerous indentations, each six inches deep and eight inches wider than a typewriter. Into these, typewriters, indestructible L. C. Smiths, were affixed in such a way that boxlike lids could be pulled over them and secured with padlocks. Rarely, however, did any reporter bother to cover his machine, let alone lock it up. He could have locked it, thereby securing personal articles with confidence—but he had little worth stealing. Booze in bottles had to be concealed elsewhere, perhaps in the watertank above a toilet or in some other out-of-the-way cache.

There were perhaps twenty of these typewriters in the room situated along the walls. Wooden chairs with hard seats were provided. The whole would have been monastic if it hadn't been so sloven. The walls had once been white but had faded to a dirty ivory. On them were pasted calendars, lists of commonly used telephone numbers, postcards with slightly obscene messages, photographs of pinup girls, amusing bits of verse (some ribald, by aspiring Eugene Fieldses), and typographical bloopers marked by hilarious comments. At the rear of the room were two massive windows coated with grime that left them eternally opaque. The lights in the ceiling, cupped in huge porcelain reflectors vaguely reminiscent of hospital urinals, were naked bulbs that shone night and day.

Although only one of the *Post* buildings rose six stories, all had cellars that went five stories into the ground. Here the giant presses in the early hours of the morning ground out hundreds of thousands of newspapers, which were carried on moving belts up to street level and put on other conveyor belts that bore them to the ranks of trucks parked in Newspaper Row. The labyrinthine passageways in those subterranean pressrooms, with their incredible mass of machinery and curious tunnels, rivaled the notorious basements of the Paris Opera House. The *Post* had to go deep to find bedrock to bear the presses, and more and more presses were needed as circulation mounted. So deep did those cellars go that the water table, when harbor tides were running high, backed up into the lowest level and kept pumps churning along with the presses above them.

When Grozier bought the *Post* in 1891, the circulation was 20,000. By 1919 it had risen to 600,000. After his death in 1924, the paper ran on this momentum; even when it folded, it still had the largest morning circulation in New England. The peak of circulation came in 1928 on the day after Herbert Hoover defeated Alfred E. Smith for the presidency; that day the *Post* printed 674,490 papers. The *Post* had backed Smith, who had carried Massachusetts but just one other state above the Mason-Dixon line. It was a proud day for the *Post*, but it was all downhill from there, although the paper would have moments of glory. In the wake of genius had come the ineffectual.

Grozier was a man of parts: part publisher, part psychologist, part phenomenon. He had already been dead four years on that proud day in 1928, but it was his ghost that brought the circulation to its highest figure. Had his son, then in charge, remained in good health, the paper might be alive today.

CHAPTER FIVE

Promotion Stunts

Stunts were a constant tactic with newspapers once the drive for mass circulation began. They were designed, of course, to lure new buyers to a given newspaper. They remain in use today, too, with some newspapers. The *Boston Herald*, for example, now runs contests with money prizes in an endeavor to increase its circulation. Successful papers normally look to more dignified promotions, however, chiefly because advertisers are wary of circulation depending on stunts.

Even as Grozier outdid Pulitzer in circulation, he also outdid him in promotion stunts. The stunts devised by Grozier were unique in American journalism. One of his most successful was the daily giveaway of a Ford automobile. At that time a Ford cost $750, a handsome prize for anyone. To win one, a reader had to submit an outstanding human-interest story. Thousands of stories poured into the *Post* offices, and hundreds were printed. The daily winner got the Ford; the runners-up, one dollar each. One staff reporter was assigned to sort out the stories, select the best, and bring them to Grozier for the final selection. Once the winner was chosen, another reporter was assigned to deliver the automobile. Since the *Post's* circulation extended to the Canadian border, some unlucky reporter found himself driving all night in the winning automobile over roads that were never meant for automobiles. It is a miracle that they all reached their destinations.

There was one hitch, however, that brought this promotion to a grinding halt, mostly through fear of recurrences and irritated claimants. It seems a daily winner had been chosen and the automobile delivered, only to have Grozier learn that this winning story had a week before been offered to the *Post* and its originator awarded one dollar. Thus the automobile had to be reclaimed from a disgruntled reader and given to the rightful winner. The difficulty had not been anticipated, but the reporter making the initial selections, not having kept a file, simply didn't recognize the story. However, while the contest and giveaway lasted, it proved a circulation builder.

Another promotional enterprise that endured a good deal longer than the automobile giveaway—and, indeed, all other *Post* promotions and even the *Post* itself—involved the *Boston Post* cane. In 1909 Grozier came into possession of 431 canes, all made of black African ebony or malacca with 24-carat rolled-gold heads. He decided to give them to 431 New England towns (excluding those in Connecticut, where the *Post* didn't bother to sell newspapers), where they would be given to the oldest male resident and then, on his demise, passed to his successor. The task was entrusted to the selectmen of the towns, and with each presentation, the *Post*, if informed, ran a photograph and a story. If names make news, this did. The men who held the canes, the *Post* wrote, "will present an interesting galaxy of the vigor and longevity of New England manhood." The gold heads were duly engraved with the appropriate information, which read, "Boston Post Cane," and "The oldest resident of [name of town]."

The *Post* printed three editions daily: the first, second, and city editions. Many a story pertaining to an event "upcountry" appeared in that first edition and disappeared thereafter. Most of the *Post*'s cane presentations fell into this class, but they were created to please the holder, his family and friends, and the community in which he lived and to keep the *Post* name alive in their hearts—not to make news.

Over the years some of the canes vanished. Perhaps they were lost in closets, taken out of New England, sequestered against the rules, burned in fires, or buried with the holders. Even before the demise of the *Post* in 1956, Mrs. Eleanor Burns of Dorchester began a check of how many of the 431 canes could be located. She has made it her hobby for more than thirty years and has located 400 of them. Most are still being passed along. In two instances, however, the family refuses to give them up. In one or two other cases, she believes the present cane is a substitute. But the fact is that the vast majority are still doing what Grozier desired.

In the town of Manchester, Massachusetts, for example, Mrs. Randolph Knight found, on the death of her husband, the broken end of the cane in a closet, its gold head somewhat battered and worn but its message still legible. It had been awarded to her husband's father; but for one reason or another, perhaps because it had been broken, it was not passed on when he died. Louis Barrier, then chairman of the board of selectmen, gave it a new shaft, and it is now awarded each year to the oldest man attending the annual clambake of The Elder Brethren, a unique all-male organization of elderly men. The nature of the club would seem to insure the perpetuation of the transfer of that particular cane.

The first recipient of a *Post* cane was Solomon Talbot, ninety-five, of Sharon, Massachusetts. Although originally intended for men only, by 1930 the cane was being passed along to women as well.

In 1983, *Yankee* magazine, that monthly compendium of New Englandiana, recounted the story of the *Post* cane. Timothy Clark, the author, declared,

> It is not surprising that the circulation gimmick outlasted the newspaper. Grozier may not have been aware of it, but he had tapped into a vein of ritual and superstition as old as humanity. The cane, or staff, is an ancient symbol of deference to age and reverence for ancestors. It is a fertility symbol as well; the passage of a sacred staff from the oldest member of a group to the next upon the first one's death is a way of defeating death. "The king is dead; long live the king."
>
> It is no more surprising that such a powerful piece of magic should become invested with its own superstitions. In some towns, as the years went by, people came to believe that the cane was hexed. Residents who were hale when they received it were said to wither suddenly and die; in many towns the oldest resident refused to accept the cane.

Over the years the cane scenario provided the *Post* with a number of stories, as each recipient was interviewed and asked the secret of his longevity. Almost always, it was put down to abstention from alcohol and tobacco or to the daily use of the same. The death of a *Post* cane holder was always dutifully reported on the obituary page.

Other promotions ran daily—essay contests; the selection of the starting line-ups of World Series teams, sometimes to match the choices of Babe Ruth; the selection of the scores of football games; limerick contests; and contests in which the readers were asked to name the persons whose silhouettes only appeared in the paper. Rarely did a day go by under Grozier when some such contest was not running. The ingenuity of it all drove the *Globe* to a very wise promotion. It simply announced that it never ran a contest.

With Grozier gone, the genius for contests diminished. One of the last *Post* contests foundered in near-disaster and certainly in a sort of comic hubbub. The *Boston Herald* lured away the *Post*'s outstanding sports columnist, Bill Cunningham, with the promise that it would syndicate his material, a practice the *Post* refused all its writers. To offset an anticipated loss of circulation (which did not occur), the *Post* launched a seemingly ingenious plan to get people talking. Each day one hundred dollars would be given to the first person who would accost a *Post* employee walking in a designated area, which would be shown on a map accompanying the story. The employee, unnamed but usually a reporter, would be walking in the area with a copy of the *Post* under his arm. The first person with a *Post* under his arm as well who approached and said, "Good morning, have you read the *Post* today?" would win the prize. On the first day, the designated area was the Tremont Street side of Boston Common. The size of the milling crowd that day should have given the *Post* warning of future danger. Thousands were walking or running back and forth like the tragic shades in the first circle of Dante's *Inferno*, everyone shouting, "Good morning, have you read the *Post* today?" A winner was soon acknowledged and photographed receiving the check.

The events of that day intensified the interest. On the second day an even larger crowd was in the designated area. The contest had not run a week when the designated area was Malden Square, center of a busy suburban city. Two reporters were sent out in an automobile. It was intended that the driver would release the other man, Frank Kinsella, in the area pictured in the morning map. Kinsella, of all *Post* reporters, was the most modest, the most retiring, and the least combat ready. As the automobile stopped near the square and Kinsella began to emerge, hundreds descended on him. There was no possible way to pick a winner amidst the babble of voices. The second man left the sedan to hold off the lusting mob, but finally both had to abandon the automobile and take to their heels, race to the police station, and there seek sanctuary, the eager *Post* readers hot on their heels. The police dispersed the mob. The promotion was abandoned. By that time, it was clear that Cunningham's departure would cost the *Post* a negligible amount of circulation anyway. All promotions after that eschewed physical contacts.

The most famous *Post* promotion of all still serves the common good. Known now as the *Globe* Santa, it began in 1906 as the *Post* Santa. Grozier felt that the poor children of greater Boston were neglected in one way by all the charitable institutions of the area: None provided toys for children. At Christmastime they might provide food, clothing, heat, and perhaps a Christmas tree; but Grozier asked, "What is a child's Christmas without toys?" He called upon the public to donate to a fund administered by the *Post*, which would use it to buy toys and distribute them to the children. Every penny donated would go to buy toys; all administrative expenses would be borne by the *Post*. The fund was instantly successful.

On the demise of the *Post*, the *Globe* bought the name and the good will and continued the promotion as the *Boston Globe* Santa. Many of the most generous donors today are men and women who, when children, received their Christmas toys from the *Boston Post* Santa and remember.

Like the *Post*, the *Globe*, too, indulged itself in promotions. Some of them were high-minded, such as the first sponsoring by a newspaper of an airplane flight. In 1909 Louis Bleriot, a French pilot, flew an airplane across the English channel—21 miles—in 37 minutes. That bit of news topped even the controversy between Admiral Robert E. Peary and Doctor Frederick Cook regarding who had reached the North Pole and, locally, the $6 million fire in neighboring Chelsea; both incidents had occurred earlier that year. The *Globe* offered $10,000 for the fastest airplane flight from Quincy around Boston Light and back. Claude Graham White, an Englishman, won the 33-mile race, which became, up to that time, the longest flight on record over water. The next year the *Globe* sponsored the longest flight over land.

Another *Globe* promotion tapped the vein of greed in its readers by offering money for the best estimate of the vote in the Cleveland-McKinley 1892 presidential race. A bookkeeper won five dollars a week for life by coming closest to the correct vote. He had clipped 200 coupons from *Globe*s to make that many submissions. Before he died, the *Globe* had paid him $14,500. Another contest, offering a ride on the new electric cars at the

THE "MIRROR OF CITY LIFE,"

Given every day in the **BOSTON GLOBE,** is one of the most interesting, entertaining and humorous features ever introduced in a daily paper. READ IT. Price 2 Cents.

The *Globe* eschewed contests and relied instead on promotional material, such as this early advertisement, to bring in the readers.

Globe's expense, cost far more than the paper anticipated. The *Globe* found it could get along without contests and abandoned them. The *Post*, however, continued them. In 1913, it found one that developed into a news story that not only had circulation jumping but had the whole nation on edge and was to make Joe Knowles a national hero (see the following chapter).

The *Globe* in another regard also left the way open for the *Post* to endear itself to the ever-increasing host of Democratic voters in Greater Boston. General Taylor and the *Globe* had been defenders of the Irish-immigrant population in Boston and the outspoken advocates of the Democratic party. The silver-coinage policy of Democrat William Jennings Bryan, however, was a platform General Taylor felt he could not support. The *Globe* did not endorse him in 1896 and indeed gave up endorsing political candidates in national, state, and city politics. Grozier grasped the opportunity and regularly endorsed candidates in various contests. The *Post* described itself as an independent Democratic paper and remained so. Its endorsement was eagerly sought by candidates, and the practice wound the paper deeper into the heart of the community and gave even greater pertinence and popularity to the *agora*.

CHAPTER SIX

★★★★

The Primitive-Man Caper

The weirdest feature story that turned first into a news story and then into a promotion stunt was the Joe Knowles exploit, which was more or less thrust upon the *Post* by its central figure and still ranks as a unique episode in the annals of American journalism. (This tale is referred to briefly in the prologue.) In his introduction to *The Call of the Wild, 1900–1916*, Roderick Nash, author of *Wilderness and the American Mind*, cites the exploit as a significant "protest for his generation" against mounting industrialism.

Knowles, forty-four years old in 1913, was a competent commercial artist who had worked for the *Post*, drawing illustrations and retouching photographs. Having been with the *Post* under Grozier but directly under Charles L. Wingate, the editor of the *Sunday Post*, he offered the latter a series of stories in which he would be the central figure.

He proposed that he walk naked and unarmed into the Maine woods and live as a primitive man for sixty days. He would get a story and his own illustrations to the *Post* each week by concealing them in a prearranged cache, where an intermediary would find them. The stories would be written and the illustrations drawn on birch bark with charcoal. During the sixty days he was to have contact with no one, to be seen by no one, to talk with no one, and to seek help from no one. It was later disclosed that he had tried to sell the story to a newspaper in Maine and, more importantly, to the *Boston American* (Hearst was known to spend big money) but, after being turned down by both, had appealed to his old boss.

Wingate agreed to use the stories, and several Sundays went by with the Knowles stories buried among the usual features in the Sunday paper. Grozier soon sniffed great human interest in the man's ordeal, however, and determined to give it everything the paper had. He moved it to page one of the daily paper, summarized its details, and assigned staff men to the scene. Before the sixty days were up half the world was watching the progress of the fabulous "nature man." When he emerged from the woods, he was a national, if not an international, hero.

What made Joe Knowles such a sensational figure? Psychologists interviewed later attributed it to his "aloneness" in the forest. He had the same appeal to the public as Robinson Crusoe on his deserted island, Charles Lindbergh over the Atlantic, and Admiral Richard E. Byrd at the South Pole. One thing was certain: The average *Post* reader, along with thousands who had never bought the *Post* before, identified with that lonely figure in the Maine woods.

Skepticism and efforts to discredit Knowles's story surfaced long before his ordeal began. Six months earlier, he had sat at a campfire with friends and fellow guides, said he would like to undertake such an experiment, and felt sure he could do it.

"How would you get shoes?" one skeptic asked.

Joe replied that he would weave the first pair from cedar bark until he could tan a pair from the hide of a deer.

"What about clothes?"

He would make them from animal hides. He declared that he would also be able to make bows and arrows and fashion cutting instruments such as stone tomahawks, stone skinning edges, and even bone knives. The proposal caused a debate around the campfire, some saying it could be done, some saying it was impossible. That night, Knowles lay awake thinking about it; by morning, he had determined to try it. It took some weeks to sell the idea. At length he was promised a modest fee by Wingate, but he was as much interested in the experiment as he was in the money. Neither he nor the newspaper realized what was coming.

Knowles went into the woods without fanfare. Indeed, he was six days in the woods before his first story appeared. The story recounted that he had gone in as naked as the day he was born, nothing with him but his knowledge of woodcraft, his acquaintance with wildlife, and his native intelligence. That his mother was part Indian didn't hurt the story. The site of his adventure was near Spencer Lake, not far from the Canadian border. He set forth in detail how he planned to live during his sixty days of ordeal.

Berries, wild onions and wild artichokes, and frogs' legs and fish
caught with nets of fiber were to be his food until he managed to
forge weapons. Then he would dine on deer meat and bear meat
cooked over a fire made with Indian techniques.

The first story told how he would illustrate his own stories,
which the *Post* planned to run once a week. He would both write
and draw on birch bark with the charcoal made in his fire. These
materials would be left at the secret cache, and a Maine guide
would retrieve them and forward them to the *Post*. Knowles
would not see the guide, nor would the guide see him.

Doctor Dudley A. Sargent, whose name came to adorn a famous school of physical education and who was a faculty member at Harvard University, examined Knowles before he entered
the woods, pronounced him fit, and praised the experiment for its
"scientific value." A group of more than twenty woodsmen,
sportsmen, and hunters signed an affidavit describing Knowles as
he made his nude entrance into the August woods. When
Knowles finally emerged from the woods, the *Post* led the daily
paper with the story and could not supply enough papers to slake
the demand.

No sooner had he gone than several skeptical sportsmen tried
to spy on him. In one or two cases, woodsmen who either didn't
care for him, envied him his notoriety, or more likely had wagered money he couldn't do it tried to track him down toward the
end of the sixty days. He became, in brief, a hunted man and
legally an outlaw. (The state of Maine had refused him permission
to kill game out of season; when one of his stories reported that
he had done so, game wardens took after him.)

Their efforts only heightened the interest in the story. The
Hearst papers, which had mounted many a fraudulent promotion
stunt in their day, became outraged at the *Post*'s success and determined to discredit the story. Assigned by the Hearst editors to
get at the facts was Bert Ford. He was one of the city's most
distinguished reporters and had all the dignity and integrity that
his newspaper, the *American*, lacked.

"He's not in those woods," one Hearst editor was quoted as
saying. "He's in some cabin or duckblind playing cards with his
buddies."

Once the story caught the public fancy, there were all sorts of
conjectures as to what Knowles might or might not be doing.
Scoffers with no regard for the truth protested that they had seen

him here, there, and everywhere: in a Portland, Maine, hotel; in the Château Frontenac in Québec; in a private home. Any such claim was a sure-fire way to start a conversation anywhere because everyone was reading about Knowles. One rumor ran that he was holed up in the bowels of the *Post* buildings, writing his stories there.

Bert Ford turned up a man named Hall who said he had sneaked up on a cabin in the woods near Spencer Lake and flung open the door to find the startled Knowles within. People who knew Hall doubted his report. The cabin in which Hall claimed to have surprised Knowles was owned by Thomas McKehoe, who was the guide relaying Knowles's reports to the *Post*. He had by that time become a sort of unofficial manager and spokesman for Knowles, and he hotly denied Hall's charge. The Hearst papers pressed the matter, and suddenly Knowles's struggle with nature in the raw was matched by a raw struggle between the newspapers that would become known as the "Battle of the Affidavits." That battle would continue even after he left the woods.

The first story from Knowles started off quietly enough.

After leaving the party of sportsmen and guides on the shore of Spencer Lake on Monday, August 4, I entered the forest alone with absolutely nothing to aid me in my new life in the woods.

It was raining hard when I started, and the rain continued to fall all day. It was slippery under foot along the trail, but with no clothing or burden to hamper me I felt the full freedom of the life I was to lead.

At Lost Pond a deer stood in the water on the opposite shore feeding on bottom grass. She looked good to me and for the first time in my life I envied a deer her hide.

My legs looked as if they had been in a fight with a wild cat to say nothing of the soles of my feet. Cat's claws were never more severe than the bull thistles and underbrush I had waded through.

I left the deer to the bottom grass, for I had decided to live within the game laws of Maine and not to molest the protected animals during the closed season. So crossing the outlet of the pond on a beaver dam, I went in search of shelter for the night.

I had not eaten since morning and did not even think of food. The smarting of the thistle and brush scratches on my legs were the severest trial.

Such was the general tone of his material. His fellow guides
had agreed before he set out that perhaps the hardest trial during
the sixty days would be the complete absence of human company. Someone quoted Scottish poet Thomas Campbell:

> I am out of humanity's reach
> Must I finish my journey alone
> Never hear the sweet music of speech
> And I start at the sound of my own.

The lines are from the *Soliloquy of Alexander Selkirk*, a
poem that relates the real-life adventure that provided Daniel
Defoe with the material for his imaginative reconstruction
Robinson Crusoe.

"I hear the voices of woodland neighbors," Knowles wrote,
"and feel the presence of my mother. It was she who guided my
footsteps along the trail that has led me to nature. It was through
her that I inherited my Indian blood."

Nothing that he wrote from the woods caused more skepticism, doubt, and debate than the story that he told of trapping
and killing a bear in order to clothe himself, his early pledge of
not molesting protected animals apparently forgotten. He recounted that he had dug a pit near the richest berry patches,
covered it with rushes, and then waited patiently for prey. Later,
he told the *Post* readers of his success.

> A yearling bear fell victim to my pitfall last night. I looked
> at the pit yesterday and nothing had passed on the trail lead-
> ing to the trap. The pitfall was a mile from my camp [a rude
> shelter he had reported building] in berry country, where
> bears are feeding at this time of year. I was returning to the
> camp near nightfall when I heard a crash in the direction of
> the trap.
>
> The noise led me to believe the animal was a bear, but as it
> was growing dark and I had one mile to go before reaching
> camp, I did not go to the trap.
>
> Now that I had the bear the next thing was to kill him. If
> he had been a young cub I would have tried to bring him to
> my camp and tame him. But the yearling was too husky for
> one man to handle and he was beyond the taming age. So I
> decided to settle with him in the pit and take no further
> chances.

I secured a stout club and, leaning down the pit, waited my opportunity. Once, in the mix-up, the rim of the pit crumbled under my feet and I nearly fell into the pit with the bear. I finally landed a blow on the bear's head and that put an end to him.

I left the skinning process until tomorrow. Here is where I needed a new implement in the way of a substitution for a skinning knife.

Later he reported:

For three days I have worked on the hide and carcass of the bear. I cut it and stripped a quantity off the meat, which I tore into strips with the grain and the hung it in my smokehole. This I ate because I needed it, not because I liked the taste of it.

I did not forget the sinews of the bear when I was mutilating the bear meat. I have hung them to dry for a later time. Aside from the comfort afforded by night by the bear skin and the abundance of meat which the bear supplied, I have secured in the sinews a lasting cord for my fire-kindle, which had given me trouble because of the lack of something more durable than roots or the lining bark from trees.

How empathically the readers responded when he wrote:

I am now paying the price that nature demands for the privilege of living an independent life among her wild creatures in the forest. I feel I must do something to keep my mind from rotting for want of word from the outside world. While my bodily needs are supplied, my mind is starving.

After that, letters poured into the *Post* city room, offering sympathy and encouragement, along with a few offers of marriage.

When Knowles finally emerged from the woods, the writing of the story was not left to him. Grozier was organizing for what he knew would be a tremendous climax. He hired a special train and had it standing ready. Paul V. Waitt, one of the *Post*'s staff writers and a man frequently used on promotion stunts and public-service programs, was sent to Megantic, Québec, to meet Knowles when he emerged. The *Post*'s coverage, which had begun as a quiet feature, was its lead story that day. Never mind

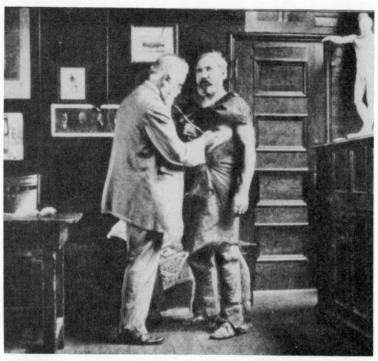

Joe Knowles, still clad in his bearskin, being examined by Dr. Dudley A. Sargent on his arrival in Boston after sixty days of primitive life in the Maine woods.

what President Wilson might be up to; never mind America's Congress and the tariffs; Joe Knowles had come out of the woods!

By Paul V. Waitt

Megantic, Québec, Oct. 4 (1913)—Joseph Knowles, the Boston artist, came out of the woods at 4 o'clock this afternoon at a point 14 miles south of Megantic, on the railroad track of the Canadian Pacific.

Clad in the rudely dressed skins of black bear and deer, carrying in a pack on his back his precious fire-machine and other of the forest-made tools he fashioned to aid him in his two-months fight for existence in the forests of Maine, Knowles stepped into the 20th century a replica of what the cave man must have looked like when the world was young.

Thus ended a test of hardihood and endurance, of skill in conquering a hostile environment, of woodcraft, that rose superior to the mightiest of handicaps—a feat so novel, so startling that all over the world people have been waiting for the issue.

On the fourth day of August, Knowles plunged into the forests near Spencer Lake in Somerset County, Maine. He was naked, he had no weapons, no tools or implements of any kind, no food. He promised to come out of the woods on the fourth day of October, fully clad, in good health and physical condition. He has kept his promise inviolate in every detail.

Knowles is in good physical condition despite the fact that his final week in the forest involved the test of endurance that was completely unforeseen and equally unnecessary in his dread that the game wardens of Somerset County might seek him out in his forest lair and bring his struggle to nought by arresting him for breach of the game laws. He left his domain near Spencer Lake and struck out across un-tracked wilderness seventy miles for the boundary mountains of Canada overlooking Lake Megantic.

With his rude pack on his back, clad in the skins of wild animals his skill had won to his uses, in constant danger of being the target of some sportsman's rifle, he traversed seventy miles of the most inhospitable country in the State of Maine.

He has lost 30 pounds of weight in the two months, dropping from 204 pounds to 174. His appeerence clearly tells the tale of the hardships he has undergone. From head to heel he is scratched and bruised by the briars and underbrush in which he has lived for sixty days. He is tanned like an Indian, almost black.

Over his tanned neck and arms was a black bear skin, cleverly fashioned with thongs of deerskin. His trousers were of deerskin, made Indian fashion, with the hair inside. His feet were encased in moccasins of buckskin, sewed with sinew. He wore no hat, no sleeves, no underwear. On his back was a knapsack of woven lining bark. It was filled with trophies from the forest. Slung over his arm were his bow and arrows. Sheathed in buckskin, a crude knife hung from his belt.

Just as the sun, after a three days' absence, poked its warm rays through a rift of clouds shortly after 4 o'clock today, Knowles came forth from the Canadian wilderness fourteen

miles south of Megantic on the railroad track of the C.P.R.
[Canadian Pacific Railroad] like a man who had traveled back
to civilization from a land of hundreds of centuries ago. No
human being was there to greet him, but a dozen miles away
a dozen parties were scouring different points along the Lake
Megantic shores in search of him. In those parties were
prominent men of Maine and Canada joining hands in the
plans to welcome him back to the world and its people.

One little girl, Frienie [sic] Gerard of Lake Megantic, a 14-
year-old child of the woods, was the first privileged person to
greet him. She had wandered far out of town, down the track
where the houses were left behind and where gaudily colored autumn trees swept with unbroken line on either side.

What must be remembered is that, such was the public hyste-
ria created by the Knowles adventure, Waitt's story did not seem
in the least high-blown.

And then she stopped suddenly and gazed ahead. Walking
toward her with long swinging strides came a creature of fur,
came a different animal than she had ever seen before. She
did not run, for somehow, she afterwards explained, she
thought it was a strange man in spite of the fact that, in the
distance, the figure appeared like a great bear.

She saw a figure not of the Rip Van Winkle nor the Robinson Crusoe type, but a man-animal creature whose black-
ened cheeks and arms showed in strange contrast to a
sweeping tunic of black fur and wild animal skin trousers of
a lighter brown. Only a nose and a pair of blue eyes could be
seen peering from out a mass of black and gray hair and
beard. The child of 14, wild-eyed, stared at him, and into her
mind came the memory of a picture of a man of the stone
age in a history book.

Knowles, who had been walking deep in thought with his
head down, suddenly saw her. It was a human being. Something in him rose and forced a cry from his throat, and kindly
tears came into his eyes.

Tens of thousand of *Post* readers in those innocent days wept
as they read those lines.

He smiled and the girl saw the gold in his teeth flash.
"He is a real man," she said to herself.

"Hello," stammered the girl bravely.

"Where is Megantic?"

A musical flow of words followed but they were not English. However, they were wonderful words to Joe Knowles. He was hungry for just such words—literally starving for them, and he understood little French. Again he listened while the girl talked. She had faced about and was walking by his side.

He saw her eyeing his queer sack of bark containing his trophies. Then her eyes traveled to the long, sweeping bow in his hand which he used as a walking stick. It was seven miles or so to Megantic, she told him, and she said she would walk only part of the way with him.

First they came to a house where ten other children, the offspring of Mrs. U. N. Roy, were playing in the country yard. Catching sight of the strange man, the whole ten ran shrieking with fear into the low-roofed white house.

The girl left him here, still staring wide-eyed but still unafraid. She watched him disappear down the track in the direction of Megantic.

Next Knowles saw a freight train panting and stationary on a siding. Again joy took possession of him, for he was weary and his feet were tired inside those thin deerskin moccasins. Here was a possible lift.

Engineer C. F. Fisher of Brownville, Me., who was oiling the engine, suddenly saw the modern aborigine and he gasped and started back. However, he had read of the Knowles experiment, and the thought flashed into his mind that this was the man.

It was verified a second later when Knowles smiled and said, "My name is Knowles."

The other members of the crew were introduced, and Fisher suggested flagging the passenger train which was about due. . . .

The siding was about five miles outside Megantic, where gala preparations had been made for Knowles's coming. Conductor Vickers, brakeman Corben Chase and Henry Adair of the crew, assured him that the passenger train would be stopped, and so the engine came tooting around a curve. It was stopped, for the men of the train crew stood directly in its path.

As one can see, no detail of the story was missed, no point, however trivial, left out.

As Knowles climbed the steps of the passenger train and entered the coach, tremendous excitement prevailed. It seemed as if everyone had read of his exploit and he was immediately surrounded and a reception followed in the car.

The news swept from one end of the train to the other and all the people in the other cars crowded into the Knowles car. Knowles was, at first, speechless at it all. He seemed dazed. He answered questions in a mechanical sort of way and seemed as if he were awakening from a long sleep.

Among others aboard the train were newspapermen and they too joined the reception. At Megantic the whole town was out to greet him. With hundreds of enthusiastic people behind him and in front of him, he was escorted to Queen's Hotel.

The hotel was ablaze with English and American colors from top to bottom in honor of the event. Hundreds of people, hearing of the arrival, choked the street in front of the hotel. In that picturesque parade were businessmen, the mayor of the town, the district representative in parliament, game wardens from Maine and Canada, guides, sportsmen from the Maine country and from Canada, and women and children. The ovation was tremendous. Every sort of vehicle lined the streets, and throngs of people. They cheered as Knowles made his way to the hotel piazza. Then the photographers took countless pictures of Knowles together with Mayor Genreau and Dr. Gregory, M. P., and other dignitaries.

A short time later he was hustled upstairs to a private room. The first thing he did was to remove the great bearskin covering. Then he saw a bed, a bed, a real bed. "Let's see how it feels," he said, and he threw himself full length upon the mattress.

"How are you feeling, Joe," asked the reporter for the first time.

"Never felt better in my life! Say, is there a cigarette around here?" he said quickly and in a moment, Knowles, stretched out and comfortable, stripped to the waist, was literally devouring the first smoke for many weeks.

"How about your eating, Joe?"

"Had a spruce partridge yesterday morning. Nothing much since."

"Are you hungry?"

"Not a bit."

However, Dr. Gregory, M. P., who happened to come into the room a moment later with the mayor and the Maine and Canadian game wardens, prescribed a glass of milk, which

Knowles drank with great relish. Knowles as he lay on the bed looked literally copper colored. He was the picture of health and power, but his eyes looked strained. He stared in a peculiar way when the husky game wardens, dressed in the garb of the woods, entered the room.

"Joe, these are the Maine game wardens," introduced the Post man.

"And instead of making trouble we have come to congratulate you and to escort you back through Maine," greeted Chief Durgin as he extended his hand.

Gratitude shone in Knowles's eyes and he proceeded to shake hands in turn with the other wardens, H. C. Templeton, James R. Cox and L. F. Comber.

Then came congratulations and words of welcome from F. N. Roche, the Canadian inspector of forest protection in the province of Québec. "As Americans and Canadians we are brothers," greeted Roche. "We congratulate you and are proud you have come out of the wilderness at this place."

Perhaps one of the most impressive scenes of the day occurred when Knowles, in the chamber of the Queen's Hotel, asked the Maine wardens what they were going to do with him. He was immediately reassured that members of the greeting party had agreed to pay his fine and that he was not to be molested but rather honored and respected. "I want to explain just why I came to Canada, gentlemen," began Knowles with gratitude in his voice. "It was because I feared that I would be molested in my experiment just at the close by [Maine] wardens who I thought might hunt me down. It was not to escape the fine. It was simply because of what I have told you. I seem to have made a mistake.

"I knew friends of mine had wagered money that I would win out and if I had been apprehended before my time was up they would have suffered. It took hold of me terribly and it preyed each day more and more on my mind. I am sorry, gentlemen, to have caused you all this trouble."

Once again the wardens assured him of their kind intentions and the best of feeling prevailed. Chief Durgin explained that the whole trouble had started from one warden who had been in the Maine woods as a guide and not as a warden. He made several boasts which had been juggled around the country from mouth to mouth.

Too tired to tell a connected story, Knowles talked with the *Post* man of his experience.

"My food consisted largely of fish, fresh deer meat, bear meat, spruce partridge and berries," he said. "As late as last week I found blueberries in the burnt lands.

"I am feeling in fine condition. I do not believe every man can do what I have done, but I feel confident that a man with good health, a knowledge of the woods and resourcefulness can accomplish the same thing. I believe anyone of these game wardens could do it. I have satisfied a curiosity.

"The hardest thing of all was the awful lonesomeness because of which I came near coming out twice. The isolation almost drove me crazy. Several times I heard voices far off and that made it only the harder.

"The eating question is nothing, neither is the dress. I have not suffered any to speak of from the cold. It was the awful lonesomeness.

"For the last 10 days I have done but little. Up to this time I constantly aspired to accomplish something, but ambition left me. During the past 19 days I believe I have lost 10 pounds because of this.

"On my trip to Canada, I simply used the moss on the north side of trees to guide me. I have worn my furs but little lately. I just dressed to come to town.

"Last night I didn't know whether I camped in Canada or in Maine. It was somewhere on the other side of Beattie. I did not sleep any because the rain was falling heavily. Perhaps it was about two hours I sat with my back against a tree. I have not been able to build a fire for two nights.

"I started for this march to Canada the day I waved the torch on the shore of King and Bartlett Lake. When I got out today I was not sure whether it was Saturday or Sunday. It was a pretty rough country but my trip today was largely down hill all the way

"I came through the deepest forest because I did not dare to strike the roads for fear of being seen before time. Then from up in the mountains I heard a wonderful thing. I heard the whistle of a train. I pressed toward it and finally came out on the railroad tracks. Someone told me later it was a little after 4 o'clock.

"I was amazed at the wonderful reception and am very grateful for it." When questioned regarding salt, he said that he missed it very much for the first few weeks but after that he never thought about it. Yet tonight when he was asked what he would have to eat he ordered fried salt pork and potatoes, the first food he had seen in 33 hours.

Thus ended the lead story of the hero's exit from the woods, Orpheus up from Acheron, the hunter home from the hill. Meanwhile, the "Battle of the Affidavits" continued. Grozier had half a dozen reporters gathering affidavits all over Maine, turning up five for every one that the Hearst papers produced. One shrewd guide sold affidavits to both sides. A public debate raged on whether or not a man was able to capture and kill a bear under the circumstances reported by Knowles. Later on, to prove his expertise, Knowles killed another bear in the woods the same way. He explained carefully that to kill a bear with a club, one had to hit it not on the skull but on the nose. His club, he said, was made of hornbeam (a tree of the birch family).

His return from Megantic to Boston in the special train that Grozier had hired matched in noisy acclaim the triumphal return of a Roman conqueror. Waitt, the Post reporter, slept in the train with Knowles. Stops were made at every tank town in Maine and every other city en route, while Knowles made his appearance on the back platform, to the uproarious cheering and applause of his fellow "Mainiacs." Waitt remembered very well in after years that the stench of the bear skin and the deer skin trousers was such that Knowles could scarcely bring himself to wear them, now that he had been able to wash up. Waitt also said it was almost impossible to live in the same railroad car with the skins, and they kept them covered in a far corner. When a stop was made Knowles would resignedly don his animal skins, while Waitt, holding his nose, would open the door to allow the hero to move to the rear platform. For the reception in Newspaper Row, the bear skin and the dear skin trousers were of course mandatory.

As fantastic as Grozier knew the public response to the story to be, neither he nor anyone else was prepared for the crowd that turned up in Newspaper Row to see the nature hero. Newspaper estimates are notoriously exaggerated, but somewhere between 150,000 and 400,000 persons jammed Washington Street that day. Certainly the scene ushered in the years that Westbrook Pegler christened the "Era of Wonderful Nonsense." By the end of 1913, the Post circulation (more than 200,000) was double that of the previous year. The Knowles story was surely the major single contributor to the increase.

Knowles subsequently went on the B. F. Keith vaudeville circuit for $400 a week, big money at the time. The editors of the

Hearst papers in Boston, not knowing when they were licked, continued the "Battle of the Affidavits" even as Knowles was packing the B. F. Keith theater on Washington Street, one hundred yards beyond Newspaper Row. William Randolph Hearst, who knew the best when he saw it and usually tried to buy it up, finally stopped the uncertainty surrounding the "Battle of the Affidavits." He hired Knowles to go to California and *repeat* his adventure there for one of the Hearst papers. Knowles did so and was well paid; the weather was warmer, too. Newspaper Row would not see his like again.

CHAPTER SEVEN

A Man without Rancor

Not by promotion alone did newspapers of that day live and prosper. Campaigns and crusades also counted, so Grozier had them going constantly as well. The *Post* agitated for lower gas rates, for lower telegraph and telephone rates, and also for universal transfer on streetcars from one branch to another. The *Post* editorials were generally pro-labor, some marked by an enthusiasm that would have made them at home in any union periodical. And the *Post* supported those candidates who supported labor. In brief, the *Post* under Grozier showed an ongoing concern for improvement in working conditions for the laboring man, including a reduction in his working hours. It was the mark of the changing attitudes of the *Post* executives that, when Franklin D. Roosevelt's New Deal brought in a shorter work week, the *Post* sought at first to evade it and then accepted it reluctantly.

Grozier had made an early announcement to his readers: "By performance rather than by promises, the new *Post* seeks to be judged. By deeds rather than words, its record will be made. From one source only can come the verdict. The new *Post* appeals to the sovereign people. It aims to be the people's newspaper not in empty phrases but in fact."

In 1899, Addison Archer, an advertising man, published a brochure on the newspapers of Boston and interviewed Grozier. The latter told him: "The *Post* almost unaided and alone advocated and achieved $1 gas in Boston, reduced the subway lease from 50 to 20 years, reduced the guaranteed dividend to the West End road under lease to the Elevated road from 8 to 7 percent, [and] brought about the large and growing system of free transfers." These were all burning issues in that day.

Although a competent business man, Grozier brought in his brother William as business manager so he could concentrate on editing the paper. He had a crisp, vigorous writing style and wrote editorials himself. Like many another publisher who found himself locked into publishing, Grozier, as a young man, had aspired to being a writer, a poet, and a novelist.

While his editorials could be stinging, his news columns were never partisan, if he could help it; he strove for fairness and balanced views. He supported David I. Walsh for governor (Walsh became the first Irish Catholic to hold that office) and later for senator. He supported Woodrow Wilson in both his presidential campaigns. The only time Grozier endorsed a Republican candidate for president, however, was when Calvin Coolidge ran for the office in 1924.

Despite the many campaigns that Grozier carried on in the columns of his paper for one sort of cause or another, he himself was never a public figure. He stayed assiduously at his desk. (General Taylor of the *Globe* was, in contrast, one of the most popular public speakers in the city and very much in demand.) It is a mark of his modesty in this regard that he never met Calvin Coolidge.

He had great vision. One story is told of him that, when he took over the *Post*, he signed a long-term contract for paper with the Great Northern Paper Company. The terms were so favorable to him at the time, and the *Post's* quota of paper grew so, that the paper company was losing money in supplying him. His suppliers never anticipated the incredible rise in circulation that marked the Grozier regime. The result was that one day the president of Great Northern walked into Grozier's office and offered him the keys to the Millinocket plant. Grozier had the contract redrawn to give the company a fair market profit on the paper it sold the *Post*.

Early on he bought property in another part of the city and there installed extra presses so that, in the event of a disaster or other emergency, the *Post* could still get its papers to its readers. Once a year, pressmen would go to the plant to run papers off and keep the presses primed. The *Post* itself never had such an emergency, but during the New England flood of 1938, other publishers were happy to be the guests of the *Boston Post*.

He was, like General Taylor of the *Globe*, a man without rancor or envy. When the *Boston Herald* left Newspaper Row in

1906, Grozier bought the building it had occupied, the only one on that side of Washington Street that had been built for the purpose of publishing a newspaper. So rapidly had been the mechanical developments in the business that the *Herald* building had become outmoded in thirty years' time. Grozier was able to couple it with his other properties and make it useful. The *Herald* remained a very lively rival to the *Post* and the *Globe*, but its shifting managements were not always as high-minded as were Grozier and Taylor. Nevertheless, when the *Herald* won a Pulitzer Prize for an editorial urging a review of the Sacco-Vanzetti case, with the result that Governor Alvin T. Fuller appointed a special commission, Grozier ran the story of the award on the front page of the *Post* along with a photograph of Frank Buxton, who wrote the editorial.

Grozier's character shone through his paper, and even the hoopla of yellow journalism could not obscure it. The *Post*'s pursuit of yellow journalism, like that of most newspapers, was comparable to a young man's sowing his wild oats and then marrying and settling down. The early *Transcript* had once given over all its pages to a sensational murder case. The *Globe* had had its fling but was so badly burned in the Lizzie Borden case that it backed off entirely and adopted an attitude of "cautious coverage." The Hearst papers tried to compete with the *Post* in toe-to-toe sensationalism; but even after Grozier was gone, the *Post* maintained its lead as the most aggressive paper in the city.

The *Transcript*, an early defender of the Irish immigrants of Boston, made no effort in its columns to appeal to them and developed a bias the other way. For a while the *Globe* was the favorite paper of the Irish-Americans; although it remained in the affections of the Irish, however, Grozier took the lead. He made a distinct effort to appeal to the Catholics of Boston, who comprised, by the start of the twentieth century, a majority of the population. William Cardinal O'Connell's every interview was front-page material. All major Catholics events were covered. Since the Democratic party and the Irish were practically one and the same, the path was an easy one for Grozier. He also found it worked.

In his espousal of these causes, there was no hint of hypocrisy. He had an honest concern with the underdog, a stout conviction in the principles of democracy, and all the instincts of a decent human being. Many of his private concerns were not revealed until after his death.

Calvin Coolidge, president of the United States when Grozier died in 1924, promptly wired the *Post*: "Like hundreds of thousands of others, who have felt the force of the man, I never saw Mr. Edwin A. Grozier. Yet I felt that I knew him. His influence was so constantly manifest that it was impossible for anyone in public life to fail to observe it. He had that indescribable power that we call character. He was a great newspaper publisher, a patriotic American and a great man. He made a mark upon a wide territory. He had a broad faith and a wonderful courage. It was a privilege to behold his accomplishments and an inspiration to feel that he was a friend. He is gone but the influence for good which he so nobly represented will live forever."

When Grozier took over the *Post*, Frederick E. Goodrich was on the staff, writing editorials and serving in other capacities. In a letter to him on the fiftieth anniversary of his service, Grozier wrote: "I have never regarded the paper as merely a piece of private property, to be conducted for mercenary ends, but rather as an institution to be managed for the public good, and to be made a force in the community, for the promotion of the welfare of our city, State, section and nation."

He closed with the following remarks, which those who knew him knew were heartfelt: "I hope that through these many years you have come to regard the *Post* not merely as a place to work, but in a certain sense as an industrial home, and have come to regard the members of the *Post* staff who are so zealously working with you, not merely as co-workers for a weekly stipend but as members of the *Post* family all interested in the welfare and happiness of each other."

Few knew of his interest in the Boston Chess Club. He had been a devotee of the game and, with no publicity, had provided a trophy for local matches and maintained a membership in the club long after his routine prevented him from attending. His generosity towards the club lasted through the years. Similar generosity to the city of Cambridge resulted in a street being named for him. Former workers, as well as public figures of every religious and political stripe, also paid tribute to him on his demise. In a day when equal rights for black citizens of Boston was a low priority for most public men, Grozier won from William Monroe Trotter, editor of the *Boston Guardian*, a black-oriented newspaper, the following tribute: "Sadness and a sense of loss for their race fell upon all of us Americans of color when the grievous news [came] . . . that Grozier was dead. He conducted the biggest, most widely read New England daily on a policy of identical justice, freedom and civil rights for all, regardless of race, of creed or color. Though Democratic in political faith, the *Post* under Mr. Grozier never hesitated to oppose colorphobic policies. Despite the increasing unpopularity of our cause for equality, his newspaper never failed us when our title to identical public privileges was challenged by however powerful an enemy . . . "

Although tributes came from statesmen, politicians, college presidents, financiers, and, indeed, from persons in all walks of life, the tribute of William Trotter would have pleased him as much as any and more than most; it marked the equity of concern that was at the heart of the man.

CHAPTER EIGHT

Munsey, Hearst, and Mrs. Eddy

The early years of the twentieth century saw the rise of the newspaper chains. Joseph Pulitzer never thought of a chain, but William Randolph Hearst did from the beginning. The first chain in the modern sense, however, was organized by Edward W. Scripps, who founded the *Cleveland Press* in 1878 and went on from there. He was the preeminent newspaperman in an extraordinary family that contributed much to the history of American journalism.

In 1873 his half brother, James E. Scripps, founded the *Detroit Evening News*, and Edward went to work for the paper. It was after a tour of Europe that he founded the *Cleveland Press*. He and James then acquired the *St. Louis Evening Chronicle*, the *Cincinnati Post*, and the *Covington* (Kentucky) *Post* to form the first newspaper chain. Political differences, however, split the two in 1889. Edward took charge of the chain, while James continued solely with the *Detroit Evening News*. Edward, with another half brother, George, formed the Scripps-McRae League of Newspapers, out of which evolved the United Press. Edward's sons took over in 1914, and the partnership with Roy Howard was made in 1922, two years after Edward was in retirement and completely out of the business.

The independent papers were always concerned that some chain would come into their bailiwicks. At the beginning of this century, Frank Munsey, a name in publishing to be acknowledged and feared, began to form a small chain of newspapers, some thought with a view to running for high office. In the fall of 1902, when Grozier had the *Post* more or less on its feet, Newspaper Row was given a double dose of excitement. Munsey bought the

Boston *Journal*. He could be a formidable and dangerous competitor. At that time he was the nation's most successful publisher of magazines, but he also owned two newspapers, the *Washington Times* and the *New York Daily News*, and was intent on forging his chain on the east coast. He was formidable because his income was estimated at close to $1 million a year. He was dangerous because he was erratic.

When Grozier bought the *Post* in 1891, Munsey bought the *New York Star*, turned it into a tabloid, changed its name to the *Continent*, and folded it within six months. During his career he would own eighteen newspapers in all and earn a reputation as an assassin of newspapers. His practice was to buy out any competitor and merge that paper with his own, with a consequent reduction in the number of jobs. He was not an able publisher of newspapers, however able he may have been as a financier or as a publisher of magazines. Still, two of his New York newspapers, the *Evening Sun* and the *Evening Telegram*, survived him. After Munsey's death, E. W. Scripps bought the *Telegram* and attached to it the name of the *World*, having bought the remains of that institution after it folded in 1931. In any case, when Munsey bought the *Journal* in 1902, his presence wasn't welcome to the other publishers in Boston.

Munsey was born in Mercer, Maine, on August 21, 1854, and grew up in Lisbon Falls, a town celebrated decades later in articles and books by another distinguished New England journalist, author and *Post* contributor John Gould. Munsey began his career, like many an editor and publisher, as a telegraph operator; at the age of twenty-eight, he was in charge of the Western Union office at Augusta, Maine, but dissatisfied. He set off for New York with forty dollars in his pocket to make his fortune. He made that fortune forty times over.

Munsey's first venture was *Golden Argosy*, the nation's first successful pulp magazine, which survived as *Argosy*. Soon he established *Munsey's Magazine*, which, when he invaded Boston, had the largest audience in America. This alone made him a famous and formidable fighter. He was in himself a fantastic figure, a brilliant, arrogant, highhanded man bent on making money and making it big. He was a bachelor and a loner who never seemed to enjoy life, a martinet who browbeat his employees yet paid them well—and was hated by them. He showed little affection for anything but regarded New England as home.

A reporter at his job in the old *Globe* building, 1886.

Grozier was naturally apprehensive. He had a vivid memory of the brutal circulation battle in the late 1890s in New York City between Hearst and Pulitzer. Now, besides the news that Munsey had bought the *Journal*, came the rumor that Hearst as well had his eye on Boston. Grozier could remember Hearst spending money as if it were water and luring many of Pulitzer's staff from the *World* with extravagant salaries. Munsey, he knew, had millions of dollars behind him to do the same if he chose. Both Taylor and Grozier felt they were in for a battle.

Why Munsey decided to invade Boston was never made quite clear. While living in Maine he had read the Boston papers, however, and entry on the scene was in a sense, perhaps, a homecoming. Also he was launched on a spree of buying newspapers, and with a Boston paper, the *Washington Times*, and the *New York Daily News*, his incipient chain would blanket the Northeast. Indeed, before he gave up on the *Journal*, he would also purchase a newspaper in Baltimore. The news that he had bought the *Journal* from Stephen O'Meara rocked Boston's journalistic circles. The *Globe*, with thirty years of publishing behind it, did not feel threatened as much as Grozier did. For the *Post*, with only eleven years' experience in fighting for mass circulation in the Greater Boston and New England markets, it was an ominous piece of news. The *Post* circulation at the time was under 200,000.

While Munsey imagined himself to be an inspired newspaper publisher, he was not. He wanted immediate results and was used to getting them from his subordinates; but the public that he wooed could not be intimidated nor bulldozed into buying his papers. He had two solutions for journalistic problems: quick change and more money. He surprised O'Meara by giving him far more money for the paper than he thought he might get. Munsey immediately threw even more money into modernizing the appearance of the paper—then staunchly Republican, staid, and oversized (extra large)—and into completing the new plant already under construction. He had the money to do it. In the year he purchased the *Journal*, his annual net earnings from other sources were over $700,000, and they would double within ten years.

The *Journal* both before and during the Civil War had made a name for itself, thanks mostly to reporters Stephen N. Stockwell and Charles Carleton Coffin. Stockwell was a stenographic whiz, and his account of Daniel Webster's speech for presidential candidate Zachary Taylor in 1848 was a sensation when the *Journal* published it in an extra edition the day after it was delivered. Coffin gave New England its first account of the Battle of Bull Run and reported subsequent battles throughout the Civil War. The *Journal* was at a low ebb when O'Meara took it over and restored its circulation to something more than 50,000. O'Meara was tiring of it, however, and offered the paper to Munsey, who made his excessive offer without waiting for O'Meara to speak. O'Meara retired from publishing and ended up police commissioner for the city of Boston.

The spruced-up and modernized Munsey *Journal* proceeded briskly for four months, after which the owner decided it was not making sufficient progress. After a personal analysis of the situation, he started off his once-sedate old newspaper "on an irresponsible career."

His first conclusion was that it was a mistake to issue two separate newspapers, morning and evening, each day from the same shop. The evening edition, he declared, was a drag. So on April 18, 1903, he killed the *Evening Journal*. Three days later, in order to preserve the valuable Associated Press membership for possible sale, he started the *Boston Evening News*, publishing from the same shop and lifting the price to two cents. Two weeks later he put back the price to one cent.

Nine months later he stopped the *Sunday Journal* and started instead an enlarged, fifty-page *Saturday Evening News*, with comics and magazine insert. At this time, as always, the *Transcript* printed no Sunday paper but rather an enlarged Saturday evening paper. After seven weeks Munsey revived the *Sunday Journal*.

Next he killed the *Evening News* a year after it had started, allowing the Associated Press membership to lapse. Then he changed the price of the *Sunday Journal* to two cents. Then, on September 11, 1904, he killed the *Sunday Journal*.

That was the same year that William Randolph Hearst began the *Boston American*, which would remain a major force in Boston until 1961, when it was combined with the *Record*. Hearst set up shop 200 yards from Newspaper Row, but the competition he offered at first was low key; he was too busy with political campaigns in New York. Still, his Boston papers (for he would acquire two more) would outlive the *Post*.

It was Munsey who was causing real trouble for the *Post* and the *Globe*, but he also had a gift for causing trouble for himself. He outraged the news dealers by making the *Journal* nonreturnable. The dealers were already dizzy from his kaleidoscopic changes. He had dropped the wholesale cost of the *News* to ten copies for one cent and then jacked it back up to five cents. But declaring the *Journal* nonreturnable was too much.

Six years went by, with the Munsey publications in Boston making little headway. He then brought out a Sunday paper again, this one without the usual accouterments and looking for all the world like a daily. Then, seventeen months later, he killed his Sunday paper for the last time.

In November 1911, he followed a former policy of the *Transcript* by eliminating all illustrations from the *Journal*. The *Transcript*, however, had abandoned that policy about six years earlier. No sooner had Munsey done this than he offered the *Jour-*

nal for sale. He kept tinkering with the makeup and the price of the paper until he sold it in 1913 and left Boston forever. Four years later the property was acquired by the *Herald*, which had already absorbed the *Traveler*, and had departed from Newspaper Row for quarters at 171 Tremont Street. Long before that, Grozier knew that neither the *Journal* nor Munsey was a threat. By the time the *Journal* folded, it was also evident that Hearst was too busy elsewhere to start in Boston the sort of war he had waged in New York and Chicago.

Munsey had assembled an able staff headed by Charles E. L. Wingate, who had been the general manager of the *Journal* and who had suffered greatly under Munsey's mercurial and domineering behavior. He was happy finally to go over to the *Post* and to end his days there as editor of the *Sunday Post*, showing thereafter a determination never to take a train to New York, which Munsey had had him doing every other day. Wingate had his eccentricities, too, one of which had made it doubly difficult for him to respond to Munsey's repeated demands that he come to New York and confer. Wingate had an acute fear of fire and always carried in his suitcase thirty feet of rope to get him down from a hotel window in the event of fire. Once at the *Post*, he was never again asked to travel and remained content. Munsey rocked the city of Boston for eleven years; but although he died a much richer (and lonelier) man than either General Taylor or E. A. Grozier, he was no match for them in the matter of publishing a daily or Sunday newspaper. The newspapermen who worked for Grozier and those who worked for General Taylor wept when those gentlemen died. Those who worked for Munsey wouldn't go to his funeral.

The excitement caused by the Munsey foray into Boston journalism was matched to a degree by the foundation of a new, and novel, newspaper. Experimental papers were being tried in various parts of the country but seemed to die like mayflies. In 1908, however, the *Christian Science Monitor* began printing in Boston. The aspiration of Mary Baker Eddy, founder of the Church of Christ, Scientist, the paper was almost a protest against yellow journalism, which was declining but still vibrant.

On July 28, 1908, William B. Johnson, clerk of the board of directors of the Christian Science Church, received from the hands of a messenger a scribbled note from Mrs. Eddy that read: "NOTICE So soon as the Pub. House debt is paid I request the

C. S. Board Directors to start a daily newspaper called *Christian Science Monitor* This must be done without fail and after Pub. M B Eddy." There were few periods, the word *Notice* was underlined, and the words *Christian Science Monitor* were doubly underlined. In March of that year John L. Wright, a *Globe* reporter had written to Mrs. Eddy about such a possibility, but the idea was already in her head. Wright became the *Monitor's* first city editor.

What was more remarkable was the speed with which the board of directors brought the paper into print. The first steps were kept secret; but on October 17 the trustees, subordinate to the directors, announced that the church planned to publish a daily newspaper, and the board of directors announced plans to enlarge the new publishing house, which had been completed and paid for that August. A fund drive went ahead. Contracts were signed for printing equipment. As early as September 15, a sample newspaper had been printed at a job-printing house in Boston. The title was left off because the name, *Christian Science Monitor*, was still a secret. From all over the country, newsmen who were Christian Scientists applied for work.

In his book *Commitment to Freedom*, Erwin D. Canham, once a *Monitor* editor, recalls the statement of purpose:

> "It is the intention of the trustees to publish a strictly up-to-date newspaper in which all the news of the day that should be printed will find a place, and whose service will not be restricted to any one locality or section but will cover the daily activities of the entire world . . ."

Later it continued:

> "To those who have inquired whether the Monitor is to be a real newspaper, we say, Yes. To those who have asked whether it will be simply a Boston newspaper, we say No, except that a special New England edition, which will give the current local news of that section, is to be issued each day."

The paper would carry no crime news or scandal, all of which Mrs. Eddy deemed "unhealthful." Its aim was "clean journalism." Grozier saw quickly that it would be no threat to the rising circulation of the *Post*, which in a few years would be ahead of the field again in coverage of a murder case that won international interest.

By 1919, the *Monitor* had a circulation of 123,080, a large portion of it outside New England. Typographically, it was the most attractive newspaper in Boston; it eschewed the banner headlines that had become so popular and presented a more attractive front page than the *Transcript*. Its publishing house was far from Newspaper Row, and the paper was little regarded there as a competitor.

Then, in that same year, a dispute between the board of directors and the board of trustees landed in the courts, almost ruining the paper entirely. The issue revolved around which board controlled the Christian Science Publishing Society. The dispute was complicated by a disruptive member of the board of directors and the paper's brilliant and ambitious editor, Frederick Dixon, who sided with the trustees. The legalities lasted three years until the Supreme Judicial Court of Massachusetts decided in favor of the directors. During these troubles, the paper's circulation dropped to 20,939. By 1924, however, the circulation had climbed back over 100,000.

The genius of Mrs. Eddy showed in her determination that the *Monitor* be a newspaper and not a propaganda sheet for Christian Science, although daily it carried an article presenting some aspect of the religion's mystique, often in a foreign language.

Among the experimental newspapers that had been tried throughout the United States up to that point, the overwhelming majority had been devoted to a cause, like those of William Lloyd Garrison. One of his newspapers stressed temperance; another, the abolition of slavery. In all these cases, the cause came first and the news second. With the *Monitor*, however, it was the other way around, even though its choice of news was determined by its refusal to acknowledge the evil in the world. Grozier's view, on the other hand, was that of a New York editor: Whatever the Lord allowed in the world would be subject for the columns of his newspaper.

Mrs. Eddy, like many a woman of genius, was no feminist radical. She had a wide-ranging knowledge of what was going on in the world and was probably well aware of the numerous suffragette newspapers that came and went, such as *The Idaho Woman*, which appeared in 1897 with the slogan "Equality Before the Law." Furthermore, in view of her strictures against the use of alcoholic beverages, she had no doubt seen the newspaper published by Carrie Nation, the temperance shrew who chopped up bars and lectured with a hatchet in her hand. Her paper bore an appropriate name, *The Smasher's Mail.* Mrs. Eddy, nevertheless, was bent on having a newspaper and not letting the news be stifled in propaganda. She achieved her aim even though her publication is legally a house organ of the Church of Christ, Scientist, and not a newspaper. Its approach to the news is generally objective; its feature articles, excellent.

In the last two decades of the nineteenth century and the opening of the twentieth, women were quietly taking their place in journalism. True, Cornelia Wells Walter had been editor of the *Transcript* from 1842 to 1847, but she was an exception, and it would be 140 years before another Boston daily (the *Monitor*) had a woman, Mrs. Catherine Fanning, as editor. She had owned and edited her own newspaper in Alaska before being asked to take the job. William Randolph Hearst's founding of the *Boston American* in 1904 was a different, and persistent, problem for the other Boston newspapers. Hearst at that time never gave up any newspaper that he started, even if it was losing a lot of money. In that year, however, he was busy with his political ambitions: serving in Congress, running for mayor of New York City, and seeking the Democratic nomination for president. Not until later did he turn his attention to Boston. In 1917 he bought the *Advertiser* and took it out of Newspaper Row; in 1920, he bought the *Record.* These purchases gave him a morning, an evening, and a Sunday paper.

The *Post* and *Globe* were the only newspapers left in Newspaper Row as the *Post* entered its greatest decade. Hearst's first plant was on Summer Street, a quarter of a mile away from the Row; and his second plant, where he consolidated all his papers, was on Winthrop Square, even farther off. With his three papers, though, Hearst became a formidable competitor.

CHAPTER NINE

Murders Most Foul

Like the *Post*, the Hearst papers gave priority to murders. Hearst had not been in town a year when the *Post* gave his editors a lesson in yellow journalism and how to cover murder cases. The sensationalism of the Susan Geary murder, one of the *Post*'s reportorial triumphs of yellow journalism, may well have been a reason why Mrs. Eddy determined to give the public something better.

Violent crimes were always in the news. As circulation builders, few articles could surpass those about murder. Given its touch of mystery, a murder story would stay on the front page of the *Post* for months. If the victim were a woman—or better still, if the murderer were a woman—the story was deemed to have an even greater appeal as news. Whether or not a slain woman was beautiful in fact, she became beautiful in type. Age was not crucial, but youth could be a plus. On one occasion the *Post* confronted the age factor by running the headline "Seventy-two Year Old Girl Murdered in Woburn." Another sparkling headline read "Most Savage Gangland Killing in Recent Weeks." No matter that the gangland slaying was not, as gangland slayings go, all that savage and that there hadn't been another such slaying for months, if not years.

Murders were not only news, they were news that entertained. Grozier, knowing the appeal of Sherlock Holmes and other fictional detectives, knew as well that what worked on the library shelves would work on the newsstands. Joseph Pulitzer had shown the way in this regard as he had shown the way in others. Newspapers throughout the country found murders front-page news. There was something very democratic about it, too: The poorest prostitute got almost as much space as the society belle.

Publishers were always exploiting crimes. In its early years, the staid *Transcript* was criticized not only for once giving the entire paper over to a murder story but was also for giving too lurid a description of the 1849 hanging of Doctor John White Webster, a Harvard Medical School professor of chemistry, for the murder of Doctor George Parkman. The murder occurred before the days of the banner headline, but the *Transcript* put the story on page one, with a one-column headline that read "Supposed Discovery of Dr. Parkman's Body! Horrible Suspicions! Arrest of Prof. J. W. Webster." The trial and hanging were front-page news. The criticism of the *Transcript's* coverage centered on the description of Dr. Webster's body swaying at the end of the gallows' rope and mention of the "spasmodic drawing up of the legs."

A description even more lurid was prompted by the most historic murder case in Massachusetts and is contained in a four-line verse that, for many years, every school child seemed to learn outside class.

> Lizzie Borden took an axe
> And gave her mother forty whacks.
> When she saw what she had done
> She gave her father forty-one.

The verse is demonstrably inaccurate in at least one regard: It was Lizzie Andrew Borden's stepmother who was slain. How many times the murderer struck Andrew Jackson Borden or his second wife, Abby Durfee Gray Borden, however, could not be determined. One fact about the sensational case is demonstrable, too: The case gave the *Globe* a near mortal blow and opened the way for the *Post* to become the foremost newspaper for crime news in Boston and New England.

The Borden case, which began in October 1892, attracted national attention from the start, and all the Boston newspapers were giving it front-page priority. At the height of the case, a *Globe* staffer with the ironic name of Henry G. Trickey, who had made a name as a crime reporter, wrote an exclusive on the story. He had bought it from a private detective, Edwin D. McHenry, who had been hired by the Fall River, Massachusetts, police department to investigate the case. At the time, it was a common practice for small communities with few police and no detectives to hire a private detective on major cases. McHenry was trickier than Trickey. Trickey did not trust him and was afraid that he would two-time the *Globe* and sell the big scoop to some other paper.

Claiming he had had a police officer privately check the story given him by McHenry, Trickey persuaded the editors at the *Globe* to rush it into print.

On October 10, 1892, the *Globe's* headlines read:

LIZZIE HAD A SECRET
MR. BORDEN DISCOVERED IT
THEN A QUARREL
STARTLING TESTIMONY OF TWENTY-FIVE WITNESSES.

Column after column, page after page, the *Globe* detailed what was presumably the police case against Lizzie. Lizzie was said to be pregnant and her father to have ordered her to "name the man or leave this house by Saturday." The story appeared to be an incredible scoop. Monday evening the *Globe* printed it again in its entirety and boasted:

ALL NEW ENGLAND READ THE STORY
***GLOBES* WERE BOUGHT BY THE THOUSANDS**
LIZZIE BORDEN APPEARS IN NEW LIGHT
BELIEF IN HER INNOCENCE SADLY SHAKEN.

But that same evening, the headlines in the *Herald* read:

A $500 FAKE
ASSAULT ON MISS BORDEN'S HONOR IS PURELY A MYTH
STATEMENTS GIVEN AS EVIDENCE UNTRUE
PUBLIC SYMPATHY AROUSED FOR THE ACCUSED.

The *Globe's* story, supplied by Trickey, was all the more startling because until its appearance, all the pre-trial publicity had been most favorable toward Lizzie.The *Globe's* story came as a thunderbolt, and it is difficult today to imagine the excitement throughout New England at the *Globe's* dramatic revelation. The excitement intensified with the *Herald's* counterthrust. The *Globe* hung on for a while, clinging to its illusion. On October 11, its headlines read:

DETECTIVE MCHENRY TALKS
HE FURNISHED THE *GLOBE* WITH THE BORDEN STORY
IT HAS PROVEN WRONG IN SOME PARTICULARS
***GLOBE* SECURES BEST DETECTIVE TALENT AVAILABLE**
TO FIND MURDERER.

In the evening edition, the *Globe* capitulated entirely. On the front page in large type was an admission.

> The *Globe* is, first of all, an honest newspaper. To err is human—as newspapers have to be edited by men and not by angels, mistakes are inevitable.
> The *Globe* feels it a plain duty, as an honest newspaper, to state that it has been grievously misled in the Lizzie Borden case. It published on Monday a communication that it believed to be true evidence. Among all the impositions which newspapers have suffered, this was unparalleled in its astonishing completeness and irresistible plausibility. Judging from what we have heard, it impressed our readers as strongly as it did the *Globe*. Some of this remarkably ingenious and cunningly contrived story is undoubtedly based on facts, as later developments will show. The *Globe* believes, however, that much of it is false, and never should have been published.

The apology went on at twice that length. Henry G. Trickey was indicted on December 2 for interfering with the administration of justice by the same grand jury that indicted Lizzie for murder. He fled to Canada and on December 4 was killed in Toronto in a train accident. The episode no doubt played a part in increasing public sympathy for Lizzie, who was generally believed innocent, as persons of nice family "didn't do that sort of thing." Also, from that moment on, both the *Globe* and the *Herald* were favorable to her.

No woman had been executed in Massachusetts since 1778, when Bathsheba Spooner was hanged in Worcester for her part in the murder of her aged, cantankerous husband. As the late Judge Robert Sullivan points out in his book *Goodbye, Lizzie Borden*, there had always been, after the Spooner incident, a "great reluctance to convict a female defendant of a crime requiring the imposition of the death penalty." In Lizzie's case, the jury had two choices: to find her innocent or send her to the gallows. There was no finding of second-degree murder possible in her case. She was found not guilty more than likely because the jury didn't want to see her hanged, not because they believed in her innocence.

The effect of its blunder altered the *Globe's* attitude toward crime news. To whatever extent it had felt the allure of yellow journalism, it now eschewed it. This gave Grozier and the *Post* a free hand to "yellow" up the main staple of such journalism—murders—as we shall now see. On September 22, 1905, the *Post* carried an eight-column headline: "Mutilated Girl's Body in Dress Suit Case." "Headless and Limbless," the subhead cried. What must be remembered is that headlines running the entire eight columns of a newspaper's front page were an innovation of Joseph Pulitzer, and Grozier had learned the idea on the *World*. Before that, only one-column headlines, later called tombstones, were the rule of the day. Such modest headlines generally adorn stories in the *New York Times* today and, in 1905, were an absolute rule on the *Transcript*. When the *Post* was offering headlines running eight columns, the *Transcript* still used only one-column heads on the same story.

That headline in the *Boston Post* telling of the mutilated body was the beginning of a murder mystery that was to engross the public for three months. The story would provide the *Post* with the opportunity to bring off several of its great scoops (or beats or exclusives, as they are called now) and a chance to pat its own back as a public-service-oriented newspaper, not just a sensational journal.

Of the 192 column inches on the front page of the *Post* that day, all but sixteen were given over to the gruesome find. The other news stories, allotted a mere eight inches, dealt with a jail break, the tribulations of a failing insurance company, and an account of Dan Patch's breaking the world record for the mile. The remaining eight inches went for advertising pickles, pianos, and a business school. The runover from the lead story consumed all of page two as well, except for some cigarette and medical advertisements, the latter guaranteeing to cure cancer by "absorption," to extract teeth without pain, and to relieve without surgery all men who were ruptured or all persons with piles, fistulas, and God knows what else. In the meantime, coffee was selling at fifteen cents a pound.

The lead on the story was in the high tradition of journalistic flamboyance or yellow journalism.

> Winthrop, Sept. 21—Believed to be the victim of the foulest and most despicable crime in Massachusetts' criminal records, the victim of a surgeon's knife, either used in malpractise or by a scientific fiend who sought to acquire knowledge at the expense of life, the trunk of a well-formed and developed woman, with head, arms and legs gone, plainly cut away by a knife in the experienced hand of a surgeon, and completely disembowelled, disclosing the fact that the woman was about to become a mother, was found packed into a big leather suitcase found floating in the waters off the Winthrop Yacht Club pier at 5:30 tonight.

The editors of the newspaper would, of course, have preferred the work to be that of a scientific fiend, even though experience taught them that the torso was most likely the end result of an illegal and tragically concluded abortion.

The story continued with exquisite rhetoric.

> Not a single clue, not a single bit of cloth, not a single name or a single mark was on the case, nor could the new piece of white oil cloth in which the body was rolled help the police in the work of identification of the woman, nor in their pursuit of the perpetrator of the crime.

The age was one in which each gruesome detail was valued. Thus the story related how the torso, still in the suitcase, was packed in ice and left in the receiving tomb of the Winthrop Cemetery until the medical examiner could make a thorough examination the following morning. Eight separate small stories, or sidebars, were printed on the front page along with the lead story. One of them mused as to whether the crime was committed in Boston. The Winthrop police chief, W J. McNeil, was quoted as opining, "This is a more horrible crime than appears on the face of it." Another story gave a detailed description of the suitcase, another a description of the bloody torso, and still another revealed the medical examiner's intentions. A companion piece offered the opinion of the harbor pilot as to the spot whence the suitcase might have been heaved into the harbor waters.

Another story summarized the case.

> Two men on Winthrop Yacht Club float see a floating suit-
> case in the water about 5:30 o'clock, and small boys tow it
> ashore. Contents prove to be dismembered and eviscerated
> trunk of a woman less than 32 years of age. Police, State
> detectives and medical examiner at once called. Body and
> case taken to vault. Autopsy and inquest to determine if case
> is revolting murder or dismemberment to hide a crime will
> be held today.

On an inside page the *Post* presented a drawing of the suitcase and explained that it had to be held closed by a strap, since
the pathetic contents were so bulky the clasps could not be
locked. Club member Rudolph Pollard, who sighted the suitcase,
provided a brief first-person story of how it caught his eye. A
diagram of a female form showed in black the portion of the
anatomy enclosed in the suitcase and in gray the portions that
were missing. A paragraph reminded readers of the parallel between this case and a similar one of "years ago."

The next day the story again led the paper, and the *Post*
announced that "*Post* readers may aid justice in solving the Winthrop Mystery." The paper asked the readers to check the list of
missing women printed within and report if any they knew tied in
closely with the estimated description of the remains of the dead
woman. *Post* reporters were everywhere, questioning and quest-
ing. Frank M. Belcher, a railroad conductor, gave a false clue that
he had heard a man tell another, "I dropped it overboard," inti-
mating that the suitcase had been thrown from one of the cars of
the narrow-gauge railroad into the harbor. Belcher provided a
first-person story as to how this might have been done.

First-person stories on all occasions were a favorite practice of
the *Post*. Major and minor figures in any big story were asked a
series of questions and the replies put into a first-person account.
Such stories were usually dictated to an imaginative and literate
reporter who put them into suitable "journalese." The winner of
the Boston Marathon each year had his first-person story, usually
an exclusive, on the front page of the *Post*. Such stories were
deemed to give an exciting immediacy to the facts.

Belcher's clue was worse than worthless. It was quite wrong and got a Revere man, utterly without connection to the case, into hot water. The *Post's* Sunday edition of September 24 covered its eight columns with the headline "Police Have Winthrop Man Hours on Rack." The story, besides naming the wrong town, also helped besmirch the name of a young woman, missing from her home at the time, who for a few editions was believed by the *Post* to have been the victim. A note was uncovered hinting that she had gone off to have an abortion. But the next day the *Post* blithely announced, "Martha Halverston is Found Alive After Saturday Search."

The rhetoric now accorded the case was worthy of a world war or the landing of the first spaceship on Mars.

> The young man is suspected of the ownership of the suitcase, and by a series of brilliant and rapid detective work by Chief Inspector (William B.) Watts, the matter was put directly to the young man, who, by the way, was acquainted with Miss Halverston, the East Boston girl who is believed to have been the victim of the awful mutilation.

Anyone familiar with the reportorial techniques of that day will recognize that the brilliant and rapid detective work upon the part of Chief Inspector Watts was the result of *Post* reporters' egging him on to act on the false clues published in the *Post* in an early edition. The *Post* reported:

> It was three o'clock this morning when, as announced exclusively in an early edition of the *Post* this morning, Chief Watts and Inspector Armstrong arrived at Winthrop in a big automobile. They immediately went into conference with Chief McNeil. A half hour later Chief Watts fractured all speed laws in a wild dash to the Revere police station. [The automobile was new to police work and deserved special mention in any given story.]
> "There he called for a police officer. Inspector Stewart was aroused from bed and was soon whirled away with Chief Watts. Arriving at the station, they picked up McNeil and Armstrong and sped to the Prospect Street home. To allay suspicion, the automobile was left a block away. The officers quickly walked to the house and, after a parley, were admitted. The young man was visited in his bedroom, and then began the five-and-a-half-hour interrogation.

The unfortunate young man, who, of course, had not seen the midnight edition of the *Post*, had no idea that the police were about to descend on him. He was merely one of the victims of the fallout from the newspapers's explosive interest in the case, which was causing consternation in some quarters and panic in others. A doctor and his wife, who was also a doctor, disappeared from the West End of the city, and a woman named Margaret Norton but familiarly known as Mrs. Doctor Bell or Doc Temple was arrested for malpractice on a Marblehead, Massachusetts, woman. More than one of the women listed as "missing" were off seeking abortions, which were then illegal. Arrested along with Norton was the sweetheart of the Marblehead woman.

The *Post* was now determined to have the mystery solved and, better still, to be the one to solve it. Chief Watts no doubt was hoping that the *Post* would lose interest, which it might well have done if a better story came along, and leave him to pursue the investigation at his own pace. He had already lost one night's sleep questioning the Revere Lothario. But the *Post* was relentless and began to print a daily advertisement in a variety of juxtaposed type faces that read:

CAN YOU RECOGNIZE THIS SUITCASE
WHOSE PECULIARITY IS SHOWN IN TODAY'S POST?

Readers were then urged to telephone, write, or personally call on the city editor of the *Post* with all pertinent information.

In the meantime, bloodstained clothes were found along the yacht-club shoreline, along with gauze bandages and absorbent cotton in wrapping paper bearing the name of a Mrs. Burnham. Like the unfortunate Revere man, Mrs. Burnham was routed out of bed by reporters and detectives. She recognized the wrapping paper as some she had discarded behind her small Back Bay shop, and she would be in the news for some while before those materials proved to be irrelevant.

Then Grozier got a break. Joseph Berkman, proprietor of a pawnshop known as the Subway Loan Company, wrote a letter to the editor of the *Post*: "Dear Sir: By a picture in the *Post* I was able to postively identify the Winthrop dress suit case as one sold by me. The *Post* printed the most accurate description of any paper. Signed, Jos. Berkman."

Here indeed was a scoop. The letter, in Berkman's handwriting, was printed on page one. Beneath it was the daily summarization, which, except for one entry regarding the letter, had little or nothing to do with the case. Because of the letter, Mr. Berkman would be roused more than once in the middle of the night and rushed to study the physiognomies of suspects or to examine photographs. His distress, however, was slight compared with that of William A. Haynes. A clerk employed by a steamship company, Haynes was a graduate of a southern medical school but had never practiced medicine, at least legally. Some casual remarks of his were quoted by a friend, Samuel R. Wingfield, and overheard. Someone telephoned the *Post*, which sent reporters and detectives to Haynes's rooms, where he was arrested on suspicion of being an accomplice in the suitcase mystery. The *Post* boasted in an eight-column headline: "Arrest in Suitcase Tragedy Made on *Post*'s Evidence."

Haynes's friend Wingfield deserved closer scrutiny than either the *Post* reporters or the police gave him at the time. Had they done so, they would not have taken his remarks seriously. He was an optician by ambition who worked two nights a week as a waiter and days at S. S. Pierce, the famous Boston grocery firm, to keep himself alive. Four nights a week he received customers at his rooms in the role of an optician fitting glasses. He liked to call himself a doctor. He was also an alcoholic with a touch of St. Vitus dance and had a habit of leaving his rooms by the fire escape, an eccentricity for which he could not account. He described Haynes as his "most intimate friend." His testimony all around was worthless, and Haynes was quickly released.

Meanwhile, the *Post* told about its own ceaseless efforts.

> *Post* reporters, who have been covering the city for the last ten days, searching every nook and corner, working often times twenty-four hours without rest, seeking, always seeking some clue to the terrible tragedy, have neglected none of the notorious doctors in their rounds.
>
> There are few of them whose reputations are not unscathed who have not come under this ceaseless surveillance.
>
> For days past the case has hung where a word might mean its solution, a look even might convey a meaning, which would lead to the untangling of the bloody skein.

Several weeks of more false leads dragged by. Then, on October 27, more than a month after the suitcase had been found with its horrifying contents, another suitcase was found, this one pulled from the waters of the Charles River, on the edge of Boston Harbor. It contained a woman's severed arms and legs but no head. The *Post* was restrained in displaying this story on page one. It confined itself to a three-column head, with drawings of the three rings taken from the right hand.

The front page also informed readers that Teddy Roosevelt, then president, had had a brush with death in a shipwreck, that the local political pot was brewing, and that Philadelphia Jack O'Brien had knocked out Al Kaufman in the seventeenth round of a classic boxing match.

Inside the twelve-page paper, the *Post* went hog wild over this second gruesome find. Of the sixteen columns of two interior pages, all but two were given over to the new horror. The rings, greatly enlarged in the drawings, were presented again. A map showed where the suitcase had been sighted. A six-column drawing depicted Edward Fraser, a deckhand on a lighter (a bargelike vessel), catching it up with a boathook, with Engineer Thomas A. Madden standing by. Another drawing showed the placement of the rings on the right hand, while a photograph showed nine members of the harbor police posed in a line, with the suitcase on the pier before them. Diagrams showed the location of the lighter and the proximity of the second discovery to the first, a sweep from the Winthrop Yacht Club to the Charlestown bridge. A doctored photograph presented a facsimile of the rubber sheeting in which the detached limbs were wrapped.

The next morning the paper carried an exclusive on its front page: a large photograph of the victim, whose arms and legs had been found in one suitcase and whose torso had been found in another. She was Miss Susan Geary of Cambridge, known in the theater world as Ethel Durrell. This was the major scoop of the year, not the sort they give Pulitzer Prizes for, but the sort that catches readers. That day the case consumed all the front page of the *Post* save for a two-column, eight-inch whiskey advertisement, a one-inch weather report, and another small advertisement for a cough medicine. The headline again ran the full eight columns: "Mother Says Susan Geary of Cambridge Is Winthrop Suit Case Mystery Victim." Suitable subheads galore draped down from the leader.

Then came the lead story:

> Ethel Durrell, in stage parlance, of the Shepherd King
> Company, Susan Geary in plain life, was the Winthrop Suit
> Case victim, according to her mother, Mrs. Catherine Geary
> of 685 Main Street, Cambridge, who late last night told the
> *Post* that the rings found on the arms in the second suitcase
> were her daughter's.
>
> Miss Durrell's sweetheart, Morris Nathan, manager of the
> theatrical company, in Pittsburgh last night told the *Post*
> what he knew of the case.
>
> The bereaved mother's and the sweetheart's statements
> follow.
>
> The State police are now working on the evidence given to
> them last night by the *Post*. State Detective S. P. Smith is in
> direct charge of the evidence and he hopes today to go far
> toward clearing up the entire mystery.

Beneath this lead in 24-point type was the inevitable first-
person story by Mrs. Catherine Geary. On the opposite side of the
page was a two-column story, the interview with Morris Nathan,
Susan's boy friend. He told of their engagement and Mrs. Geary's
blessing on it despite religious differences.

What happened in the *Post* on October 30 must be unmatched in the annals of journalism. First of all, the paper told its
readers that on the previous day, a Sunday, it had sold 200,200
copies, a record for the *Post* and the city. The Suit Case Mystery
was indeed a circulation builder. Evidently the people of Greater
Boston and New England could not get enough detail.

That Monday, the *Post* did its best to provide it. Beneath an
eight-column headline, six columns of the front page were given
over to the Susan Geary story. The headline reported: "Mrs.
Geary Faints Identifying Winthrop Suit Case Victim as Her Daughter." A subheadline under that told of the arrest of Morris Nathan
in Pittsburgh. His picture and a new picture of Susan adorned the
front page. Inside, the *Post* provided a four-page circus. In brief,
almost half of the twelve pages the paper published that day were
given over to the case.

The *Post* had brought the world the identification of the suitcase victim! To prove that it had scooped the town, the *Post* repro-
duced on page four the front pages of the October 29 issues of the
Sunday Herald, the *Sunday Globe*, and Hearst's *Sunday Ameri-*

can. Above those facsimiles was the story on "How the *Post* 'Beat the Town' in Suit Case Mystery."

While the Post headline read "Mother Says Ethel Durrell Is Winthrop Suit Case Victim," the *Globe's* read that nobody tried to identify the rings, the *Herald* said the police were dragging for the head, and the *American* read that the mystery was near solution and that it was expected that the rings would lead to the victim's identification. Because Mrs. Catherine Geary was a *Post* reader, however, "The Post Had It Alone"—always a proud boast for a newspaper.

On the inside pages the paper presented more pictures of Susan Geary, a very pretty girl: one of her dancing, another with the troupe of actresses in the Shepherd King Company, still another in the pose favored by her mother. Her life story was recounted. Her sister's picture was run, as was yet another picture of the waterfront where the arms and legs were found. In one story, the father of the benighted Nathan was being grilled by the police; in another, he was prostrate with grief. *Post* readers were told in detail how the mother and sisters of Susan identified the rings. The paper also reprinted Susan's last letter to her mother, signed with her stage name, Ethel, and presented it in facsimile. In yet another story, another doctor was routed out of bed in the night to see if he was the man who bought the suitcases. He was not. Friends of Susan were questioned, and the search for the doctor went on. Even the recitation of these items becomes tedious, but *Post* readers couldn't get enough of it.

On November 1, the *Post* wrote almost laconically, "The Winthrop suit case mystery, solved in the essentials by the *Post*, will, in all probability, be totally cleared up within 48 hours, when the police expect to have completed their chain of evidence around a Boston doctor whose name was furnished to the authorities by the *Post* several days ago, along with those of his wife and another doctor, all of whom will be accused as accessories before and after the fact."

Meanwhile, a *Post* reporter had gone to Pittsburgh to accompany Morris Nathan and police back to Boston. The man's confession would lead to more arrests.

With information provided in part by Nathan and the *Post*, two men were arrested in New York and soon after confessed to having thrown the suitcases from the East Boston ferry into Boston Harbor. One of them was Louis M. Crawford, the son-in-law of

Jane Bishop, to whom Nathan had appealed for assistance. Crawford in turn had solicited a friend, William Hunter, to help dispose of the suitcases, paying him or promising to pay him one hundred dollars. When the first suitcase was found, the two men slipped town, went to New York, and sought rooms under assumed names. *Post* reporters suggested to their superiors that the New York police be tipped off to watch theatrical-employment agencies. The tip worked.

The *Post's* biggest scoop in the Suit Case Mystery was, of course, the story announcing the identification of the torso and limbs in the suitcase. Throughout the case, the *Post* was ahead of its rivals. The misinformation that the *Post* printed and had to retract was also exclusive, of course. The major stories, however, made readers forget the foul balls. It's the home run that counts. The rival papers took consolation in their failure to print the names of William A. Haynes, Martha Halverston, and Samuel R. Wingfield.

The rival papers, however, observed the *Post's* mounting circulation figures with chagrin. In November, the Susan Geary story was still on page one and would not leave the front page until the *Post* scored one more "beat," this one of a unique nature.

Grozier was told that the culprits in the case might not be brought to justice unless the victim's head were found. His reporters badgered Chief Watts to engage a diver and scour the bottom of the harbor. Chief Watts, although more grateful than resentful at the *Post's* intrusion into his life, was reluctant to put the city to the expense of a diver. Grozier decided to hire his own, whatever the police did. This course was urged on him by Clifton B. Carberry, his youthful managing editor. Always a crafty newspaperman, Carberry did not want the same diver the Boston police had hired in the past, lest the news of whatever was found get to the police before it got to the paper.

At any major metropolitan newspaper in those days, newspapermen being, more so then than now, the individualists and eccentrics that they are, there was no field of human activity on which some reporter could not throw light or in which one or another failed to have a connection. Carberry turned to his staff. In the field of aquatics, Ernest "Deacon" Jackson proved to be the right man. Carberry remembered that Jackson had once helped solve a murder upcountry by getting into his swimsuit and doing some diving himself. While the word moonlighting wasn't in use in 1905 for the work a man might do outside his trade to supplement his income, most reporters had one sideline or another: writing publicity, advising politicians, handling small advertising accounts, writing speeches, or teaching English or journalism or shorthand at one place or another. One *Post* reporter was said to have been the judge in the kangaroo courts of the underworld; several others were members of the bar and practiced law quite legitimately. Still another taught dancing.

Deacon Jackson's sideline was different still: He had a troupe of women divers in the midway at Revere Beach. All were well-formed young ladies who stood in their bathrobes outside their aquacade while Deacon gave his spiel, emphasizing the athletic prowess of his charges while hinting lubriciously at what lay concealed beneath the bathrobes. If the Deacon had done some diving himself and had a troupe of women divers, he should undoubtedly know a professional diver.

Deacon produced Fred Wallace, who in turn produced Captain W. D. Duncan. Fred, a professional diver, worked for Duncan, whose general business it was to clear wrecks from Boston Harbor and contract for underwater-demolition work. Duncan signed a contract with the *Post* for his boat and equipment and Wallace to search the ferry slip where Hunter confessed he had thrown the head of Susan Geary in her own Gladstone bag, weighted with shot, into forty feet of water. Duncan also submitted a plan of procedure, whereby Wallace would cover the area where Carberry now believed the bagged head would lie. Duncan and Wallace knew that the water near the ferry slip would be so murky that Wallace would more than likely have to feel his way along. Visibility would be nil. For Wallace it was a unique assignment but not that different from jobs he had done before.

The search began at 6:30 A.M. on November 5. Police boats were already dragging in the same area, but Carberry was confident that a diver would have a better chance. Both crews were working from the information provided by Hunter and Crawford. By late morning a crowd of 1,000 persons had gathered to watch the operation, among them newsmen from all the Boston papers and half a dozen more publications from outside the city and the state.

To facilitate Wallace's work, Duncan weighted the ends of several 100-foot lengths of rope and dropped them into the water. When Wallace reached bottom, he felt his way along the ropes to keep track of the ground that he covered. At first, he poked around with a stick as he went. Finally, he decided he would have to crawl on his hands and knees if he were to find anything. It was tedious work, but after several hours and several returns to the surface to rest, he was rewarded. His head bumped into the Gladstone bag.

Carberry had instructed him on what he was to do in the event he did find the head in the bag. Wallace tied the bag to the bottom rung of the ladder on the stern of Duncan's boat. He then surfaced. He had difficulty disguising his excitement as he reported to Duncan that he had found the head. The crowd was simply told that the search was over for the day, and, while the police boat continued to drag, Duncan moved his boat slowly to Constitution Wharf some hundreds of yards away across the harbor. The newspapermen left the pier when the police quit. The *Post* was telephoned, and Carberry had on his hands the biggest scoop of the case. Grozier decided to do the noble thing. He gave the information to the police and so to all the opposition papers.

The next day, however, the *Post* was careful to take full credit for the work: "Missing Head Found By the *Post's* Diver." Beneath the headline was a picture of the bag. Beneath that was a four-column lead story.

> Divers employed by the Editor of the Post recovered the missing head of Susan . . . Geary from the bottom of Boston Harbor.
>
> By direction of Mr. E. A. Grozier, Editor of the Post, full information of the gruesome discovery was immediately placed in the hands of the police on the ground that the furtherance of the demands of justice was of vastly more importance than a great newspaper exclusive.

Then came a story on "How the *Post* Recovered the Missing Head." The story absorbed half the front page and three full pages inside, or nearly one-third of the twelve-page paper. On one of the inside pages was a facsimile of a typewritten letter from William H. Pierce, superintendent of police, to Mr. Grozier, thanking him "for your latest invaluable aid to me in the finding, by the *Post* diver, of the head of Susan Geary . . . . Through the *Post's* instrumentality, the body of the dead girl is now complete. This finishes and makes possible the legal identification of the chorus girl victim of the 'Suit Case Mystery' so called, as reported alone by you in your paper a week ago."

The lead story dealt predominantly with the difficulties encountered by Wallace in combing the harbor bottom. The remainder of it was given over to the condition of the Gladstone bag and to Superintendent Pierce's thanking the *Post* for its "invaluable service" and remarking on it as "a powerful ally of the police." The superintendent closed with the remark, "I am glad this ordeal is over."

Some of the *Post*'s readers also must have been glad it was over if they reflected on the florid coverage given the crime by the paper. But the majority of readers were evidently howling for more. Pictures were thus provided of Jane Bishop, Louis M. Crawford in a bowler hat, and his colleague Hunter, alias Howard, who turned out to be "the mysterious Dr. Roberts wanted in Philadelphia . . . for complicity in the death of a Miss Maud Gilpin, a choir singer."

A picture was also presented of Mrs. Mary Dean, who had begun the ill-starred abortion at her home in Roxbury. Doctor Percy McLeod, the physician called in to repair the damage done by Mrs. Dean, fled the state. Crawford and Hunter went to jail. Mrs. Dean skipped town. Doctor McLeod was cleared by the jury. At the end, the court case had receded to the back pages under the goiter ads. In 1936, the *Boston American* recounted the story in 10,000 words without ever mentioning its rival, the *Post*, which still had the largest circulation in Boston. Such are the inimical techniques of journalism.

CHAPTER TEN

☆☆☆☆

Murder and the Minister

Murders were less frequent before World War I than they are today. Handguns were less common, and the "Saturday-night special" was not on the market. Murders, however, occurred with sufficient regularity to keep the front page of the *Post* lively. Nevertheless, not until 1911 did Boston have a murder to rival in public interest the Susan Geary case and have the *Post* again play a key role in the solution of the crime.

The Clarence V. T. Richeson case had the story-book ingredients of a minister's illicit romance with a choir singer, his wealthy debutante fiancée left at the altar, so to speak, and a poisoned corpse. Oswald Garrison Villard was one of a small minority in thinking that there was no place in newspapers for entertainment; one of the objects of yellow journalism was to make the news entertaining.

Clarence V. T. Richeson was a Virginian who, in 1906, came to study at the Newton Theological Seminary. One of its trustees, Moses G. Edmands, had a fashionable home in Brookline and a beautiful daughter, Violet. In September of that year, Mr. Richeson visited the home and met Violet. Two years later, while still a student, he was called to the pulpit of the Baptist Church of Hyannis, then more a fishing village than the crowded summer resort it is today.

In June 1908, Richeson met Avis Linnell, a choir singer still in her teens, when he presided at the marriage of her sister to William McLean of Brockton. A romance grew between the divinity student and his parishioner, and on December 17, her seventeenth birthday, he gave her a plain gold ring, which was understood to be an engagement ring. The following June, he was graduated from the theological school, ordained, and continued to serve the Hyannis church and another in neighboring Yarmouth.

He was a vigorous preacher, and his rousing sermons, marked as they were by the exuberance of youth, annoyed the good people of Hyannis. Their resentment contributed in part to his resignation in April 1910. The next month, he was called to the pulpit of the Immanuel Baptist Church in Cambridge, and on June 1, 1910, he began to serve there. He went to Brockton to visit Avis at the home of her sister, Mrs. McLean, in August. Complaining of a malaise, he asked Avis to fetch him a glass of water. When she returned with it, he was gone. He had said at the time that on occasion he suffered from amnesia, and this seemed to authenticate the claim.

Avis and he had planned to marry in October 1910, and the month before that, following suggestions he made earlier, she came to Boston, took a room at the Y.W.C.A. on Warrenton Street and enrolled at the New England Conservatory of Music. On March 13, 1911, the newspaper in Hyannis, the *Barnstable Patriot*, carried a story announcing the engagement of the Rev. Clarence V. T. Richeson to Violet Edmands. The news came as a shock to everyone in Hyannis excepting Avis Linnell's mother, who earlier had received a letter from her daughter in Boston stating that she had broken off her engagement to Richeson at his request. The events of Richeson's life immediately subsequent to these were never quite sorted out by the newspapers or the courts. He evidently had one of his nervous attacks, begged off from evening services, and got a substitute clergyman. He then moved into the home of a friend but spent a good deal of that summer at the Edmands summer house in Dublin, New Hampshire, although he continued to visit Miss Linnell in Hyannis.

That September she returned to Boston for her second term at the conservatory and took a room again at the Y.W.C.A. There on October 14, 1911, in the early evening, Avis Linnell was found dying in the bathroom near her room, partly undressed and with her feet in a tub of hot water. Fellow residents hearing her groans broke open the door. She was found slumped in a chair, the water still hot in the tub. It was evident she was dying. Medical attention was summoned but was of no avail, and the woman was pronounced dead. The medical examiner, one Doctor Timothy Leary, soon determined that Miss Linnell had died from an ingestion of cyanide of potassium. She was believed to have been a suicide and was so recorded in the police records. It was then that the *Post* got hot on the story.

Police investigating the case learned that two days before she was found dead, she had been called to the telephone at the Y.W.C.A. and had a long talk with—she told her companions—her "gentleman friend," as she referred to Richeson.

On October 14 she met him, and they walked together in the Fenway (a park on the city's southwest side) on the banks of Muddy River, quite near the conservatory where she was studying. It was then, the *Post* assumed, he gave her the "medicine" to take to abort the child he had fathered. On October 20, 1911, at 7:00 A.M., Reverend Richeson was arrested in the Brookline home of the Edmands and charged with murder. Four hours later he pleaded not guilty to first-degree murder and was held without bail.

He might have escaped justice entirely if it had not been for the *Post*'s tenacious investigating. This role of the paper actually arose from a newspaper practice that had its roots with Lord Northcliff in England. He was convinced that there was usually one story that dominated the public mind and that a paper could not print too much about it. With this conviction and his *Evening News*, Northcliff became England's foremost publisher. Pulitzer was motivated by this principle, too, and developed what was known as "the wrecking crew."

Once Pulitzer decided which story was dominant or was going to be a potential circulation builder, every man in the office within reason was assigned to all aspects of the story. Grozier adopted the same technique. When police learned of the connection between Reverend Richeson, the fiancé of a wealthy Brookline woman, and the tragic soprano dead in the Y.W.C.A., he was the obvious suspect in her murder.

Only the *Post*'s stubborn insistence that the woman's death was not a suicide but a murder led to the solution of the mystery. This was not due to any particular newspaper practice of the *Post* but to the ongoing conviction of all editors at that time that a murder was better copy than a suicide and that no suicide should be declared without being examined closely for evidence of foul play.

The *Post* pushed the theory of murder with the medical examiner and with the police. Pressed by a newspaper, and presented with a cogent explanation of the facts and some probable deductions, the police will not shirk their duty. So the search began for evidence. The key clue was seen to be the origin of the poison. Whether or not the police were pursuing all possible leads is a question. They were moving around, but it was a member of the *Post*'s wrecking crew, Walter "Dutch" Mahan, who came up with the vital information.

Post reporters were sent throughout Massachusetts to find out, if possible, whether Reverend Richeson had bought cyanide of potassium and, if so, where. Or had Avis Linnell bought it herself? Hundreds of police had been alerted to the quest in Boston and in surrounding towns.

Post reporters had an advantage over the police in the search because each reporter was armed with photographs of Richeson and Linnell. Mahan, a veteran staffer, doggedly going from one pharmacy to another, turned up the salient information. He found a druggist in Newton who recognized a photograph of Richeson and identified him as the man to whom he had sold cyanide of potassium. He had told the druggist he wanted "to kill a dog that had pups."

Unlike its boasting in the Susan Geary case, however, the *Post* made no public claim of credit this time; instead, it traded with the authorities for favored treatment that kept the paper one jump ahead of its rivals for a while. The reason for this restraint was that yellow journalism was already on the wane. Frank Luther Mott, a leading authority on newspaper publishing, cites the year 1914 as the end of the yellow-journalism period. The modification and moderation of news presentation and news writing can be observed in the contrasting coverages of the Geary case and the Richeson case. Although the *Post* was generally ahead of the other papers in the city with the facts in the latter case, no boasts were published and no contrasts made between the *Post*'s pages and those of the opposition. The "journalese" had moderated somewhat, too, although not all that much. The headlines still screamed in large type, and an excessive amount of space was given over to the story and its details of prison scenes. In the space of five years, however, the circus had become somewhat more circumspect.

On December 11, 1911, the *Post* ran a lengthy summary of the case, describing Richeson as thirty years of age, an Apollo and a Virginian with the voice of a well-trained actor. "In the month of roses," the *Post* rhapsodized, the couple met as he preached "words of truth and love." She was then sixteen. He suggested voice lessons, and he persuaded her to go to Boston to study. A rift came after an announcement was published of his engagement to Violet Edmands of Brookline and a date was set for their wedding, which was to be a "society affair." He denied the story to Avis's mother. Then wedding invitations went out. Just eleven days before the wedding date, however, Richeson was arrested in the Edmands home and charged with the murder of Avis.

The *Post* then recounted how the death of Avis had been first listed as a suicide. The paper also related a telephone call that was highly significant.

No sooner had Avis Linnell been pronounced dead than Miss Ines Hanscomb, connected with the Y.W.C.A., called a drugstore near Mr. Richeson's boarding house in Cambridge. This was at 9 o'clock Saturday evening. After a time Mr. Richeson came to the phone and was told that Avis was dead.

When Miss Hanscomb began talking with Richeson, she said, "This is Miss Hanscomb of the Y.W.C.A., Boston. I called to inform you that Miss Linnell has died here and that we want you to come immediately so that you may arrive by the time the medical examiner gets here."

"Miss Linnell is dead? Why did you call me?" replied a voice.

"Because you are the only friend of the girl near at hand."

To this the voice replied: "I remember that I baptized Miss Linnell at Hyannis three years ago. I know her folks at Hyannis, where I used to preach but I do not know why I should be called in regard to this matter."

Miss Hanscomb said in reply, "We felt that, since you are her fiancé and that as she was out to lunch with you during the day, it is right that we should notify you."

In an almost indistinct tone the voice came over the phone from the man: "Did she say anything before she died?"

Taken by surprise, although treating it lightly at the time, the young attendant at the home said, "No."

This ended the conversation. It should be remembered, though, that this took place two hours after the death of the girl and before the arrival of the medical examiner. When he came, he ordered the body removed to the City Hospital morgue, where he said he would perform the autopsy later.

William McLean, brother-in-law to Avis, came to Boston as a family representative but refused to accept the examiner's finding of suicide. Undoubtedly, he had been urged to do so by those *Post* reporters who told him of the callous attitude of Richeson during the telephone call. The autopsy had shown the girl to be pregnant. The medical examiner pushed on with his investigation. There was, of course, only one suspect. The search was then on to find who had bought cyanide, Avis or Clarence. In its summation, the *Post* did not credit Walter Mahan with finding the pharmacist who sold Richeson the poison. It settled for using this information to give itself an inside track with the authorities, who were, of course, grateful for such help.

Some concern for libel made the *Post* refrain from saying that Miss Linnell was pregnant and also made the paper underplay the contretemps at the Edmands home when the police first tried to enter. (The family had barred the doors and pulled the telephone out of the wall so that they could not be called.) Knowing Richeson was inside, however, the police had the home surrounded. When they finally gained admittance, police arrested Richeson without incident. The next day, he was arraigned and held without bail.

The newspapers hardly knew what to do with Richeson's so-called suicide. On December 20 at about 4:00 A.M. in the Charles Street Jail, where he had been removed, Richeson attempted to castrate himself with a tin cover from a can of marmalade, which he had sharpened against the wall of his cell. He had reread the Gospel text in Matthew 19:12, which talks about eunuchs and some men making themselves such for "the kingdom of God." He may have also reread the text offering the admonition, "if thy eye offend thee, pluck it out." The *Post*, which managed to descend to all sorts of vulgarity in the Susan Geary murder case, found itself at a verbal loss in dealing with Richeson and could only refer to "the prisoner's peculiar wound inflicted with a crude, jagged cutting instrument fashioned from tin . . ." A three-column drawing illustrated how one section of the can cover was bent down, enabling Richeson to hold it in order to mutilate himself. His attorney promptly announced that the defense would be insanity. An eight-column headline read, "Guard Richeson to Prevent Another Attempt to Die."

That day one-quarter of the paper, four full pages (excepting advertisements), was given over to the Richeson case. The opinions of psychiatrists, then called alienists, were solicited. Clergymen were asked for their opinions. One story dealt with the details of his arrest, his arrival at the Charles Street Jail, and the visit of his father and concluded with his remaining unmoved despite hymn singing by a visiting troupe of Salvation Army.

The *Post* reported:

> Another Sabbath service was held. On this occasion it was conducted by the Salvation Army. Old familiar hymns were sung and the gospel of life preached. Throughout the service Richeson sat unmoved and huddled over the edge of his cot. Nothing in the service stirred him. As the army captain prayed, he did not change his position. As the lassies sang "Where is My Wandering Boy Tonight?" and "There Is a Fountain Filled with Blood," two selections that had been his favorites, he remained unmoved. When the little band had left the jail house, Richeson still huddled over the edge of his cot.

Neither hymn would appear designed to cheer up an imprisoned man. Richeson's mood, however, changed the next day. The *Post* told its readers that he was singing hymns at the top of his lungs, reciting passages from the Gospels, and talking so loud the other prisoners complained to the guards. Richeson told them he was "suffering from an ingrowing nail which . . . caused sleeplessness."

"Within the last few days," the *Post* reported, "he was given absorbent cotton, a roll of bandage, and material for the treatment of the nail. He saved the cotton and the bandage until . . . he used them in the mutilation [the already mentioned castration] of himself." His picture adorned the front page that morning, a studio portrait in which he did seem "of the Apollo type of mankind."

The *Post* reported on December 22 that, when Richeson was carried from his cell after his self-mutilation, a Bible was found open to Matthew 19:12, the passage that talks of eunuchs self-made for the Kingdom of God. The passage is generally believed to refer to celibacy rather than castration. Whether or not the Bible was opened in his cell to that particular chapter and verse, the information certainly left no doubt in the minds of the *Post's* readers just what Mr. Richeson had been up to.

In a touch of black humor—while the unfortunate man was still in the death house awaiting execution—the baggy-pants comedians at the Old Howard, Boston's celebrated burlesque house, rolled two bowling balls across the stage at the mention of Richeson's name in a vulgar routine.

The next day, December 23, the Richeson case was driven off the front page of the *Post* because two women were found murdered in the city, one in an abortion clinic in Forest Hills, the other in front of her Hyde Park home, stabbed to death—evidently by a total stranger, as she had been in this country only six months.

So, for about five months, while Richeson waited in his cell at Charles Street Jail, news about him was confined to the inside pages of the paper, excepting for his confession. He made the confession in January 1912 and repudiated it when he was condemned to death, saying that he had made it on the advice of his attorneys, who thought it would save him from the electric chair. He was never tried but executed on his own confession, a juridical occurrence practically impossible today.

The insanity plea failed. Alienists agreed that he was abnormal and subject to seizures that read like epilepsy, but they declared that he knew the difference between right and wrong. It was the findings of the alienists in May 1912 that brought Richeson back on page one day in and day out until he died.

On May 17, the *Post* headline read: "Richeson Declared Sane; Foss Says He Must Die." The day before that, the headline had read: "Richeson Would Convert Convicts." The subhead declared: "Tells Sheriff He Would Be 'Living Example' and an Effective Teacher—Told Alienists He Did Not Intend to Kill Girl." The story was accompanied by a drawing of the death house at Charlestown State Prison, the location of Richeson's cell, with him in it and two guards seated outside.

Inside, a full page was given over to the case. The sheriff told how Richeson had a horror of death, showed no signs of insanity or moral degeneracy, and always acted in a way "that suggested southern gentlemen." Another sidebar spoke of his stoicism in the face of death. The lead story gave an hour-by-hour description of his daily activities in the jail.

On May 18, the headline took up six columns of the front page: "Richeson Shrieks Like A Madman in His Cell." The subheads were extensive: "Condemned Man's Screams Arouse Prison—Doctor Called, Finds Prisoner Raving Madly—Guards Find it Difficult to Control Him—Later Becomes Unconscious"; "Collapse Came after Lawyer's Visit—Terror Causes Richeson to Ask Clergymen to Stay With Him Night and Day"; "Richeson Denies Confession—Says Avis Congratulated Miss Edmands on Engagement—Feels Himself a Martyr."

The front page of the paper bore a large three-column box running up half the page under the lead story and announcing that the *Sunday Post* would present exclusively on the next day "The First Photos of the South Pole, Just Received from Captain Amundsen from Hobart, Tasmania." In small type at the bottom of the advertisement was the message, "It will be recalled that the *Boston Post* was the first New England paper to print the Photos of the North Pole Expedition."

On May 20, Monday, the *Post* headline read: "Richeson Dies Tuesday, Preaches Last Sermon." One subhead read: "Conducts Complete Service in Death House—Wanted to Preach to Prisoners but Warden Could Not Allow It—" The two-column lead on the story was the Twenty-third Psalm of David, which Richeson had chosen as the text for his homily. The story described a death-cell scene rivalling that of Socrates.

> In the death cell at Charlestown State Prison, the condemned man, propped on his couch, with trembling voice, read from the Bible and drew a lesson of life from the verses he had carefully chosen.
>
> "The Lord is my shepherd, I shall not want," was the text Richeson had selected from the 23rd Psalm.
>
> It was a strange, even weird scene, that was enacted there in the gloom of the death house. Within the cell, his left hand holding the Bible, and with his right gesticulating feebly, sat the man who is soon to meet his Maker. Outside, drawn in a small semi-circle, interested spectators of the unusual ceremony were the two prison guards, the Rev. Dr. Herbert S. Johnson, who is Richeson's spiritual advisor, and the Rev. Herbert H. Stebbins, the prison chaplain.

The *Post* of May 21, 1912, was, at eighteen pages, average in size for the time. Approximately four of these pages were given over to the electrocution of the Reverend Clarence V. T. Richeson. The four-column front-page headline read: "Richeson Went to His Death Singing." The subheads went on to recount: "Electrocuted at 12:10 This Morning," "Only Given One Shock," "The Rev. Mr. Johnson With Him," "Smiled Bravely When Warden Came To Lead Him From His Cell to Chair," "'I Am Willing to Die,' Are Last Words as Warden Raises Cane for the End," "Passed Quiet Day Reading Bible," "Body Will Be Sent to Old Home in the South."

The lead story, two columns wide, read:

> Clarence V. T. Richeson expiated the murder of Avis Lin-
> nell in the electric chair at the Charlestown State Prison at
> 12:13:02 o'clock this morning.
> He went to his death singing, unflinching, brave to the end.
> He left the death cell and entered the electrocution chamber
> at 12:08 A.M.
> The current was turned on at 12:10:02 with 1,900 volts of 8
> amperes and left on for 1 minute and 8 seconds.
> He was declared legally dead at 12:17 o'clock.

This clinical approach, which measures in a way the development into a more restrained prose as yellow journalism waned,
was soon abandoned for the flamboyant, imaginative style.

> Warden Bridges called upon him at 12:06 to start for the
> death chamber. He arose, and to the wonderment of all as-
> sembled in the grim chamber just beyond his cell, the sound
> of singing was heard.
> With his head erect the condemned man walked before
> the two clergymen . . . singing in a loud voice, "For I know
> whate'er befalls, Jesus doeth all things well."
> As he entered the cell, the last word of the song died in his
> throat and in one flash his roving eyes took in their first
> glance of the instrument of death and those assembled to see
> him die. He did not flinch. He walked to the chair unassisted
> and sat down. While the guards were adjusting the straps on
> his legs and the leather cap on his shaven head, Dr. Herbert
> Johnson began to talk with him:
> "Would you like to confess Christ as your saviour before
> these witnesses?"
> "I do confess Christ my saviour," replied Richeson, moving
> slightly to aid the guards in their work.
> "Does Christ give you the strength you need in this hour?"
> "Christ does give me the strength I need in this hour,"
> came the answer, the voice trembling but slightly at the last
> word.
> "Do you repent of your sin?"
> "I do," in a strong voice.
> "Do you forgive everybody?"
> "God will take care of my soul and I pray for all," replied
> Richeson, his voice weaker.

"Are you willing to die for Jesus' sake?" asked the Rev. Mr. Johnson, his own voice hoarse.

"I am willing to die," were Richeson's last words. Richeson's body leaped into the straps almost as his last word left his lips. For one minute and eight seconds the current was, at first, 1,900 volts of eight amperes to as low as a few hundred, and then back again to 1,900.

But two shocks were administered, and at 12:17 o'clock—a trifle less than seven minutes after the switch was first thrown—the two doctors stepped to his side, opened his collar and shirt, and pronounced him dead.

The witnesses sat as though carved of stone when the two doctors stood back from the lifeless body and nodded to each other and then to the warden.

"He is dead," they said.

The *Post*'s stories went on for column after column. The next day, the paper went looking for more excitement.

The day of Richeson's execution, a two-column box at the bottom of the page told an interesting story:

Boston Post	128,291
Boston Globe	100,307
Boston Herald	62,267

These were not circulation figures. The *Post* had taken the lead in circulation sometime between the Susan Geary murder case and the Richeson case. The figures printed that day were for display-advertising lineage, at that time the most desirable. Grozier had learned well what Pulitzer had taught him: Profits follow circulation.

CHAPTER ELEVEN

Newton Newkirk: Genius

For the first three decades of the twentieth century, some columnists had tremendous readerships without even being syndicated. Because they were regional, these readerships were intensely loyal as well. No other columnist in the history of Boston, however, had the appeal of Cyrus C. Newkirk, who, under the byline Newton Newkirk, conducted the *Post*'s "All Sorts" column for thirty-three years (1901 to 1934) until his death in an asylum. He was an extraordinarily funny man and, like so many humorists, went about with a lugubrious face. His daily column was deemed the first such in the country, rivaled in that claim only by Eugene Field's "Sharps and Flats" in Chicago. The *Post* had a predecessor to "All Sorts" called "Bon Bons" by B. J. Shillinger, but its readership was minute compared with Newkirk's, and its appearance was irregular.

No other columnist of this period had such a grip on so large an audience in the New England area. He was a major contributor to the *Post*'s rapid rise in reader reception, and Grozier remained grateful even after Newkirk had a real challenger in Kenneth Roberts, who worked at the *Post* from 1909 through 1917.

Newkirk's imaginative inventiveness was boundless; the extent of his production, awe-inspiring. Besides writing a column six days a week for the paper, he put together an entire page of humor for the Sunday paper, writing it practically all by himself and illustrating it as well. On top of that, he edited the *National Sportsman* for a good many years; it was a monthly magazine devoted to rod and reel, dog and gun. He also appeared regularly on the lecture platform. There as elsewhere his imagination ran riot. One of his zany constructs was the Post-Hole Company, which sold postholes by mail and involved some of the daffiest correspondence ever to grace the pages of a newspaper. His inventiveness seemed inexhaustible.

His achievement was done in the days before radio and television, in an age more leisurely than ours, when the average newspaper reader had a good deal more time, was undistracted by electronics, and expected a large number of words on the page. Newkirk obliged. Humor, by nature, is likely to be evanescent and thins quickly with the passage of the years. Yet in 1957, when the *Boston Globe* carried a series of stories entitled "The Best of the *Boston Post*," it included a sample chapter of one of Newkirk's celebrated series, the one involving his indomitable Stealthy Steve, the Six-Eyed Sleuth. A generation had passed since Stealthy Steve had disappeared from the pages of the *Post*, and even the paper itself had disappeared. The presentation of the first chapter, somewhat shortened from the prolixity so admired in the pre-radio days, brought a storm of letters to the *Globe* asking that the entire Stealthy Steve story be run. It was one of a score Newkirk had written over the years for the *Post*. Many of his humorous figures of speech have become old hat or even cliches but were startlingly fresh with him. This sketch is worth reprinting if only for the reason that, in it, Newkirk fired the first Polaris missile ever from a submarine. Entitled "A Maid of a Million, the Great Porkenlard Mystery," it bore the subhead "Stealthy Steve the Star, in some new stunts." Stealthy, we will see, anticipated Inspector Clouseau, the magnificent Parisian bungler brought to life on the screen by Peter Sellers, but there is also a touch about Steve of James Bond and Superman.

A MAID OF A MILLION

It was a blustery evening in March, 19—, that Stealthy Steve, the great six-eyed sleuth, sat before the fire in the library of his cozy home in Suburbington-on-the-Hudson. The hands of the clock on the mantel pointed to the midnight hour. Outside the wind moaned through the nude branches of the trees or sighed about the eaves of the house, pausing now and then to rattle a window shutter or whistle down the chimney. The members of the family had long been abed. . . .

As he lapsed into a nut brown revery he became conscious that he was sitting on something which gave him an uncomfortable feeling and arose and examined the chair with eagle eyes. Nothing was visible except the cushion.

"There is some mystery here," hissed Stealthy Steve with a professional hiss.

Cautiously he felt behind him and as he did so the stern rigidity of his face relaxed into an expression that might have been a smile. Then he removed from his pocket his trusty six-shooter and placed it on the mantel.

"I never could sit on a loaded gun and feel comfortable," he mused as he reseated himself and resumed his cigarette.

At that instant the doorbell rang violently. The six-eyed sleuth sprang to his feet and snatched the gun from the mantel shelf.

"Ah, ha," exclaimed Stealthy Steve, "probably a book agent who learned his trade at night school."

With that the great detective tiptoed to the door, gripping his revolver for instant use.

Book agent or burglar, Stealthy Steve was a man who took no chances. He had once taken a chance in the Louisiana State lottery years before, which had drawn nothing, and this experience had taught him a lesson.

"Who goes there? I mean, who comes here?" he demanded, inclining his ear to the keyhole.

"It is I," said a firm voice.

"It izzi?" repeated Stealthy Steve. "Are you a Jap or a Russian . . . and if so . . . why?"

"Please open," persisted the voice.

"Give the password."

"What is it?"

"Nux Vomica."

"Nux Vomica."

"Enter," said Steve, throwing open the door. A prosperous-looking business man stepped inside. Having closed the door, Stealthy Steve waved him into the library.

The stranger was a rotund man of perhaps 60 years of age, with a bald head and face save for a grizzled goatee.

"My good sir," began Stealthy Steve kindly as he lighted a fresh cigarette. "What can I do for you?"

"Are you Stealthy Steve the Six-Eyed Sleuth?" asked the visitor.

"I am the same," said Steve nonchalantly.

"My name is Porkenlard—August Porkenlard of New York and Chicago. I desire your services in clearing up one of the deepest mysteries that has ever baffled the hawkshaws of two continents—a mystery that has prostrated me with grief

because it involves something I prize more than anything
else on earth."

"Is it your reputation?" gasped Steve. "Quick, man, answer.
Can't you see I'm all hetted up with curiosity?"

"No. Not my reputation," responded Mr. Porkenlard. "Ah, if
it were only my reputation I would be happy, for I could build
up another one just as good. No, my loss is even greater than
a reputation."

"What have you lost?" shouted Steve, his face contorted
with curiosity.

"My daughter!"

"Your daughter! Give me the facts," hissed Steven, whipping out his notebook and pencil.

Thus far Newkirk took his reader in the first chapter. The
column, of course, carried a tag line that told the reader the story
would be continued the next day.

CHAPTER TWO

In a voice cracked and broken by emotion, Mr. Porkenlard
related to Stealthy Steve all he knew about the mysterious
disappearance of his daughter.

"To begin at the beginning: I was born of poor but proud
parents in the town of Milwaukee 51 years ago. Owing to the
fact that my parents were in a continued financial embarrassment, they could not afford to educate me, so I tried to educate myself. . . .

"I followed the brewing business in Milwaukee for several
years with indifferent success. I found the brewing business
was not what it was cracked up to be—one year the boll
weevil would destroy the hop crop, and the next year perhaps a large majority of my patrons would desert me and get
positions on the water wagon.

"So in the end I got tired of helping to make Milwaukee
famous and migrated to Chicago and engaged in a small way
in the pork-packing business. I became prosperous, and one
evening I balanced up the books and found myself a millionaire. It was then that. . . ."

"Pardon me for butting in," broke in Stealthy Steve, "but
after following you closely thus far, I fail to see the connection of all this dry-rot with the disappearance of your daughter. It is now 1 A.M. and if you think I am going to sit up until
morning listening to the history of your life, you are more of
a lobster than you look."

"I am coming to the point," resumed Mr. Porkenlard. "After becoming a millionaire I married a good cook in Chicago and we went housekeeping on the lake front. As time passed there was a child born to bless our union, a girl. She weighed ten pounds on the hoof, and it seemed but a few years until she budded and blossomed forth into a beautiful girl of 17 years. Heavens, how time flies. We called the child Agatha.

"Well, it was about this time that my wife got the New York bug in her bonnet—she insisted on going to New York to live. She argued that as long as we remained in Chicago, we would never amount to a hill of beans socially, but with our burden of wealth it would be a small matter to break into New York's Four Hundred and thus bestow upon Agatha the social prestige she craved. So we moved to New York.

"We sent Agatha to a seminary, whatever that is, and after she got through with it, Mrs. Porkenlard and I talked the matter over and decided we would send our daughter on a trip abroad, so that when she returned she would be able to say that she had seen some of the world.

"This idea was really first suggested by Prince Itchi-Scratchi of Constantinople, who at the time was visiting this country. He met Agatha at some social function, and after he had looked up my rating in Dun's, he began to think a good deal of her.

"The prince said that a trip abroad would widen her horizon. I thought her horizon was wide enough. Agatha wore a number 23 corset, but her mother insisted on our darling going abroad and so we arranged it.

"Of course, it was out of the question to let her go abroad alone, so as her traveling companion and chaperone we selected my wife's sister, an old maid aunt, by name, Clarissa Schnitzel.

"Last September Agatha and Clarissa left New York for a tour of England and the continent. We bade her a fond good-by and I told her to cable us every day during her absence at my expense. This injunction she followed faithfully. We heard from her by wireless until her arrival in London, and daily thereafter I received a cablegram from her until . . ."

Here Porkenlard broke down and started to sob.

"What was the import of the message?"

"She wired that her aunt and herself were going to take a trip inland from there."

"And you have heard nothing from her since?"

"Nothing directly. Yesterday in response to my inquiries, I received a message from the American consul at Constanti-

nople to the effect that he had ascertained my daughter and
her aunt, Clarissa, had left for the interior, as advertised, but
they had not returned and he could learn nothing of their
whereabouts."

At this point Mr. Porkenlard leaned forward and began to
weep copiously into the cuspidor, at the same time making a
noise a good deal like a bathtub drain in the last spasm of
strangulation.

"Brace up, old man," cried Stealthy Steve, springing to his
feet and raising his hand toward high heaven. "Brace up and
be a man. I will restore your daughter or bust my suspenders
in the effort. I swear it."

They parted, but Stealthy Steve agreed to go to the
Porkenlard home in New York to examine the documents in
the case.

Scarcely had Stealthy Steve left his own door to catch the
early morning express to New York than he heard the shrill
blast of the locomotive. The station was a half mile distant.
He knew that he would have to do the half mile in a little
better than a two-minute clip. Steve settled down to an amazing speed. But his movements were hampered by the suitcase he carried. Slowly the train began to move away from
the station, with Steve still a quarter of a mile distant.

Lightly jumping a six-foot fence, the great detective sped
across lots. His idea was to head off the train. After running
swiftly for some few seconds, the sleuth came out upon the
right of way and looked up and down the tracks. The express
was not in sight. He sat down beside the tracks and lighted a
cigarette. He smoked leisurely for perhaps two minutes,
when there was a rumble along the track. The next instant
the train burst into sight and came booming along at sixty
miles an hour.

Holding his suitcase lightly but firmly in one hand, the
great detective braced himself. When the train was 2,000
yards away, Steve sprang into the air. He calculated with such
nicety, he alighted on the platform of the last coach as it shot
past and, opening the door, walked inside. He was perspiring
freely but was otherwise unmarked. . . .

Arriving in New York, Stealthy Steve jumped from the train
into a hansom and ordered the jehu [speedster] to drive with
the utmost speed to the residence of August Porkenlard.
When he gave the cabman the address, Steven noticed that
the man was addicted to stammering. Steve was consumed
with impatience lest he arrive a couple of minutes late. Presently his eye caught the number of Mr. Porkenlard's resi-

dence, which was 237 Fifth Ave. To the detective's amazement the hansom did not pause. After traveling two blocks, Steve lost his temper and, reaching out with his strong right arm, he seized the reins and with one yank brought the horse back on its haunches. He turned angrily to the cabbie.

"Why didn't you stop at 237?"

"I cu-cuh—I cu-cuh-couldn't su-su-say wuh-wuh-wuh-wuh-wuh-whoa!" explained the cabbie.

Steve felt ashamed for having upbraided him and gave him a five dollar bill.

"Thu-thu-thu . . ."

"Thanks. Oh, you're welcome," said Steve and, picking up his suitcase, dashed to the Porkenlard mansion.

Conducting Steve to the library, August Porkenlard placed before him all the cablegrams he had received from his daughter, Agatha, following her departure for Europe. . . .

But on reflection, Steve could find nothing . . . that threw any light on Agatha's disappearance, and he was almost at his wit's end.

"I ought to have a stock of canned clues for an emergency like this," he muttered to himself.

At that moment, the doorbell rang and the butler announced, "Prince Itchi-Scratchi."

Mr. Porkenlard sprang forward and grasped the prince's hand heartily.

"My dear prince," he said, "Agatha is missing."

"Missing!" shrieked the prince in faultless English. "You do not mean that she is a dead one?"

"Alas, we do not know. We last heard from her at Constantinople and since then no word has came, I mean, has come."

The prince was visibly pained at this sad intelligence, and it did not require much astuteness to see that there existed on his part a feeling for Agatha which was a few degrees warmer than friendship. Mr. Porkenlard, reminded of the presence of Stealthy Steve, who coughed audibly, introduced the two men. At this moment, the butler entered the room, bearing on a psilver psalver a telegraph message. The whereabouts of Agatha was no longer a mystery. She was not dead, but perhaps it would have been better if she was.

The message disclosed that she was being held by Turkish brigands, who wanted $1,000,000 in ransom. If it was not delivered, they would kill her after 15 days. Prince Itchi-Scratchi was all for paying the ransom. Stealthy Steve was against it. Stealthy suggested going to Washington to have

the Secretary of State John Hay make representations to the
Turkish government. As soon as the three men agreed,
Stealthy Steve clapped on his hat, snatched Prince Itchi-
Scratchi's umbrella from the hall rack, and rushed from the
house.

Hailing a passing cab he jumped inside and directed the
driver to rush him to the Liberty Street Ferry with all possible speed. After what seemed a period of about six years'
duration, the cab came to a stop and the cabman flung open
the door. He advised the great detective that the ferry was
leaving the slip. Stealthy Steve sped toward the departing
boat. The ferry was already drawing away.

When he reached the edge of the landing, Steve gave a
wild yell and sprang into the air. As he described a semi-
circle in his mad flight, he placed a cigarette between his lips
and lit it. After traversing a space of 72 feet, he alighted
nimbly on the deck of the boat and, without losing a step,
walked forward smoking.

When the boat reached midstream, a horrible thing happened. The chain against which Stealthy Steve was leaning
gave way without warning, and the great detective fell headlong into those dark abysmal waters. He disappeared beneath the boat and was carried backward toward the paddle
wheel, which was churning the sea into foam.

"Well," said the sleuth to himself, "I will sell my life as
dearly as possible." The next instant, a great arm of the
wheel grazed his shoulder. Wheeling about with a lightning-
like movement, Stealthy Steve grabbed the arm of the paddle
and held it in a vise-like grip. The boat listed sharply to
starboard from the recoil. Stealthy Steve had not only
stopped the paddle-wheel, he had stopped the powerful engine.

Holding the wheel still, the great detective grabbed the
deck and clambored aboard. His clothing was damp but otherwise he was unharmed. The ferry got underway again. He
flicked the water from his clothing, and when the boat
touched shore, he sprang nimbly from the deck and caught
his train to Washington. At the office of the Secretary of
State, Stealthy Steve passed the boy his card. When the youth
read Stealthy Steve, he shrank back enraptured. He bowed to
the ground and saluted the prince of hawkshaws. Then he
telephoned the cabinet session and told the Secretary of
State John Hay to return at once, that Stealthy Steve desired
to see him on important business.

After Secretary of State Hay and Stealthy Steve entered the Secretary's private office, the great detective plunged into the business at hand. He explained that Miss Agatha Porkenlard was in the hands of Turkish bandits who were holding her for $1,000,000 ransom and that, if this was not forthcoming in 15 days, she would be brutally killed.

The detective then went on to state that her father, August Porkenlard, was a man who could ill afford to pay the ransom demanded by the bandits. Steve told Hay that Porkenlard had only $50,000,000, and if he should pay $1,000,000 for the recovery of his daughter, he would have left only $49,000,000. Hay, who is quick at mental arithmetic, had to admit the truth of this. But he explained that he was powerless to help recover Agatha because war was too costly. When he said this, Steve said, "Very well, I shall take the matter directly to the Supreme Court, and if the Supreme Court turns me down I shall go to Turkey, fight the nation single-handed and bring Agatha home myself, alone."

He lost no time in reaching the White House. There a messenger told him that President Roosevelt would see him in the gymnasium, where Teddy was taking a private jiu-jitsu lesson from a Japanese instructor. President Roosevelt, in prize-ring attire, greeted Stealthy Steve heartily and asked him if he had ever taken lessons in jiu-jitsu. Steve replied in the negative. Mr. Roosevelt then introduced the Japanese instructor Professor Kee-o-kuk, and asked the professor to throw Steve down a couple of times just to demonstrate to him the wonders of jiu-jitsu. Steve demurred but the President insisted. At length Steve took off his coat, spat on his hands and told the Japanese to wade in. The professor then asked Steve to defend himself with all his strength so as to make the bout more interesting. Then the Jap jumped on the sleuth. Like a flash, Steve seized the Jap by the neck and, swinging him around his head a couple of times, threw him against the ceiling with a thud. The professor then fell limply to the floor, and it was some minutes before he could sit up and take notice.

The President was amazed at the dexterity of Stealthy Steve and told Steve to look out, for he was going to take a fall out of him. As the President rushed Stealthy Steve, the great detective side-stepped, and, as Teddy passed Steve, [he] seized him by the black belt and held him at arm's length, kicking and struggling helplessly.

Mr. Roosevelt then admitted that the average human being had no more show with the six-eyed sleuth than a young lamb in Wall Street.

(Footnote: A jump of 72 feet was nothing for Stealthy Steve. The great sleuth has a record of 87 feet for standing jump without weights. This stands as the world's record never having been approached by any jumper or jumpist.)

The column that day closed with what is known in the business as a teaser:

Will Teddy Roosevelt declare war on Turkey to retrieve Agatha Porkenlard, meat-packing heiress, or will Stealthy Steve have to go to Constantinople and single-handedly bring back the kidnapped girl? See tomorrow's chapter.

CHAPTER THREE

"No," said President Roosevelt, "nothing would please me more than to kick up a little war, but I would be ashamed to pick on a moth-eaten little one-horse-power dynasty like Turkey. I'm sorry, Stealthy Steve. If I were to bring about war with Turkey, there would be a lot of newspaper talk about a big stick, and that sort of thing annoys me.

"Now if you wanted a fourth-class postmastership or something of that kind, I could fix you up, but what you ask is impossible. And now, if you will excuse me, I will bust a trust or two before lunch."

Steve returned to his hotel but was no sooner in his room than a note was slipped under the door. Always on the alert, he sprang to the door with one fell spring and threw it open. The corridor was bare, empty and echoless.

The note read, "To Stealthy Steve: If you know what is good for you, you will keep your nose out of the Agatha Porkenlard abduction case. Do not interfere at your peril. I have been watching you and unless you attend to your own business, I will carve you into sixteeen different slices and nobody will ever know what has become of you. I don't like you very well anyhow. You done me dirt once and if you don't look out, I'll get even. Yours for blood. Signed, Nick the Knock."

Nick the Knock was to Stealthy Steve what Professor Moriarty was to Sherlock Holmes.

Disguised as a workman, Stealthy Steve set out from his hotel to find Nick the Knock and try issues with him. He took

up a post before the post office, thinking that Nick the Knock
might stop by for his mail. He had been waiting about half an
hour when a beautiful woman dressed in black approached
him. Her sweet face was lined with sorrow.

"O, sir," she said, "my chee-ild is dying! What shall I do? I
am a stranger in town and have just run for a doctor. O, I fear
my little one will die before I can return."

"Calm yourself, Madam," said Stealthy Steve soothingly.
"Conduct me to your apartment. Perhaps I can render temporary aid to your offspring. I am not a physician but chance
to have some knowledge of medicine."

"You are so kind, sir," she said, and hurried off with
Stealthy Steve at her heels. And so Steve was led to a little
form covered with comforters in a second story apartment in
a squalid court. He threw down the coverlets. Instead of a
baby he uncovered merely a bundle of clothing. At the same
time he was seized from the rear by a pair of powerful arms.

"At last," a voice hissed in his ear, "you are in my
power... r... r... r... r."

Steve knew the voice as soon as he heard it. It was the
voice of Nick the Knock. Then began a fearful struggle. Back
and forth across the room the two men swayed, locked in
deadly embrace. Presently, Steve by superhuman effort
whirled around and in a flash clutched Nick the Knock by
the throat. Pressing his thumbs deep into the flesh of Nick
the Knock, Steve heard the man's Adam's apple crack with a
loud report. He seemed undisturbed. The man had two Adam's apples!

Suddenly, the woman who had enticed Steve to the apartment sprang at him. The next instant she plunged the long
blade of a dagger deep into the detective's heart. The detective sank weakly to the floor. The woman had lost some of
her paint and powder in the struggle, and Stealthy Steve
recognized her as the notorious Slippery Sal, known to the
police of two continents.

"Good-by, Stealthy Steve," she sneered. "You won't get the
reward offered for Agatha Porkenlard, but Nick and I will
come in on the ransom."

The dying sleuth turned his head feebly and saw Nick the
Knock struggle to his feet. Whipping a heavy pistol from his
pocket, Nick bent over the prostrate detective and emptied
six bullets into his body.

When Stealthy Steve opened his eyes, he found himself
lying on his back gazing upward at a small barred window in
the ceiling through which came a shaft of daylight. He re-

called his desperate struggle with Nick the Knock and of having been stabbed through the heart by Slippery Sal. To his great joy, the blood had coagulated and the hemorrhage had stopped. He also noticed that his clothing was punctured at various points. This puzzled him until he remembered that Nick the Knock had fired six bullets into him. The barred window was 15 feet above him. He knew he was in the repository for the victims of Nick the Knock and Slippery Sal. He knew now that they were in on the Agatha Porkenlard kidnapping. At this thought the great detective raised his hand high above his head and hissed, "Be it so! I will foil them yet." Saying this, Stealthy Steve buttoned his coat tightly and, crouching low, sprang into the air. He shot upward like a sky-rocket and grasped the bars of the opening 15 feet above. Holding on with one hand and reaching into an emergency pocket, he brought forth a file and began to file the bars as he hung there. In a short time he had filed away two of the bars and was walking away over the flat roof. Out from behind a chimney stepped a man who stood directly in Stealthy Steve's path. It was Nick the Knock and in his hand was a flashing knife.

Nick the Knock drew back the knife and launched it through the air at Steve with a whizz. Although the sleuth was not prepared for this emergency and was still carrying six bullets in his body and a healing wound in his heart, he met it with rare presence of mind. He stepped aside as the knife came and seized it with a snap, being careful to take it by the handle rather than by the blade.

When Nick saw how the issue had terminated, he sprang upon Steve with a low musical oath. It was against Steve's principles to fight an unarmed enemy so he cast the knife to one side. The men clinched. The street was 75 feet below. Nick charged Steve hoping to cast him into the street. Stealthy Steve held Nick the Knock at arm's length and kicked him heartily in the seat of the pants. Nick shot through the air and plunged headlong through a window in the opposite block, carrying sash and glass with him.

Steve dusted off his clothes, slid down the fire escape and went to confer with the Secretary of the Navy. When he returned to August Porkenlard's in New York, he was able to say:

"I have chartered a submarine from the Secretary of the Navy so as to sail to Turkey without being seen to recover your daughter. I have a few purchases to make before I go aboard the submarine. Be of good cheer. If anyone can find your daughter, it is Stealthy Steve the Six-eyed Sleuth, and I don't want to brag either."

Don't miss tomorrow's chapter, in which Nick the Knock almost prevents Stealthy Steve's submarine from getting to Constantinople to recover the missing heiress.

CHAPTER FOUR

Taking his seat in the operating room of the submarine, the S.S. *Loon*, Stealthy Steve pressed the depressor button and the boat sank beneath the waves. Then he threw the forward lever. Once past Sandy Hook, he headed for Constantinople. He was lying on the observation couch, looking through the glass roof of the submarine when he was about half way across the ocean, when he saw a strange object that seemed to hang in midair above the submarine.

"By heck, it's an airship," he said. And so it was. He gazed at it through the marine glasses, and presently a chortle of amazement escaped him. From above the edge of the basket which hung suspended from the airship, a human face appeared—the face of Nick the Knock. That Nick the Knock meant him no good was evident.

The great detective leaped into the operating room of the submarine and turned on full power, the equivalent of 57 knots. The airship was falling rapidly behind. At this the great detective gave a loud haw, haw. The laugh had scarce died on his lips when Stealthy Steve was thrown violently to the floor with his head in a cuspidor. The S.S. *Loon* quivered from stem to stern. As soon as Steve clapped his eye on a porthole, he saw what had happened. A monster whale had gotten in the way of the *Loon*. The speed of the submarine was greatly reduced and the airship was overhead again.

When Stealthy Steve looked up at it again, Nick the Knock was dropping a round bomb. It was a terrible moment. Steve made a flying leap into the operating room and pressed the depressor. Down, down, down, went the *Loon*. The next instant the bomb hit the water with a thunderous report. The *Loon* was thrown on her side by the shock. So was Steve. He decided to give Nick the Knock a taste of his own medicine. Rushing forward where the flat-headed torpedoes were kept, the great detective, with a superhuman effort, seized one and pushed it into the tube. When he had adjusted it ready to launch, by a manipulation of the levers he held the *Loon* vertically in the water with the torpedo pointing upward. There was a swish and a roar. The torpedo shot upward through the surface of the water and cleft the air in its vertical flight. It missed the bag of the airship by only a few inches. The desperate villain, who was really a coward at heart, was seized with a paroxysm of fear. He fled in his airship.

The great detective turned to right the *Loon*. To his amazement the machinery refused to respond. He uncased a porthole and looked out. The *Loon* was imbedded in nine feet of mud, standing on its nose, due to the recoil when the torpedo was fired upwards. Water was pouring into the ship through a gaping hole in the nose. Stealthy Steve went out one of the portholes, locking it carefully behind him. Once the damage was repaired, he found he had lost the key. He was searching for a skeleton key when a shark attacked him, and it was only when he had disposed of this blood-thirsty fish that he was able to reenter the porthole. The water was a foot deep in the submarine but it was back in operation and was not leaking. And so it was that Stealthy Steve came to Constantinople after difficulties that would have broken the heart of a less stalwart man.

The American consul declined to aid in the search for Agatha Porkenlard, and so did the Sultan of Turkey. Steve showed the Sultan a picture of Agatha. "By cracky," exclaimed his majesty, "she's a peach." But he was afraid to act against the brigands. So Steve moved into the interior with a native guide named Rah-Rah-Hooray. It was in short order that Steve found Agatha and her aunt Clarissa. Nick the Knock tried to stop him but Steve married him off to Aunt Clarissa. He was aided by a young man named William Weeks, who turned out to be in love with Agatha. Steve brought them together on the return trip to the *Loon*. But imagine Steve's consternation when he returned to the home of August Porkenlard to find the great man widowed and remarried to Slippery Sal, Nick the Knock's beautiful but unscrupulous accomplice. Agatha was disappointed, but Weeks turned out to have a few million dollars of his own.

Thus it was with mixed emotions that Stealthy Steve returned to his home in Suburbington-on-the-Hudson to his seven children and his wife, Genevieve.

"I'll surprise Genevieve," he said. With this thought in mind he tiptoed along the hall to the sewing room. Inside, Genevieve was sewing the children's socks. Her back was to the door. Steve entered softly and, creeping up behind her, put his hands over her eyes and asked, "Guess who it is!"

"The ice man," Genevieve replied promptly.

The invincible Stealthy Steve, the Six-Eyed Sleuth, was ready for his next adventure.

Newton Newkirk's Sunday page leaned heavily on country-hick dialect. Called "The Bingville Bugle," it described itelf as "The Leading Paper of the County, Bright, Breezy, Bellicose and Bustling." It was also "the biggest and only paper this end of the county" whose "sirculashun books are open to nobody, yer have to take our word for it."

A typical news note from "The Bingville Bugle" read thus:

> We announce with great cheer that the Ladies Aid of the Bingville Church has decided to give a series of entertainments in the Bingville Town Hall at intervals during the rest of the winter the perceeds of which will go tords paying Rev. Samuel Moore our beloved pastor a porshun of his back salery which is now so fer back (being several yrs. back) that there ain't skeercely enny hope of getting him paid off and yet Rev. Moore shows the pashients of Job to stand there in the pulpit Sunday after Sunday and preach & holler until he is hoarse in a frantick effort to steer the wicked sinners of Bingville into the strate & narrer path while haff of them is asleep and don't hear a word he says while the other half lets what he says go into one ear and out the other.

That was the sort of thing Boston's maturing immigrant population could laugh at, perhaps because they believed it was that way up country (northern New England), and the folks up country could laugh at it because they knew it wasn't. "The Bingville Bugle" usually carried an advertisement. If it wasn't Hink Barclay offering to fill up your ice house before the thaw comes, or Silas Henderson starting a butter-and-eggs business and looking to buy some chickens, or Hank Dewberry offering to go gathering nuts rather than go back to the poor farm, which he didn't like the first time, it was a character who, like all of them, reappeared, if not in the advertisements, at least in the news notes. Bingville was more low-key than Al Capp's Dogpatch; indeed, it was almost believable. There was a time when phrases from "The Bingville Bugle" were on everybody's lips, and people of respectable mien would be heard shouting, "Hold her, Newt, she's a-rearin'!"

Newkirk, who held forth for decades, an incredibly productive major factor in the *Post*'s meteoric rise, died in a mental hospital in 1938 following a four-year illness.

CHAPTER TWELVE

Kenneth Roberts: Reporter

The most famous writer ever to work on the *Post* and to leave it for greater glory was Kenneth Roberts, whose historical novels rode the bestseller lists for years. There were others who went on to distinguished careers outside the newspaper business. George Horace Lorimer went to Philadelphia to become the celebrated editor of the *Saturday Evening Post*. In later years, Joe McCarthy left to edit *Yankee* during World War II and *Cosmopolitan* after that. Ben Ames Williams wrote for the *American* and the *Post* before becoming a full-time novelist, as did, after him, Fulton "Bill" Oursler, Jr. The list could be extended. Others worked briefly in the newspaper business in Boston and then went on to writing careers in other areas.

Other distinguished writers remained in the newspaper business and made national reputations in New York or Boston. Olin Downes was music critic at the *Boston Post* until the *New York Times* called him, and John K. Hutchens did book reviews on the *Transcript* before going to the *New York Herald-Tribune*. Elliot Norton, the *Post*'s drama critic, stayed with the *Post* until its demise and then for many years wrote for the *Record-American*. He was regarded by many as the best drama critic in the country. Numerous writers of distinction contributed to the *Post* over the years, from Louise Imogene Guiney to Edwin O'Connor, from John Boyle O'Reilly to Al Hirshberg.

Roberts, however, turned to fiction, and no other Boston newspaper writer of this era made a comparable reputation. He was born in 1885 in Kennebunk, Maine, and went to Cornell University, where his gift for humor placed him as editor of the *Cornell Widow* in his sophomore year. On graduation, he went into

Kenneth Roberts describes threading his way through the paper
trucks that blocked Newspaper Row. This photograph of the Row at
night shows what Roberts meant.

the leather business in Boston. He wanted something else. *I Wanted to Write*, the title he gave a book about his career, tells what that something was. He recounts in this book, with revelatory humor, his experiences at the *Post*, where he worked during its great days from 1909 to 1917. In the excerpt below, he was unhappy in the leather business, and a mutual friend suggested that he go to see Mr. Grozier.

That night . . . my friend and I threaded our way through the paper trucks that blocked Newspaper Row, mounted a worn flight of stairs to an office bearing the sign, "Editor and Publisher," brashly knocked upon the door of the supreme authority of the *Post*, and walked in on Mr. Grozier as if he was no one out of the ordinary.

Mr. Grozier was a small, brownish man who sat at a large desk, looking down at the roaring traffic of lower Washington Street and across at the chalk-written blackboard bulletins of the *Post*'s deadly rival, the *Boston Globe*.

Since I knew nothing about newspapers or writing, Mr. Grozier at the time seemed to me just another undersized party, rather delicate and plaintive-looking, perhaps because he wore a straggly mustache, had a rug over his knees and peered benevolently at me over the tops of his glasses.

Later when I had become aware that he was a newspaper genius, an ex-secretary of the great Joseph Pulitzer, and the creator of a newspaper property whose miraculous circulation baffled the most astute New York circulation managers, I found it impossible to enter his presence without shivering slightly at the shocking ignorance and temerity I had displayed on the occasion of our first meeting.

But as my friend said, Mr. Grozier was a nice man; and instead of having me turned out on my ear, or brusquely telling me to see the city editor or the Sunday editor, he inquired blandly as to my reasons, if any, for thinking I was qualified for newspaper work; listened as though I was saying something worth hearing; then amiably observed that if I cared to accept a position on the staff of the *Sunday Post* at eighteen dollars a week, he felt sure his Sunday editor could find a place for me.

The offices of the *Post* at that time were a sort of rabbit warren of ancient, dusty houses joined by labyrinthine passages, the whole underlain by subterranean chambers tunneled deep into the rock to hold the presses; and of all the dark and dingy rooms in those dark and dingy buildings, the Sunday Room was the darkest and dingiest.

Somehow, too, the type of news stories to which the Sunday editors of those days were addicted struck me as even darker and dingier than the room.

The *Sunday Post* was convinced (it seemed to me) that its readers were passionately interested in such things as giant squashes, two-headed calves, hundred-and-five-year-old women who ascribed their longevity to the daily chewing of an ounce of tobacco or the curry-combing of a horse.

I was completely uninterested in such manifestations; and when I sat before a battered typewriter and painstakingly tried to describe them in a fascinating manner and at unwarranted length, I found myself oppressed by an overwhelming feeling of futility. . . .

I felt hampered, too, by frequent warnings I received from the assistant Sunday editor against intruding humor into my accounts of two-headed calves and four-yolked eggs. If I persisted I'd be labeled a "one-armed man," fit to deal only with frivolous subjects. Then no city editor would work me on Big Stories.

For me the brightest day in the week was Saturday, when the Sunday staff was instructed to report to the City Room and put themselves at the disposal of the city editor.

I quickly made several important discoveries during those Saturdays in the City Room. Word seemingly had got out that I had gone to work on the *Post* by direct orders of Grozier; and the deduction had promptly been made by those in authority that I was not only somehow related to Mr. Grozier, but probably dined with him several times a week to dispense office chitchat. Thus I was viewed with alarm and suspicion: I might, perhaps, be a stool pigeon.

I found, too, that there was deep-seated distrust in Boston newspaper offices of persons with college educations. They were thought to be afraid of hard work; lacking in reportorial stamina. I never wholly understood the reason for this aversion to college graduates, and it eventually faded to such a degree that Dartmouth and even Harvard men came to be tolerated in all Boston newspaper offices; but for a year or so I couldn't pass the den in which the staff photographers played with their pans, stinks and chemicals without hearing ironic shouts within that noisome cave, of 'Rah, rah, college.'

This alarm and suspicion, however, did not extend to the assistant city editor, a young man who had bounced almost straight from office boy to the city desk by virtue of locating the rammed steamship *Republic* in a fog off No Man's Land and scooping the town with an account of the disaster. This

The city room, where Kenneth Roberts and the rest of the Sunday staff reported to the city editor every Saturday for their assignments. On the right are the antique telephone booths. The view is to the rear from the author's city desk.

young man was Mr. John F. Royal, who later became Midwest director of the Keith-Albee interests; then went to high office in the National Broadcasting Company.

Mr. Royal pointed out to me that he officiated at the city desk from 10 A.M. to 1 P.M. each day, after which the regular city editor appeared on the scene, and that, during those three hours reporters were scarce as hen's teeth, since few of them deigned to rise from their couches until high noon. Yet, if any sort of story broke while he was on the desk, he explained, he couldn't wait for the arrival of the city editor; he had to lay hands on a reporter by fair means or foul and jump him on the story.

I took his words to heart and every Saturday thereafter I was in the City Room promptly at ten o'clock eagerly anticipating the fifteen-hour day before me. Thanks to Mr. Royal's habit of finding stories that couldn't wait for the city editor, and to his repeated admonitions of "don't be afraid to josh em," I spent the first five days of the week looking forward to Saturday, and all day Sunday dreading my return to the dreary purlieus of the Sunday Room.

This unhappy situation was complicated by a difficulty
with the Business Office. The Business Office, in addition to
selling advertising space to various organizations and amusement enterprises, gave away additional space in the form of
stories about the advertised product, right in among the
reading matter. Miss Jane Cowl was then at the beginning of
her brilliant career; and when the *Post* sold space to the
management of the theater at which Miss Cowl was playing,
it did so with the understanding that an interview with Miss
Cowl would be printed just as if it were a genuine news story.
So the advertising manager sent up to the Sunday editor and
requested that I be assigned to this Business Office Must.

I went to Miss Cowl's hotel and had a long and pleasant
chat with her, after which, in line with Mr. Royal's suggestions, I joshed Miss Cowl for a column and a half. When the
results were delivered to the Business Office, there were dark
looks and head shakings. At that period no soubrette had
feelings as susceptible or as easily hurt as Boston advertisers.
When accidents took place in department stores or hotels,
no Boston newspaper ever, ever ventured to publish the
names of the hotels or stores. Any disconsolate or intro-
verted unfortunate who wished to disappear completely and
unrecorded from Boston's tribulations and repressions
needed only to cut his throat or swallow a tot of arsenic in
one of the thronged aisles of Jordan Marsh & Company or in
William Filene's Sons & Company; for the affair would be
completely ignored by all Boston newspapers. And for a Boston newspaper to mention an advertiser or anyone connected with an advertiser in a tone that even hinted at levity
was almost as unthinkable as to speak slightingly of any form
of religion. But eventually a representative of the Business
Office timorously conferred with the theater management
about the Cowl interview, and since the management saw
nothing harmful or libelous about it, the story was reluctantly published.

A few days later I was again summoned to the Business
Office. My story on Miss Cowl, the business manager said,
hadn't been all bad. Miss Cowl had liked it, the theater had
liked it; *Post* readers had liked it. Consequently he had decided to let me do more of the same; and as a starter would I
step up to the Touraine and interview the gentleman now
playing at the Tremont Theater.

Somewhat to my surprise, and certainly to the business
manager's annoyance, I refused the assignment on the
ground that this was a press agent's work, that press agents

too often had to misrepresent their wares, and that I didn't want to be a press agent. The business manager, huffy at finding his generosity unappreciated, complained bitterly to the Sunday editor, who also seemed to think my attitude was unreasonable and incomprehensible.

They were so unpleasant about it that I thought a little about attempting to storm that frowning Boston newspaper citadel, the *Transcript,* but I hesitated to do so because I felt that I was congenitally unfitted to write ponderous columns about supremely uninteresting subjects. . . .

People who knew Roberts in later life, when he was deemed the dean of America's historical novelists, were astounded to learn that he began his journalistic life as a humorist, for such soon became his role at the *Post.* He was transferred to the city staff and there created a character who led *Post* readers through a variety of nut-cake adventures. That character was the now quite forgotten Professor Morton Kilgallen. The following incident, involving the professor, is illustrative of much about the journalism of the day and of the *Post.* It seems the *Globe* carried a story that a record-breaking codfish, weighing seventy-one pounds, had been caught by the schooner *Manomet.* Roberts was sent to the fish pier to get the details on the story but, having arrived, found everybody had gone. Unable to get additional facts, he returned to the city room and wrote:

> A codfish measuring five feet three inches from snout to tail and weighing 71 pounds dressed was caught by the fishing schooner *Manomet* and pitchforked into Boston yesterday.
>
> So far as is known this codfish is the largest ever caught and brought home. It is on exhibition at Quincy Market.
>
> The eminent authority on fish, Prof. Morton Kilgallen, estimated the age of this enormous cod as 47 years.
>
> "I base my estimate of this fish's age on the length of his whisker," said Prof. Kilgallen to a *Post* reporter. "I would unhesitatingly give him ten years per inch. "
>
> The cod's whisker was four and seven-tenths inches long and was slightly mossy around the edges.

The story won Roberts a raise and more. Professor Kilgallen began to appear frequently. Before too long, however, Grozier, who enjoyed the Kilgallen stories immensely, had to put this proviso before them: "The *Post* has a deep regard for the remarkable scientific theories put forth by Professor Morton Kilgallen, F.R.S., but as the subjects are beyond the lay editor, the responsibility for the assertions must lie with Professor Kilgallen." Too many *Post* readers had been taking the professor for real. All subsequent stories stressed his being a fictional character.

In those days there was a good deal more such persiflage in newspapers than there is today, when editors and reporters are far more sober-sided. Roberts, a master of it, was chosen to fill in for Newton Newkirk whenever that worthy was on vacation or ill. This prompted Roberts to ask Grozier to give him a daily column of his own. Grozier said he couldn't do that without offending Newkirk, whose popularity had contributed so much to the rapid rise of the *Post*'s circulation. He suggested instead that Roberts have an office of his own (at the time, he shared one with Olin Downes) and a full page in the Sunday paper. Roberts took the offer and, for three years, filled a page in the Sunday paper with amusing verse, hilarious fables, short stories, burlesques, parodies, and other nonsense. But the itch to write books was not to be soothed. Roberts decided to make the break. He left the *Post* in 1917 and began writing humorous copy for three popular magazines of the day: *Life*, *Judge*, and *Puck*. Service in World War I soon interrupted his writing, but he was able to turn his wartime experiences into an article for the *Saturday Evening Post*, where, immediately on his discharge, he met George Horace Lorimer. He wrote for the *Saturday Evening Post* until 1928, then he retired and wrote his first novel, *Arundel*, which appeared in 1930. *Northwest Passage*, his best-known work, was published in 1937. Although managing editor Clifton B. Carberry at one time wired him and made a pleasant offer, Roberts never returned to the *Post*.

On his Sunday page, he instituted a number of regular features, in one of which, each week, he presented some verse of his own surrounded by sketches by one of the staff artists. Not too much journalism stands up against the passage of time, but some of Roberts's verses do. One was rather prophetic.

A PROTEST AGAINST TIGHTER SKIRTS

Skirts they tell us will be tighter
Than you've worn them in the past.

Madam, you will be a sight a
   Man will contemplate aghast.
Present styles permit a gesture
   One foot wide below the knee;
But with any lighter vesture
   Goodness gracious mercy me!

Even now you cannot hurry
   If you'd shun a bad mishap
As for running, you should worry
   Lest you fall upon your map.
Even now there's some disclosure
   When you mount a street car stair
Yet you're planning more exposure
   Madam! Madam! Have a care!

You will have to dress less thickly
   In your —well, your undercrust
Madam, when you stoop too quickly
   What if anything should bust!
Do not make our blushes brighter
   Do not take this dreadful chance!
If you must wear something tighter
   Give up skirts and take to pants!

    This sort of verse was very popular in newspaper columns at
the time and in such humor magazines as *Life* and *Judge*. So
Roberts began to send his better efforts there first; only if they
were rejected there did he put them in his Sunday page. His success with the magazines prompted him to make the break from
the paper, take off for Maine, and support himself as a freelance
writer. He never looked back, at least not with any intention of
going back, but always looked back with affection.

    Years later, when Roberts was celebrated internationally for
his historical novels, Bill Cunningham, a popular Boston sports
writer, called upon him as a friend to fill in on his column while
he was on vacation. Roberts was curiously unsuccessful. Nevertheless, he outlived the *Post*, and his books bid fair to live forever.

CHAPTER THIRTEEN

Boston "Firsts"

The story of Newspaper Row could well be told in terms of the *Globe* and the Taylor family, for they were there before Grozier arrived and were still there after his creation, the *Post* in its greatest days, had gone, along with its peak circulation of 600,000. The *Globe* story has been told, however, by Louis M. Lyons in *Newspaper Story: One Hundred Years of the Boston Globe*; *The Boston Transcript*, by Joseph Edgar Chamberlain, recounts the first hundred years of that newspaper.

The *Globe*, of course, went on to become one of the leading newspapers in the country. It is rich in Pulitzer Prizes and innumerable other awards, in circulation, and in advertising, with William O. Taylor, great-grandson of the founder, in the role of publisher today. The stability of the Taylor family—three of the founder's grandsons saw it through its transfer from Newspaper Row to its huge modern plant in Dorchester, an outlying section of Boston—stood in sharp contrast to the instability of Richard Grozier and the alcoholism and erratic genius of his successor, John Fox. The *Globe* also was blessed for almost a century with the presence of three outstanding editors: James Morgan, Laurence Winship, and the latter's son, Thomas. The succession of publishers has run from Charles H. Taylor through William O. Taylor, William Davis Taylor, and now William O. Taylor II.

Nevertheless, no story is more intimately connected with the glory days of Newspaper Row than is the *Post*'s. Grozier had been intent on building the largest circulation in New England, which he did. It began, of course, as a matter of survival. He reduced the price of the *Post* to one penny, which Adolph S. Ochs was to do in New York with the *Times*, and kept it there until 1918.

If Grozier emulated Pulitzer, Charles H. Taylor struck a course somewhere between Pulitzer, Ochs, and Charles Dana of the *New York Sun*, remembering all the time that he was publishing a regional paper and not a national one, which the *Times* ultimately became.

Persons with little understanding of newspaper publishing are forever comparing their daily newspaper unfavorably with the *New York Times*, which is similar to comparing linotype machines with foolscap. One could make the case that, as a daily newspaper seeking to serve all the people of New York City, the *Times* is a failure. It tries harder, after all, to be a national newspaper, a paper of record. As more than one critic has remarked, it has become an "international textbook on contemporary history." Regardless of how critics may dissent from its editorial policy, most recognize it as an essential American institution.

Because of New York City's position as the financial and publishing capital of the world, whatever happens there is likely to take on mythic dimensions and override what happens elsewhere. The excellence of the *New York Times* and its national outlook has helped create that atmosphere. Yet historical records seem to overlook Grozier and Taylor, who demonstrated stature equal to that of their New York counterparts. In 1893 Joseph Pulitzer announced that the *New York World* had instituted the first photoengraving plant of any newspaper in the country. The *Globe* had its own plant in 1886. Histories of journalism credit Philadelphia papers with carrying the first full-page advertisements in 1879. In 1875 the *Globe* carried two full-page advertisements, one for Jordan's department store and one for the Mason & Hamlin Organ Company. In other words, because of New York City's myth-making preeminence, Boston's accomplishments have been overlooked in such journalistic history as has been written. The *Globe*'s national "firsts" have been all but unrecorded.

Besides running the first full-page advertisements and having the first photoengraving department, the *Globe* was the first metropolitan newspaper to run a full-length serial, the first to give bylines to staff members, the first to sponsor an airplane race, the first to publish a newspaper peering one hundred years into the future (by printing a supplement dated A.D. 2002 and guessing satirically about the next century), and the first to receive a news story over the telephone.

THE FIRST TELEPHONE MESSAGE.

PROF BELL DESCRIBING HIS INVENTION AT LYCEUM HALL, SALEM, IN 1877.
(From "The Telephone.")

The first news story sent by human voice over the telephone was transmitted February 13, 1877. Professor Alexander Graham Bell is portrayed as he describes his "wonderful instrument, the telephone" that night in Salem.

That historic call was made on February 13, 1877, from Salem, Massachusetts, where Alexander Graham Bell had given a lecture, to Boston. The contents of the call and the news story it reported can be read with interest today.

Doctor Bell was a native of Scotland who, when he immigrated to Ontario, Canada, with his parents in 1870, was already an accomplished teacher of speech. In 1872 he came to Boston to open a private school and to become a professor of speech and vocal physiology at Boston University. He was teaching there when Grozier was graduated. Dr. Bell was experimenting with devices for transmitting sound along wires and with making graphic recordings of sound waves. From these experiments came the telephone, which he patented in 1876. The next year he lectured for the Essex Institute in the Lyceum Hall in Salem and gave a demonstration of the telephone, talking to his assistant, Thomas Augustus Watson, who was eighteen miles away in Boston. Dr. Bell may well have been persuaded by his assistant to give the talk in Salem, for Watson had attended school there before going on to study geology at Massachusetts Institute of Technology. Watson was later to serve as superintendent of the Bell Telephone Company but left that business to take up a career in shipbuilding.

Henry M. Batchelder, an enterprising reporter, had been covering the lecture for the *Globe*. At its conclusion, he asked Dr. Bell whether he could transmit his report of the meeting over the telephone to a colleague in Boston. Dr. Bell agreed, and the *Globe*, alerted by telegraph, sent Austin Barclay Fletcher to Watson's quarters at 5 Exeter Place, Boston. (What was the Lyceum Hall in Salem is today a restaurant, which commemorates the event with a bronze plaque.) Fletcher, also a law student at Boston University at the time, went on to a distinguished career before the bar. He is remembered best, however, for his endowment, which, forty-six years later, established the Fletcher School of Law and Diplomacy at Tufts University.

The text of the story, not reprinted since it appeared originally, makes interesting reading today.

SENT BY TELEPHONE
THE FIRST NEWSPAPER DESPATCH
SENT BY HUMAN VOICE
OVER THE WIRES
TO THE *DAILY GLOBE* FROM SALEM—PROFESSOR
GRAHAM BELL EXPLAINS HIS VALUABLE INVENTION—
AN ENTHUSIASTIC AUDIENCE—HOW THE CAPACITY OF THE
TELEPHONE WAS TESTED

Special Despatch by Telephone to the
Boston Globe

SALEM, February, 12, 10:55 P.M.—Professor A. Graham Bell, the inventor of that wonderful instrument the telephone, which has caused so much interest in the scientific world and is now becoming so popularly known, lectured at the Lyceum Hall this evening. The lecture was one of a course at the Essex Institute and about 500 persons were present. The lecture was very well received and long-continued applause showed that the audience appreciated fully the wonderful uses and the experiments made with the machines. Professor Bell briefly explained the construction of the instrument and then sketched his studies of the system of transmitting sounds. He explained that it was his first attempt before an audience to try these different experiments. An intermittent current was first sent from Boston by Mr. Thomas A. Watson, Professor Bell's associate. This caused a noise very similar to a horn from the telephone. The Morse telegraph was then sent by musical sounds and could be heard throughout the hall. The audience burst into applause at this experiment. A telephonic organ was then put into operation in Boston. "Should Auld Acquaintance be Forgot" and "Yankee Doodle" were readily heard throughout the hall and heartily recognized. Professor Bell then explained how he learned to

TRANSMIT THE TONES OF THE HUMAN VOICE

and paid a graceful tribute to Mr. Watson. Professor Bell asked Mr. Watson for a song and "Auld Lang Syne" came through the instrument almost before his words were ended. Mr. Watson was then asked to make a speech to the audience. He expressed himself as having more confidence eighteen miles away than if he was present. His speech was as follows: "Ladies and gentlemen, it gives me great pleasure to be able to address you this evening, although I am in Boston and you in Salem." This could be heard thirty-five feet distant, that is, all over the hall, and brought down the house with applause. A system of questioning was then carried on and Mr. Watson was asked if he heard the applause. The answer was, "I was not listening. Try again." The applause was given and its receipt

AT ONCE ACKNOWLEDGED IN BOSTON.

Coughing and sighing were then heard and a variety of questions were then asked from the Salem end and among them, "What news from the Electoral Commission?" followed by the distinct answer of "I don't know of any." But the news came fleeting along that the engineers of the Boston and Maine had struck. General Cogwell asked if the trains were running; the answer was clear and distinct that they were not at 5:30 o'clock. Professor Bell introduced the Rev. E. C. Bolles who said, "I shake hands with you cordially in imagination twenty miles away." The Rev. E. S. Atwood asked, "Does it rain?" "It does not in Boston," was Mr. Watson's reply. Professor Gage, the electrician, then spoke through the telephone endeavoring to have his voice recognized. This could not be done as Mr. Watson was not familiar with the voice. Mr. Shaje Zsawa was recognized, Mr. Watson being perfectly familiar with his tones. One of the assistants in Boston then said that "Hold the Fort" would then be sung in Boston and the tune which followed was readily recognized. Professor Bell closed his lecture by briefly stating the practical uses to which he was confident the telephone could be applied. Hearty applause was afforded the lecturer as he finished and people flocked about the stage in large numbers to more closely examine the wonderful instrument that had placed them in audible communication with people nearly twenty miles away.

THE LECTURE AND THE INSTRUMENT

were an unqualified success. Among those present were Dr. Henry Wheatland, president of the Essex Institute, the Rev. E. C. Bolles, Ph.D., Professor D. H. Hagar of the Salem Normal School, General William Cogswell, the Rev. E. S. Atwood, Professor John Robinson, Dr. Amos H. Johnson, ex-Mayor Williams, Dr. George H. Loring, A. C. Goodall, Jr., Esq., and many others who are identified as particularly interested in scientific pursuits. Vice President Goodall of the Institute offered an order which was adopted providing for the appointment of a committee to draft a series of resolutions to express the satisfaction of the institute and audience for the instructive and interesting entertainment offered by Professor Bell. A vote of thanks was also extended to Mr. Watson and sent to him by telephone. A vote of thanks was passed to the Atlantic and Pacific Telegraph Company for their kindness in allowing the use of their wires for these experiments. A vote of thanks was also tended to Miss Malloy, operator of the Atlantic and Pacific Telegraph Company at Salem, for her assistance during the evening. The telephone was then taken apart and explained to a few ladies and gentlemen to their great wonder and satisfaction. This special by telephone to the *Globe* has been transmitted in the presence of about twenty who have thus been witnesses to a feat never before attempted—that is, the sending of a newspaper despatch over the space of eighteen miles by a human voice—and all this wonder being accomplished in a time not much longer than would be consumed in an ordinary conversation between two people in the same room.
H. M. B.

The *Globe* put the story on an inside page; the editors could not gauge the effect that the telephone would have on the gathering of news. One man who did was Arthur Milnor Bridgman, who was in Amherst College when the historic telephone call was made. He was preparing to enter the newspaper business, and, when he was twenty-eight years old, he bought the Haverhill (Mass.) *Gazette* and started an afternoon paper that he called the *Evening Telephone*. He boasted that it was the first newspaper to adopt that name and that it was the first newspaper to receive and send news by telephone. This was ten years after the call from Salem transmitted the gist of Dr. Bell's remarks at the Essex Institute. It is interesting that, while any number of papers have borne the name *Telegram* or *Telegraph*, none remains called the *Telephone*. Editor Bridgman later became a distinguished legislative reporter at the Massachusetts State House. He more than likely had not read the story in the *Globe* when he made his brag about the *Evening Telephone*.

CHAPTER FOURTEEN

Election Night

Those persons living in the computer age can have little idea of the excitement on an election night in the days when the figures had to be gathered by hand in a thousand places, totted up at half a dozen others, and rushed into print in a mad competition to get the final results to the public first. Today, by analyzing the results in key districts, computers can predict an election outcome in the first hour of the voting, and all the cliff-hanger aspect, all the suspense, is lost almost entirely.

Before radio and television, the public learned of the outcome of an election through the newspapers, and since the alienated voter had yet to appear on the scene, interest ran at fever pitch. Those who were most intent on getting the results as soon as possible would stand all night in Newspaper Row. In the first three decades of the twentieth century, anywhere from 5,000 to 50,000 persons would be assembled on Washington Street during election night, each of them evaluating the tabulations as they were written in chalk on black bulletin boards or announced through megaphones. Later, loudspeakers were mounted in the upstairs windows of the *Post*.

It was dangerous for a candidate to go to bed without seeing the final tabulations. In 1916, Charles Evans Hughes retired for the night thinking that he had been elected president of the United States, only to have the morning papers show him different. Even Harry S Truman was not sure of his election until he read the East Coast papers. He later delighted in holding up a copy of the *Chicago Tribune*, which declared happily and with bias based on insufficient information that Thomas E. Dewey had been elected. The *Boston Post* did itself proud in the 1948 elec-

tion. It was one of the few major papers in the United States that
endorsed Truman, particularly in a famous editorial by Henry
Gillen headed "Captain Courageous."

The emphasis on local news by the leading Boston newspapers led to the creation of a network of reporters, each of whom
was assigned either to a specific district in Boston or to a community immediately adjoining the city. Called district men, they were
on a regular wage. Beyond, in the more distant suburbs and in
the countryside, were reporters who were paid by the amount of
material they managed to get into the paper in the course of a
week. On occasion, they were paid whether their stories appeared or not. They were called correspondents or stringers.

On election night, each of them was assigned to get the figures from the cities or towns that they covered regularly. Thus the
mobilization of employees of the major newspapers gathering the
election results went into every municipality, into every ward,
and, on many an occasion, into key precincts. In the days before
radio, these reporters were sent throughout New England, sometimes cooperating with reporters from the opposition papers,
sometimes competing.

Covering a national election was an expensive operation for a
newspaper in those days. The *Post* looked upon it as a public
service, an essential one, too, if it was to keep its readership. The
other papers felt the same, though perhaps not with the same
intensity—the *Globe* with more dispassion, the *Herald* with more
bias. Each competed to get the vote first, but the *Post*, which
endorsed more candidates than any other paper, had a heightened interest.

A district man or correspondent who was assigned on election night to get the vote counts from, say, four towns and telephone them to the *Post* built up, in turn, his own network of
informants. He made arrangements with town clerks or other
worthies who were close to the scene of the counting and who,
he knew, would be among the first to have the figures. Often he
would arrange to have these persons telephone the results to him
at his home or at one of the municipal buildings where he was
posted because a particularly close count was being tabulated
there. He wanted to assure himself of being the first with the
figures. Upon receipt of the counts, he in turn would telephone
them to the *Post*, where special batteries of telephones had been
installed to receive the figures and relay them to *Post* tabulators. It
was much the same at the opposition papers. The computer was

A crowd gathers to await election results in 1907.

not yet invented, but the adding machine was on hand, operated by one of the *Post*'s bookkeepers with political seers leaning over his shoulders.

Frequently, the district man or correspondent was given instructions to rush to the phone with the vote tally regarding the top of the ticket or of some particular fight that was capturing the attention of the voters and the public in general. He would work diligently to get those figures first. On such occasions, he would not get to bed as usual but would work through the night until 6 o'clock the following morning. In cases when there were shenanigans at the polls, he might be on duty for a twenty-four-hour stretch until the problem was resolved and a recount ordered or dismissed. The pay was small, but the excitement was worth it. More often than not, the correspondent was the editor of a local paper or a member of its staff. Often he was the correspondent for half a dozen Boston and New England papers. In some instances, he was even a candidate for office; at other times, he was a town clerk, a town moderator, or a selectman.

In the city of Boston itself, men were watching the polls in the various districts, but city hall was the center of the news gathering. Traditionally, the police went to each precinct and carried the ballot boxes to the offices of the election commission. When the police arrived at the polling place to pick up the ballots and carry them to city hall, they would jot down the vote and relay it to police headquarters. There, extra reporters were assigned to pick up the vote and phone it to the *Post*. When the boxes arrived at city hall, another cursory check was made and those figures were phoned in. The figures gleaned by the police were definitely unofficial; those obtained at city hall, less so. The official count would not come until days or weeks later, but it rarely changed significantly the tabulations assembled by the newspapers. Such intensive coverage continued until the arrival of not only radio and television but also the voting machine, which so accelerated the count that newspapers can now get most of the vote by telephone well before deadline.

Inside the offices of the papers, special batteries of telephones were manned by employees drawn from departments in the paper other than editorial. Advertising solicitors might manipulate the phones, while men and women from the cashier's or payroll department would be operating adding machines or totaling figures by hand. Occasionally at the *Post*, mathematical wizards from the Massachusetts Institute of Technology would be hired for the night to make lightning calculations based on comparisons of the incoming vote with those of previous elections. They would be teamed with political diagnosticians who were able to offer psychological insights into a particular close fight in a representative or senate district. At all the papers, a half-dozen political writers would be on hand to handle the main or lead story and sidebars, to preside over the tabulation of votes in the paper, and to present the human-interest side of one contest or another.

For the figures on a national election, most papers would depend on the Associated Press or the United Press; but in the case of certain contests of particular interest, the editors might make a special arrangement with a newspaper in the state where the contest was taking place. The *Post* always had a special arrangement with the *Daily News* in New York City and would depend on that paper for special bulletins. The *Herald* had an arrangement with the *New York Times*; the *Globe*, with the *Chicago Daily News* and the North American Newspaper Alliance. Two or more men would be detached from a paper's staff and put in charge of mobilizing the inside force and notifying the district men and correspondents which contests were of particular interest. The inside workers were told when they were wanted and where they would be stationed. At the *Post*, an especially wide corridor was used as the headquarters for the operation; it was close to the library—or morgue, as it was called.

The executive offices led off of this corridor, and, sacrosanct as they were the rest of the year, they were open to intrusion on election night. The sports department was close by, as was the telegraph room, where several hand-operated keys were readied for news dispatches from distant points where telephones were hard to find.

All this was for the purpose of being the first paper on the street with the names of as many winners in as many contests as possible. Minutes after midnight, the election results rolled out on the *Post*'s trucks, unless the outcome of some major battle became so obvious and was so startling in its nature that a so-called "bulldog" edition was published hours ahead of the usual deadline.

Other extraordinary events would also call for a bulldog edition, which were distributed more frequently under Mr. Grozier's regime than under those after his death in 1924. The last bulldog (May 6, 1937) published by the *Boston Post* was for the explosion in New Jersey of the *Hindenburg*. Such bulldogs were truncated editions of the paper, of perhaps no more than six pages, published hours before deadline. Replates or extras were regular events, the first involving the insertion of a paragraph or two, the latter involving considerable remaking of the paper. These occurrences, as opposed to bulldog editions, came after deadline.

Election night at the *Post* was of heightened importance for another reason: various candidates that the paper backed in local or state elections made their way to the paper's offices in the course of the night to be interviewed. Boston, after all, is the largest city in New England and a state capital as well. Consequently, the candidates for state office would also spend part of the evening at the *Post*, along with those from the city fights or the county contests.

Grozier had seen early that his audience was to be drawn from the rising lower–middle class and from the Irish Catholic majority in the city, which was solidly in the Democratic Party. The *Herald* was Republican, as was the *Transcript*, while the *Globe* was deemed neutral. The *Journal*, while it lasted, had no clout but did bring its readers to the Row on election night. The Hearst papers might endorse candidates, but their offices were not in the Row. The *Herald* left the Row in 1906 and only after that became determinedly Republican. Thus the *Post* alone significantly endorsed candidates in what became, in effect, Democratic-party fights. Such being the case, to stand in front of the *Post* on election night was to stand at the center of local history.

In the presidential election of 1928, the *Post* endorsed Alfred E. Smith, the Democratic candidate. The *Globe* clung to its policy of not endorsing, and the *Herald* supported Herbert Hoover. Smith was of course defeated by Hoover, but he nevertheless carried Massachusetts. The crowd in Newspaper Row that night was enormous. The day after the election, the *Post*'s circulation rose to 674,490 papers.

The crowd in the Row and the general public were unaware of the intense mobilization that went on throughout New England to bring in the returns. Thousands of persons nevertheless assembled in Newspaper Row on election night to be among the first to learn of the outcome of the various contests and of the success or failure of their candidates. The *Herald*'s quarters on Tremont Street and, later, on Mason Street could offer no sense of location to a crowd. Newspaper Row, with the *Post* and *Globe* and the *Journal* at its heart and the *Transcript* nearby, was the place to be.

People began to assemble early in the evening, before even the first results trickled in. There were half a dozen barrooms within easy reach, at least three right in the Row. Restaurants extended their closing time. The crowd would remain in huge numbers until the first edition issued forth from the doors of the *Post*. Shortly before midnight, of course, they had to withdraw from the center of the street in order to let the *Post*'s trucks back up to the building to load the first edition and rush it to various distribution centers.

For a four-hour period, the place was a two-ring circus, as the *Globe*, to a lesser extent, also provided information for the crowd by posting returns and announcing the vote. Partisans dissatisfied with a result given by the *Post* would move up the Row a few yards to check that figure against the *Globe*'s returns. The excitement was intense; rarely was there an election when one contest or another was not attended by partisanship and a good deal of wagering. More than one bookie moved through the crowd.

For the evening the lower end of Washington Street was closed to traffic. Police were on hand as well, not so much to prevent any outbreak of violence as to direct all automobiles that came along Washington Street or descended School Street past the lighted city hall, down Water Street, and away from the direct route. At city hall, the crowd knew, the official vote was being tallied; but those precincts were closed to the public.

The *Post* put on an engaging show for the crowd. If the weather were mild, the windows facing the Row on the second floor of one of its six buildings were removed, giving the effect of a stage. From there, vocal announcements were made, first by megaphone and afterwards by a loudspeaking system. Recorded music was also provided; indeed, on some occasions, so were live entertainment, local singers, and standup comedians with a variety of political jokes.

On the street level, blackboards were mounted and the latest returns posted on them. In quarters on the first floor, staff artists who were deemed masters of lettering would chalk up the latest figures and then replace the boards bearing the earlier figures. Meanwhile, the loudspeaking system would be blaring out statistics, returns, and news items. Occasionally, a favored candidate would be permitted to thank the voters over the loudspeaker for the support they had given him.

When the votes began to pour in, such frivolities as a rendition of "Danny Boy" from one of the windows or the canned music would be put aside; the paper would get down to the business of informing the world how the voting had gone.

Farther along Washington Street, a smaller crowd would be standing in front of the *Globe*. Persons in both crowds would drift from one paper to the other, checking returns, looking for comparisons, or perhaps hoping that the disappointing figures they got from one paper would be contradicted by those from the other.

While the crowd was generally quiet (people were reading bulletins and listening to announcements), some vote counts would bring forth ringing cheers. In the main, the crowd was Democratic simply because the city fights were almost all among Democrats. But a good fraction of the gatherers would be Republicans. In those days, after all, the Republican Party dominated the General Court of the Commonwealth of Massachusetts, the official name of the two houses of the legislature.

Crowds formed in the Row for other reasons than national and local elections—they awaited the outcome of sporting events as well. Here fans gather in 1912, when the Red Sox were riding high.

Whenever good news was posted that such and such a candidate had won, there would be a rush to his headquarters, often at the Parker House or Young's Hotel preferred because of their proximity to the Row. More often than not, when the word of victory came for one candidate or the other in a citywide fight, both would make their way promptly to the *Post* to make a statement. In state elections, Republican candidates would go first to the *Herald* but were sure sooner or later to make their way to the *Post* and the *Globe*. When all those papers were in Newspaper Row, along with the *Journal* and the *Advertiser*, a candidate's election-night itinerary was of course shorter.

Even after radio began to bring returns into the home more speedily than any newspaper could, crowds still collected on the asphalt surface of Newspaper Row, confident that they would learn more there than they would over the radio and wanting the camaraderie and excitement. The hours of their vigil were shortened by the increase in telephones, which phased out the hand-operated telegraph key; by the introduction of voting machines, which gave each precinct count infinitely faster than before; and by the presence of radio, by which the newspapers were able to help check and correct their own reports. Thus the size of the crowds diminished; but until 1956, when the *Post* died, hundreds would still gather in Newspaper Row.

At the beginning of the twentieth century and well into the 1930s, the Boston experience remained unique in the country because of the concentration of newspapers. Friend and foe alike were conscious of the Row's sense of community during elections. It was more than political, and it is lost today. On election nights now, all is in darkness, except for the activity in city hall. The drawing power of the Row was the same as the theater's appeal over film: the lure of being where the action is. But the action has gone elsewhere.

People now join one another in a private home, or supporters and friends will show up at some hotel ballroom hired for the night by one of the candidates. The mixture of characters, however, the hoopla, the noise, the conversation, the bantering, the suspense—all is gone. Election night in Newspaper Row—that mingling of bankers and bums, lawyers, politicos, hangers-on, gamblers, bookies, detectives, pickpockets, candidates, body guards, secretaries, relatives, friends, newspapermen, reporters, and editors who were making their way to the bars—is gone forever.

CHAPTER FIFTEEN

Women Arrive

Women worked in Newspaper Row from the beginning. At first, they were employed setting type. After a while, this activity became an all-male preserve on the major metropolitan papers and remains so today. Women, however, continued to set type and perform other mechanical chores at small-town weeklies and some suburban papers. But women very soon found themselves in important editorial roles. Some became correspondents; others became staff reporters, society editors, art critics, and columnists — at first society columnists, then columnists giving advice to the lovelorn. Gradually, women on the staff of the Boston papers found themselves covering something other than "the woman's angle" and were working shoulder to shoulder with men on politics, trials, murder stories, scandals — financial and otherwise— and on medical and scientific stories. Some became department heads, especially after World War II and the rise of the minority movements.

Three women distinguished themselves in the early history of Boston journalism. They were Cornelia Walter, the first editor of a major metropolitan newspaper (the *Boston Transcript*) in the country; Florence Finch Kelly, whose autobiography, *The Flowing Stream*, recounts "Fifty-Six Years in American Newspaper Life" and whose career flowered in Boston; and Mary Baker Eddy, the head of the Christian Science church, who has the distinction, among others, of being the first woman to found a major daily newspaper.

To be sure, the pre–Civil War Boston publishers let the redoubtable Margaret Fuller escape. Horace Greeley, having read her essays in the *Dial*, which she edited, brought her onto the *New York*

Women gradually came into their own on Newspaper Row, moving from setting type to covering society events to working shoulder to shoulder with men on politics, trials, financial scandals, and medical stories. Note here the lone woman, absorbed in her job.

Tribune as a critic. She performed admirably. Although he hired her to do criticism in the fields of art, theater, music, and literature, she wrote an investigation of a penal institution and performed other reportorial tasks. She was eager, however, to get to Europe, and Greeley, the first publisher to think in modern ways, promptly made her his foreign correspondent, a role she brought off very well. Fuller was, by her intellectual brilliance, the leading pioneer in opening the field of journalism to women. (She is not included with the three women whose profiles follow only because, while in Boston, she never worked on a newspaper.)

Cornelia Wells Walter was named editor of the *Boston Transcript* in 1842, the year that Fuller gave up the editorship of the *Dial* and two years before she went to New York. While Margaret attracted a good deal of attention, Cornelia was by nature retiring, except in print.

Whether or not Fuller and Walter ever met is uncertain. While it would seem likely, as a strong feminist like Fuller would have rejoiced at Walter's being named editor of the *Transcript*, the latter was of such a retiring nature that they may not have.

She came to the editorship of the *Transcript* rather through the back door. The first editor, also one of the paper's founders, was her brother, Lynde Minshull Walter. They were Bostonians of an old family and had among their forebears Increase Mather, one of the first famous Puritan divines. Lynde had suggested founding the *Transcript* and edited it with success for ten years. Then he was incapacitated by a malady that resulted from carrying a flag in a Whig parade, in the course of which he injured his groin. Cornelia, who had acted as his secretary, now found herself doing more and more of the work as Lynde conducted some of his editing from their home on Beacon Hill. In 1842, the year he died, he wrote a moving farewell to his editorial chair. On his death, Henry Dutton, his colleague and the head of the printing firm that printed the paper, offered the editorial chair to Cornelia Walter at $500 a year. This figure, incidentally, is half what Margaret Fuller had been offered to teach in Rhode Island and probably half of what she received from Greeley.

Rumbles of discontent and amusement ran through Boston's newsmen at the thought of a woman editor; but other papers welcomed her, and, where the appointment attracted national attention, it was commended. Walter soon proved herself. The offices of the *Transcript* at the time were on Exchange Street; but its success demanded larger quarters, and it found them on Congress Street, some distance from Newspaper Row. Not until 1860 would it move to Washington Street. In any event, she elected to do her work at home, where she had done her brother's work in his illness.

She was a woman of conservative views, did not support women's suffrage, disdained Ralph Waldo Emerson, and hit hard at Asa Gray, the celebrated botanist, when he lectured that the world had not been made in six days or six years but had required millions. She wrote briskly and well and never stepped away from a fight. The one that brought her national attention came as a result of her criticism of Edgar Allan Poe's performance at the Boston Lyceum. He shared the platform with a lecturer, and his part of the program was advertised as "A Poem by Edgar A. Poe." Poe at this time was well known because of his poem "The Raven."

After dismissing the first speaker in a few lines, Walter wrote,

> The address had been announced in the papers, "to be followed by A Poem . . . ," an officer introduced . . . a gentle-

man who, as we understood him to say, possessed a *raven*-ous desire to be known as the author of a particular piece of poetry on a celebrated croaking bird well-known to ornithologists.

The poet immediately arose; but, if he uttered poesy in the first instance, it was certainly of a most prosaic order. The audience listened in amazement to a singularly didactic exordium, and finally commenced the noisy expedient of removing (themselves) from the hall, and this long before they had discovered the style or the measure, whether it was rhyme or blank verse. We believe however that it was a prose introductory to a poem on the "Star Discovered by Tycho Brahe," considered figuratively as the "Messenger of the Deity" out of which Mr. Edgar A. Poe constructed a sentimental and imaginative poem.

The audience now thinned so rapidly and made such commotion in their departure that we lost the beauties of the composition. We heard the prefatory exordium however (which we took to be *in prose*) and our thoughts upon it ran as follows:

"Twixt truth and poesy they say, there is a mighty schism
I'd like to be a moral man and preach 'didacticism'—
But as truth and taste do not agree and I do surely know it
Let truth and morals go and be a critic and a poet

. . . The "Star Discovered by Tycho Brahe" was no sooner out of sight than the terrestrials who had watched its disappearance and were about to follow the same course, were officially urged to a further delay, and another small poem succeeded. This was "The Raven"—a composition probably better appreciated by the author than by his auditory, and which has already gone the rounds of the press, followed by a most felicitous parody from another source. . . .

We are sorry to record a *failure* in these opening exercises of the Lyceum . . .

She returned to the attack the next day.

A Prodigy—It has been said by "those who know" that the poem delivered by Edgar A. Poe at the Lyceum . . . . *was written before its author was twelve years old*. If the poet felt "doubts about his ability in preparing a poem for a Boston audience" at an early age, it is not to be wondered at that they were openly *expressed* (as a correspondent of a morning paper states) on Thursday evening. A poem delivered before a literary association of adults, as written by a boy. Only think of it Poh! Poh!

Poe, back in New York, responded in the *Broadway Journal* in a "churlish and vulgar tone," one historian reports. Walker won the fight. Poe's *Broadway Journal* went out of business, and she wrote:

> To trust in friends is but so-so,
> Especially when cash is low;
> The *Broadway Journal*'s proved no-go
> Friends would not pay the pen of Poe.

He later called her "that most beguiling of all little divinities, Miss Walter of the *Transcript*" and a "witch" and then became ill-mannered and scurrilous. Later she responded in kind, beginning, "He is a wandering specimen of the Literary Snob continually obtruding himself upon public notice; today in the gutter, tomorrow in some milliner's magazine; but in all places and all times, magnificently snobbish and dirty. . ." It was, as we have noted elsewhere, an era of very personal journalism. Walter had further satisfaction when the Lyceum, in its annual report, apologized to its members for the Poe performance.

While politics and national legislation were not her strong suits, she opposed the Mexican war vigorously and likewise the annexation of Texas. She remained as editor for five years and left to marry, recognized and praised by all the papers in the city. Although she was no crusader, she had opened as many doors as Margaret Fuller, and for the ensuing decades, more and more women found desks in the editorial rooms.

Florence Finch came to Boston from Chicago in 1881. In her autobiography she heads her Boston chapter "The Stone Walls of Boston." Her letters of introduction brought her to Lillian Whiting, a famous figure for many years in Boston journalism. (Miss Whiting won *her* first newspaper job in upstate New York, where she was born, by writing two essays on Margaret Fuller. In 1880, she came to Boston and went to work for the *Traveller*. When Florence Finch arrived, it was Whiting who advised her, suggesting that she submit articles to the various papers and follow up should anyone accept her material.)

An editor at the *Herald*, then the dominant paper in Newspaper Row, agreed to take a Finch article on temperance legislation and pay ten dollars *if* he published it. A day or two later, for a second piece, he paid two dollars and fifty cents. After two or three weeks, she went to him to ask about the first piece. He had forgotten it. Pressed by her recollections, he recalled it, said it was lost, and stated they didn't want it. She protested, and after some discussion, he finally paid her five dollars.

"It was," Finch wrote fifty years later, "my first, but far from my last, experience of the ruthless injustice to which my sex would submit me in the newspaper world. For I do not believe he would have tried that crooked game upon me if I had been a man."

Finch appealed to the editor of the *Transcript*, who promised her a few book reviews. They did not pay for the reviews but she could keep the books. She did and sold them at second-hand bookshops to raise some money. She had had only forty dollars when she arrived. She had more success in selling an article to Lucy Stone, the celebrated feminist, and her husband, Henry B. Blackwell, for their magazine, *The Women's Journal*. Her fortunes were at their very lowest, however, when Mrs. Annie Diggs, the social reformer and an old friend, came to Boston. They roomed together through the winter. In the spring, she was hired by the *Globe*.

The *Globe* was one of the first papers in Newspaper Row to have a woman on staff. She was Georgia Hamlen, a native of Charlestown, where General Taylor had been born. The *Globe* history records that she started in 1872, probably as a "girl Friday" doing miscellaneous chores. She was at length assigned to book reviewing. She worked at the *Globe* for five years before leaving to work with John Boyle O'Reilly, a distinguished author and orator, on the *Boston Pilot*, a Catholic weekly. For the ensuing four years, the *Globe* was without a woman on its staff. It was then that Florence Finch applied on a tip by Lillian Whiting.

Her interview is indicative of the attitude toward women in Newspaper Row at the time. Ben Palmer, the managing editor, prefaced his interview with her by saying that "Colonel Taylor [the title General would come later] . . . did not believe in women in journalism, that he had always been opposed, and was still opposed to having a woman in the office. But he had decided that a woman was needed in order to carry out his ideas the way he

wanted them treated . . . especially, he emphasized, they wanted a
woman to do millinery openings." Before she left that day, she
agreed to do that, to write a woman's column on Sundays, and to
act as art critic. Her column was called "The Woman's Hour," a title
taken from the speech of a legislator who said that "the woman's
hour had struck." Taylor was bent on making an appeal to women
readers, and Florence Finch was to be his driving force. Among
her reportorial duties were indeed millinery openings, but within a
year's time, another woman handled such things.

When Finch arrived in Boston, she was turned against the
Globe by her Boston acquaintances who spurned it as a low sort
of paper. This was probably because it was, at the time, aggres-
sively Democratic and supported General Benjamin F. Butler for
governor. Finch soon found that her Back Bay and Beacon Hill
friends were reading the *Globe* assiduously and following her
work. She stayed with the *Globe* for four years, doing some exciting assignments and some memorable writing.

Her departure from the *Globe* tells a lot about the role of
women in journalism at that time. In his history of the *Globe*,
Louis M. Lyons writes: "Soon she found that 'any door I wanted to
open yielded readily to my touch. . . .' " In her social notes she
scattered editorial paragraphs, some humorous, some mildly irreverent. The notes turned up missing, to her disappointment,
until she found them moved to the editorial page. She was taken
off society and assigned to editorial writing. She found that Colonel Taylor liked freshness and originality in editorials and that he
appreciated items of pungency and piquancy on that page, material that would give the reader a chuckle and lead him to ask,
"Did you see so-and-so in the *Globe* this morning?"

She had grown up in Republican Kansas; the *Globe* was edito-
rially Democratic, but she found it also liberal and independent. It
was of course against the Republican tariff. Having to study about
the tariff, she discovered "it was quite as much an ethical as an
economic question," and that appealed to her. She was liberal and
inclined a little toward radicalism, such as it was in the 1880s.
One Sunday in 1884 Governor Butler, who had been supported by
the *Globe* as a Democrat, announced his candidacy for president
on the Anti-Monopoly and Greenback ticket. It fell to Finch to
write the editorial regarding the announcement. She had become
politically sophisticated enough to know that Butler's platform
was a delicate matter; it had to be taken seriously but without in

the least committing the *Globe* to the new heresy. She managed so deftly that the Colonel beamed Monday morning that the editorial was "just right."

Louis Lyons does not link the incident to her departure; yet, in her autobiography, *The Flowing Stream*, she does.

> A friendly acquaintance in the business office told me that when the Colonel arrived Monday morning his usually stern, immobile face was beaming with gratification and he wanted to know who wrote the Butler editorial. While someone went to get the information, he said that he had been anxious about the matter after he saw the Sunday papers but this editorial had dealt with it in exactly the right way, and he wanted to know who had made such a good job of it. My informant told me that when he was told that "Miss Finch wrote it," his countenance fell instantly into stony lines, his mouth snapped shut and he turned on his heel and walked into his private office without another word. Colonel Taylor could not forget that he "didn't believe in women in journalism."
>
> I have told the incident at some length, partly because it is vividly illustrative of the spirit of the times, which was not only vigorously opposed to any attempt by women to do unusual things, but even more violently objected to their success when they did; but I have related it especially because it helped me to a decision that made a turning point in my career. For it let me know that I had gone as far as I could on the Globe.

She was being paid less than the other two editorial writers, one of whom, Alan Kelly, she would marry. When she asked for a raise, however, she was refused.

While Boston may boast having had the first woman editor of a major metropolitan daily, the city's paper, as Florence Finch learned, lagged far behind New York City's in receiving women into the editorial rooms and elsewhere. From 1862 to 1872, Jane Cunningham Croly, whose pen name was Jennie June, ran a women's department in the *New York World*, contributing drama and literary criticism as well. Contemporaries in the business were Grace Greenwood and Minnie Myrtle, also competent newspaperwomen. The use of pen names was a common practice among women journalists at the time, and alliteration was the style. Florence Finch was baptized with that style; yet, it had never appeared in the *Globe*, and she didn't want to continue anonymously. It was, however, that editorial that led her to leave. When she did, her fellow staff writers presented her with handsome bound copies of *Bartlett's Familiar Quotations* and *Quotations from Shakespeare*. Despite her decision to leave, she always looked back on her years in Boston as golden.

The era of yellow journalism was about to dawn. Joseph Pulitzer had bought the *World* in 1883, and E. A. Grozier was learning his trade there when Finch, by a circuitous route, arrived in New York City in 1887. Her husband, Alan, had been named an editor of the *Evening Sun*. They remained a year and then went to work in California. They returned in 1903, and in 1906 Florence happily landed a job with the *New York Times*. She had a good post from which to observe the rise and decline of yellow journalism. She felt it set the women's advances back sharply. In her autobiography, she decries it.

And then came yellow journalism and its two fearsome offspring, the "stunt girls" and the "sob sister" and the outlook took on another color. The clamorous yellow press with its incessant noxious appeal to whatever is base and evil in human nature was in itself a flaunting challenge to the development of journalism toward ideals of reputable publishing. . . . And its use of women reporters and writers in its emotional, spectacular and scandalous methods and purposes dealt a blow to the progress women were making in the profession. For some years its specious pretence of humanitarianism camouflaged too well its real purpose as to deceive large numbers of reputable readers. But it has no real interest in humanity. Its sole purpose was to gain such enormous circulations and such manipulating power through their emotions over these vast masses of readers as would enable its leaders to mobilize their millions in support of whatever scheme they chose to undertake. For some years, while it was able to delude surprisingly large numbers of intelligent and well-meaning readers, it was a hindrance of real consequence and a serious threat to the growth of respectable journalism. And the discreditable "stunting" with which it exploited women reporters was almost a knock-out blow to the progress and the inviting prospects of women in professional journalism from which their cause did not recover for nearly two decades.

For a dozen years or more women writers of high standing had been advising ambitious young women who wanted to write to enter journalism and their advice had been an important factor in sending many young women into newspaper work. But when the clamor of the stunting sisterhood began to shriek from headlines and its daring and unsavory exploits to be everywhere talked about, they were shocked into silence. Of still more importance was the fact that in the legitimate press all over the country the man in whose hands rested the fate of women applicants for work were revolted by the spectacle of those stunting, shrieking, and sobbing young women of the yellow press, and their attitude toward women wanting employment, which had become much more lenient, stiffened into antagonism. It became more difficult for women to get positions on reputable newspapers or even sell their work by space.

But the yellow press was thronged with them. It wanted them and used them, not for the ordinary and legitimate uses of the newspaper, the collection and writing of news, but for the exploitation of their sex. The kind of things they did and wrote about would have been of slight value, even in the columns of the yellow journals, as the work of men reporters, while the missions on which they often were sent achieved an added salaciousness over a woman's signature. Some of them could not write well enough even for the reporting of their own stunts, but had to have their stories written for them or rewritten by men detailed for the purpose. Nevertheless, among them were a few women who might have made good in legitimate newspaper work and even a very few who did develop into journalists of as high a grade as the yellow press was accustomed to tolerate.

Not until the end of World War I did Florence Finch see better opportunities for women.

The judgment she passes on the yellow press is exceptionally harsh. The definition implied in her denunciation does not fit the *Globe*, *Post*, and *Herald* in their scramble for circulation. The Boston papers never engaged in such warfare as marked the battle between Hearst and Pulitzer in New York or between Hearst and the *Tribune* in Chicago. The title "poor farm of journalism" belonged elsewhere. Nor did the "scarlet woman of journalism"— as magazine editor and reformer Oswald Garrison Villard called

the *Post*—ever subject its women staff writers to any more undig-
nified "stunt" than having one of them move around the city and
award ten dollars to the first man to show her marked courtesy.
During those decades when the *Post* was at its most flamboyant,
women were on the daily and the Sunday staffs; and while the
majority were engaged in the society pages, social notes, market-
ing, fashions, and feature stories, they were also called on for
general assignment.

The Hearst papers in Boston did lean toward the excesses
that Florence Finch Kelly enumerated but never with the enthusiasm for such that was shown in New York City and elsewhere.
There was a certain "Boston decorum" that restrained them.
Nonetheless, Boston's journalists during those early decades of
the twentieth century were sufficiently yellow to help stimulate
Mary Baker Eddy to found the *Christian Science Monitor*, an
action that gives her a place of distinction in the history of journalism and the feminist movement.

Not far from Newspaper Row, a woman pioneer, Katherine L.
Conway, was from 1905 to 1908 the editor of the *Boston Pilot*, a
Catholic weekly, and made a brilliant career there for herself. In
1908 William Cardinal O'Connell bought the paper, made it the
official organ of the archdiocese of Boston, and put a priest in the
editor's chair. Miss Conway had followed the distinguished John
Boyle O'Reilly, poet, orator, and journalist. She earned her spurs
by a long apprenticeship.

Cornelia Walter, the only woman that Newspaper Row ever
knew as an editor, was an accident of history. True, more and
more women were employed on newspapers after the turn of the
century. Yet they served as society editors and art critics, wrote
household columns, edited copy, and worked as general reporters; they were never advertising executives, editors of authority, or department heads. The post-war feminist movement had to
come, and Newspaper Row disappear, before they moved behind
the administrative desks and into the executive suites of Boston
newspapers, where they remain underrepresented today.

CHAPTER SIXTEEN

The Subculture

In the 1920s and the '30s and more than likely well before that, Newspaper Row had become such a community, a microcosmic world in itself, that it had its own subculture. During the years of Prohibition, the newspaper business, involving as it did a good deal of night work, also involved a good deal of hard drinking. Consequently, it was served by speakeasies and roving bootleggers who provided curb service and home-or-office delivery. Two things would combine in 1935, however, to reduce considerably the amount of drinking among newspapermen. The first was the introduction of the five-day work week by Franklin D. Roosevelt. The other was the creation of Alcoholics Anonymous. Before either of these occurrences, drinking seemed to be the order of the day or, better, the night, for the extreme tension in an editorial room as deadline approached, usually midnight or one or two o'clock for a morning newspaper, seemed to call for a relaxing libation when the paper had finally been "put to bed."

Before the arrival of the five-day week, newspapers were inclined to work reporters and rewrite men for extraordinary hours and out of necessity became very tolerant of heavy drinkers. Publishers generally underpaid their editorial employees and so were lenient toward their failings. The *Post* in the '20s and the '30s had one editor who was paid for the days he showed up.

During Prohibition there was always some employee in the bowels of the building or elsewhere who ran a little business supplying emergency liquor to the thirsty. Drinking, of course, was not permitted on the premises; but despite that edict, after the last edition had been put to bed, many a bottle party was held in the city room or the sports department.

Long after Prohibition's repeal, one man in the *Post* mailing room continued to provide such a service during his own working hours, after which "customers" had to appeal to a drug store in Scollay Square or to another shop in the Elks Hotel on Tremont Street. The shop was controlled, if not operated, by Beano Breen, a well-known gangster who was shot to death in the hotel's lobby.

The Depression served to intensify the activities of the subculture of Newspaper Row, which developed several curious arrangements. The majority of *Post* workers were, of course, night workers, as were many at the *Globe*, the Associated Press, the United Press, the International News Service, and various other satellite businesses attendant on the major papers. These men usually came to work when shops were closed and consequently had difficulty in attending to their everyday needs.

There were half a dozen salesmen, all struggling and as poor as the newspapermen they serviced, who provided what was needed. David Galler was a big man with a caricature of a face but a good head for figures. Dave could get you anything you wanted: an automobile, household furniture, appliances, tires, radios, even a house—all without a down payment. He made his money on the interest he charged but would have considered the percentage charged by today's banks as immoral.

He had any number of customers at the *Post* and presumably as many more at the other papers. On pay day, Dave stood beside the cashier's cage, and as a customer received his pay (and the *Post* always paid in cash), Dave got his weekly payment. As the burden of payments extended over years, a certain resentment built up in the payer. On occasion in the city room on pay day someone would say, "Get down to the cashier's cage at noon—so and so is going to belt Galler. He's making his last payment today."

Galler's office was in his hat. So was Sam Dryver's. Sam was a pleasant but mournful businessman who did for clothing what Galler did for bulky items. Usually Dryver, whose operation was a small one, charged no interest. All *Post* employees, certainly those in the editorial offices, knew that Sam could "get it for you wholesale." He had numerous friends in the wholesale business and would buy what was needed from them and deliver it to the city room. It could be embarrassing the first time one bought from Sam because he had to take his client to the wholesale house for a fitting, a visit these houses never seemed happy about. Sam's customer had to stand around, draped in the garment preferred, while Sam bargained with his friend. Once Sam had your size, he delivered.

Once a year, the staff of the city room, or at least those on it with a taste for elegance, would await the arrival of a man named Bradley, a Canadian who came to Boston to sell worsteds and wools and bolts of cloth for Canadian manufacturers. Before returning to Canada, he arrived at the *Post* city room intent on disposing of his samples at very reasonable prices; rarely did he leave burdened. On occasion he made a semi-annual visit.

The most familiar daily visitor, however, was Harry Victorson, a bookseller who had a "hole in the wall" somewhere on Beacon Street but actually spent his working day in the editorial rooms of the various newspapers. As opposed to Galler and Dryver, Victorson was a scholar, an anti-Communist Marxist who spent his hours in newspaper offices reading *The Nation*, books he had offered for sale, or some favorite from his own library.

He entered an office lugging two large leather bags filled with books. He spread some of these out on a suitable flat surface, to which members of the staff drifted to buy what they wanted. Always he had orders for certain books, which he provided, leaving them on top of the buyer's typewriter. The majority of the *Post* staff paid him one dollar a week. (I did so myself for more than twenty years.) But despite regularity of payment, all his customers owed him money. He kept the accounts in a small brown notebook, entering each payment with an antique fountain pen. At irregular intervals, he submitted bills that in effect were rebukes, not that one owed money, but that one hadn't bought a book in a long time. While one might haggle with Galler or even with Dryver, no one ever thought of questioning Harry—or "Vic," as he was universally called. When he died his brother, Emmanuel—"Manny"—took over. Manny was not the scholarly type that Vic was, but he was a dear, hard-working man whose death was marked by the *Globe* in a laudatory editorial. The bookselling enterprise died with him.

There was one difficulty in dealing with Vic or Manny. If by chance you once ordered a novel by Evelyn Waugh or H.G. Wells, every book he had ever published suddenly appeared on your typewriter without the entrepreneur's being on hand to receive your protest. Such impositions were usually received by the reporters and editors with resignation; but if someone ordered a book on beekeeping for his Aunt Agatha, books on beekeeping multiplied on his desk every time he left the office. Vic managed to look so grieved at their return that the customer was almost inclined to take up beekeeping as a hobby.

Gambling in the Row was as intensive as the drinking. When Prohibition ended in 1933, barrooms flourished again on the Row, and bootlegging was reduced to after-hours sales. The men who attended to the gambling instincts of the Row's denizens, however, were still legally off limits. The state lottery, with its mega-bucks and weekly and daily tickets, was still a long way in the future.

Sporting bets on horse racing, baseball games, and other athletic events were handled by a man called Army—for the simple reason that he had one arm only, and that one his left, although he was born right-handed. He was by common acknowledgment the hardest-working man in the Row. Morning, noon, and night he was on hand, servicing his customers, citing odds, providing the names of winners and losers, explaining percentages and point spreads, and providing courteously whatever information was requested. Each night he dined at Purcell's restaurant, a gathering place for *Post*, *Globe*, and *Transcript* people. Army's wife, appreciating the public-service aspect of his work, journeyed in from their Somerville home so that they could dine together and he could attend to his clients.

Army did not handle the "nigger" pool—as it was known then in street parlance—a gambling enterprise run by organized crime in which a person could wager anything from one penny up on the order of a series of numbers that would appear daily in each newspaper. When it had to be mentioned in the columns of the newspapers, it was called the "number" pool. In Newspaper Row, such bets as these were taken by a diminutive but chunky newsboy called "Nigger." Although not black, he always dressed in black woolens and was well clothed with them in summer and completely swathed in winter. His complexion, moreover, was swarthy, and he never seemed washed. He recorded the numbers on large brown shopping bags that he tore into manageable slips. He never seemed to enter anyone's name but merely the nature of the bet, with special markings for "boxing" a number or "bleeding" it. There was no such thing as a receipt. Everyone knew he was dealing with men of honor. Most of the papers at that time carried in their morning edition the "number"-pool number, although it was never so designated. It would instead be a special typographical presentation of various totals of monies bet on certain races at one of the tracks. Read vertically instead of horizontally, the arithmetical arrangement gave one the winning number. The rate of pay-off was high.

At that same time there was another pool, less favored by newspaper people, called the Treasury Balance. Another pool offered monthly prizes, the top one of which was $13,000. To be in this pool did not require an invitation, but you did have to have a ticket, which were limited in number and thus hard to get. There was a waiting list. The drawing was held in one newspaper or another once a month, and a man from the Internal Revenue Service, the tradition ran, was on hand to take the government's share off the top. The pool lasted for years. Not until the 1950s was it abandoned as a result of the Estes Kefauver Senate investigation into gambling.

That investigation also revealed that one of the major "lay-off" operations in the nation was located in Newspaper Row, to the astonishment of most newspaper people. A "lay off" operation usually was an arrangement among gambling syndicates in various cities to spread gargantuan bets around so that, in the case of a "hit," no one syndicate would suffer too grievously. The operation's quarters were called the Row Club (from Newspaper Row), with offices on School Street.

The bookie at the *Globe* was a strapping man called Monty, who used his profits to buy the barroom in the basement of the *Globe* building on Devonshire Street. One of the oldest bistros in the nation, it was known as the Bell-in-Hand. When the *Globe* finally left the Row, so did Monty, taking his establishment with him. Later, after having been shot and robbed one night near his home, he decided to retire.

Monty never operated full-time, as did Army. The latter's work required a good deal of walking around Newspaper Row and the side streets radiating from it. Army had a nodding acquaintance, if not a friendship, with Frank Dolan, who was the police officer most often assigned to the traffic detail in Newspaper Row. Army customarily carried on his public service unharassed or unmolested; but every so often, for one reason or another, there would be crackdown on gamblers in the city. This always put Army at a disadvantage. Being arrested would not only deprive his customers of his services, it would also deprive him of his livelihood. The result was that he was determined to

avoid arrest. He had more escape routes than a rabbit or a fox.
There were four buildings that he could enter and leave by a total
of twenty-one doorways, three of them leading into the subway,
where he could catch a train if pressed.

One building had a barber shop in the basement and a barroom above it. The barroom had two doors, one on Water Street
and one on Spring Lane. If he emerged on Spring Lane, he could
then enter a restaurant that ran all the way through another
building to Milk Street. If he chose another door in Spring Lane in
the same building, it gave him entrance to the subway or another
exit onto Washington Street. If he entered the barber shop from
Water Street, he knew he had an exit to Spring Lane, which permitted him to emerge onto Devonshire Street or, again, to enter
the subway.

If the police were pursuing Army and he entered the barber
shop, dodging among the chairs and the customers and the man
who refurbished hats, they—the pursuing police—suddenly found
themselves bumping into barbers and shoeshine men while their
prey vanished. Hardy indeed was the vice-squad officer who
chased Army more than twice. On this, his home turf, he was
uncaptureable.

For a while those newspapermen looking for casual sex were
serviced by a waitress in a small hashhouse that rented quarters
in one of the *Post* buildings. The young woman had discovered
that an unused door in the rear of the restaurant opened onto a
flight of stairs that led to an office on the second floor of the
building. This office had somehow become permanently barred
off as the *Post* juggled buildings and office space in the frantic
days of its growth under E. A. Grozier. It was a full decade after
his death before the woman's operation was discovered by *Post*
management. For the first time in twenty years, they were alerted
as to the presence of a locked door to an office with no legend on
its glass. They opened it and found waitress and client in flagrante
delicto.

Like the Paris Opera House, the *Post* buildings had more per-
manent residents than this waitress. During the winter, one of the
hallways was given over to a bearded alcoholic, who left it so foul
smelling by urinating on the radiator that all *Post* people including the janitors avoided it entirely, leaving him in undisputed possession. No one knew where he went in the summer. His return in

December was as much a harbinger of winter as the swallows at Capistrano are heralds of spring.

Both winter and summer the "Lung-er," so named because he seemed consumptive, lived in the Associated Press room, appearing about midnight after the first edition had been published and the more censorious editors had departed the building. He slept on the trash bags that the janitor for the editorial rooms piled in one corner and that were removed in the morning by another shift.

The Lung-er was fed by whatever editor worked the "lobster" shift—3:00 A.M. to 9:00 A.M. He must have come and gone over a period of ten years. Of all the strange inhabitants of Newspaper Row, he was the most taciturn, homeless before the number of homeless became a national disgrace. The Lung-er accepted what was given him without question and without thanks. I don't know if he ever asked for the meal he received each morning, but it was understood by whoever worked the lobster shift that he was to be taken care of.

There were more demanding dependents on Newspaper Row continually looking for handouts. They fell into two classes: former newspapermen who had drunk themselves out of the business entirely and almost out of life; and former athletes who, their heyday being past, could find no suitable living in the work-a-day world. Two of the latter had been great basketball players in the age before television, when basketball was a barnstorming sport that saw any number of teams traveling about New England.

Some of the derelict newspapermen were forever cadging money from anyone they could or trying to sell tips on news stories, usually those already known to the paper. They were quite different from stooges. The latter were young aspirants to the newspaper business who fastened themselves onto a photographer or a reporter and worked practically as unpaid servants in the hope of one day breaking into the business. They would be described today as gofers. One ended up as a librarian on the *Post*, another as a photographer on the *Globe*. Their like were familiar figures on Newspaper Row.

When the moon was full the *Post* city room, like every other city room, was subject to a barrage of calls and visits by the looney. However loudly psychiatrists may dismiss the thought that the full moon affects the half-demented, any city editor will tell you that the empirical evidence is to the contrary. This was not unique to Newspaper Row. One chap who appeared when the moon was waxing thought he was St. Paul. One irreverent rewrite man would always ask him, "How are things with the Corinthians?" "Not good," the man always replied, his brow suddenly furrowing. Another thought he was Shipwreck Kelley, a famous flagpole sitter. The paranoid were frequent, nameless, and hard to get rid of. Such characters, however, were transients and not a part of the daily picture.

One unique figure defying categorization was Timothy "Haddock" Sullivan, sometimes called "Fish." From the mid-'20s to the mid-'30s, he was a possession of the sports department, or perhaps it is better to say that the sports department was a possession of his. For many years his occupation was shoveling the fish from the holds of the draggers (fishing vessels using nets) and trawlers that came into the Boston Fish Pier. But Haddock's aspirations rose above that. He knew he was made for better things. He became the manager or at least the representative of the Irish-American Athletic Club, one of several that bore that name, which maintained quarters in South Boston and had a gymnasium and a ring on its second floor and a barroom on its first. Gerald V. Hern, a sports writer of great talent and later sports editor of the *Post*, often considered becoming Haddock's biographer but deemed the man's exploits too far beyond all norms to find ready acceptance with America's hidebound publishers. Hern's contention was always that there were more fights in the barroom than in the gymnasium.

Bill Cunningham, the *Post*'s most distinguished sports columnist, became Haddock's foremost chronicler and always described him as the manager of "divers [sic] boxers." When that description first appeared in the paper, Haddock confronted Cunningham and said that "no one of my bums ever took a dive." He was by then a familiar at the *Post*. He had made his first forays into the sports department with news releases about the fights he promoted. Even if they had been in superlative English, they would have been rewritten by one of the reporters. So Haddock made it a practice simply to drop into the paper, give some sportswriter the information, and see it written up as he waited.

He was a powerful man and could probably have licked any of the fighters he handled if the Marquis of Queensbury rules were suspended. He was also an expert and graceful ballroom dancer and handsome in a rough, masculine way. Ultimately, Haddock would arrive at the sports department to dictate a release and there would prepare himself for a night on the town roaming the dance halls. He would wash and change at the *Post* and, as soap was hardly enough to rid him of the aroma of fish from his day's work (and he used the sandsoap favored by printers), use a heavy cologne. After his toilette, he could be sensed ten yards away. The hair was coal black and greased down; the gray suit and four-in-hand tie were immaculate.

As the years went along, he took to leaving his change of clothing in the *Post* and spent more time there, it seemed, than at his home in Revere. Cunningham, the sports columnist, made good use of Haddock, quoting him on affairs of state, the condition of athletics in the United States, and on the outcome of major athletic events. Haddock had a gift for malapropisms, and one most often quoted was, "The wish is farther than the thought."

For one mad reason or another—perhaps because Fish boasted he could beat anybody at anything if he put his mind to it—a golf match was arranged between him and another fight manager named Bobby Goldman. Both these characters had become familiar to *Post* readers through the sports pages, and the match was duly announced. Neither had ever played golf before or held a club in his hands. The Wollaston (Mass.) Golf Club was the site of the event, and a group of *Post* readers numbering about fifty actually showed up to follow the competitors around. They didn't see much golf, but they weren't disappointed.

Gerald V. Hern was there to keep everyone on his feet for the duration and to prevent the players from assassinating one another or some club member by accident. He not only kept score, but he also timed them. It took one hour and seven minutes to clear the first hole. Hern called the match at the end of the fourth hole, not because of the time element but because he was sore from laughing. He declared Haddock the winner. The match was reported on the sports pages, perhaps no more inaccurately or hyperbolically than was the custom of the day. In making his own comment on the match to Cunningham, Haddock insisted he had had one great shot during the match. "With my nimlick," he said.

Haddock enjoyed the notoriety he achieved and was willing to oblige newsmen if the need arose. One bitter winter day, several photographers were waiting at the Fish Pier for the arrival of some draggers, which were ritualistically photographed when they came off the ocean and into the harbor sheathed with two feet of ice that had to be chopped off. Pictures of the crew wielding axes on the ice were *de rigueur* when the mercury dropped below zero. On a given day, the draggers were delayed and didn't appear. Tommy Watson, one of the photographers, appealed to Haddock to clown up as if he was surprised at their delay.

"Get your cameras ready," said Fish. "Are you ready?"

"Yes."

"Good. I'll go get them." Thereupon he dove into the water, splitting the scum of loose ice on the surface. The air temperature must have been, at the most, zero. The photographers provided all the hot toddy that was needed to restore him. On other occasions the hot toddies got to Haddock and he went on a bender. Such delinquency was likely to leave him idle for days, but his friends in the sports department understood and took care of him, rushing him to Boston City Hospital's K Ward, where beds were reserved for alcoholic-poisoning victims. It took four of them to do it; but once recovered, Haddock was as docile as ever.

He developed his public-relations activities as a result of the *Post*'s companionship. He was hired by Walter Brown, then the owner of the Boston Garden, as a press agent. By then he knew the ropes because of his work with prize fighters and because of friendships he had built up in the newspaper business. One of his friends was George Minot, the penny-pinching managing editor of the *Boston Herald*, who, because his acquaintance with the sporting world was less than he would have liked, was entranced by Haddock's conversation.

Fish eventually left the Pier and ended his days as a press agent. His son inherited the business. Haddock remained long in the memory of newspapermen as one of the more vivid and likeable figures on Newspaper Row. He was a type that could not exist in the newspaper business today, a type whose presence emphasized the remarkable cohesiveness of the Newspaper Row community.

CHAPTER SEVENTEEN

Hindy the *Post* Cat and Other Animals

No episode in the story of the *Boston Post* so illustrates the rapport that existed between the paper and its readers than that of Hindy the Cat and his exploits. The newspaper magic that drew a half a million people to Newspaper Row to cheer the man of the forest, Joe Knowles, was to manifest itself again, much to the surprise of the management, in the case of Hindy, who became famous as the *Boston Post* cat.

If you were to have asked any reporter from an opposition paper what most distinguished the *Post* in its heyday, he would more than likely have replied, "those damned ridiculous animal stories." Without doubt, the *Post* loved animals, and no day passed without a picture or story or both about a lost dog, a rescued cat, a sheep, a goat, a cow, or some other beast. Only two of God's creatures were barred from the paper's pages: snakes and rats. The editorial wisdom was that the mere mention of either would not set well with the average reader perusing the *Post* at the breakfast table.

Grozier was no doubt responsible for thus having sensed that animal stories built circulation. That sense prompted another of the *Boston Post's* promotion stunts, the purchase of three elephants for the Franklin Park Zoo. This came about in 1914. Molly, Waddy, and Tony were performers. They were owned by an English couple, Mr. and Mrs. William Orford, who had put them through their paces in London, Berlin, Paris, Rome, Boston, and other cities for a good many years. The Orfords sensed that the performing years were over and that it was time for the beasts' pleasant retirement. It is not known how Grozier heard that the

Orfords wanted to sell, but he determined to buy the elephants for the city of Boston.

An agreement was signed, and Grozier mounted the campaign to purchase the animals by having the children of the city of Boston raise money by contributing nickels and pennies. No large donations were to be accepted. The *Post* undertook to pay all the expenses, which far exceeded the purchase price. Once again the editors and Grozier, as in the Joe Knowles case, underestimated the power of the *Post*. Boxes were set up in shops throughout the city for the children to pitch in their mite. Every child in the city was to have a chance to say he or she had helped buy the elephants. The coins came in so rapidly that counting machines had to be borrowed from the Elevated Street Railway Company to keep abreast of the intake.

As the fund reached $10,000, Paul V. Waitt, the man who had managed the Knowles caper, was in Providence arranging for the purchase and the transportation of the elephants to Boston, a task not without its own difficulties. Waitt had to get special permits from the city of Providence (the site of the last performance) to walk the animals through the streets to the train; he also had to make arrangements with the police department, the Orfords, and the elephants themselves.

The newspaper told the public that on June 6, 1914, the animals would be presented to the city of Boston on behalf of the children at Fenway Park at 10:00 A.M. Grozier had learned from experience how a curious public could make things awkward for the coverage of news or the mounting of a promotion stunt. During the Susan Geary murder case, crowds had lined the pier, had watched the diver searching for the severed head of the woman, and then had besieged the office of the medical examiner to catch a glimpse of it. In the Knowles case skeptics had chased into the woods to spy on Knowles, whose discovery would have ruined his experiment. Grozier guessed that hundreds of curious *Post* readers would also seek an unofficial glimpse of the elephants. Thus the time of their arrival was kept secret, and they were secreted (it took a bit of doing to hide them) in a barn at an undisclosed site to prepare for the big day.

Waitt had to make certain that the floor of the barn was sufficiently reinforced to support the weight of the elephants; then, under cover of darkness, he had to spirit them from their hiding place into Fenway Park. The Orfords were brought to Boston at the *Post*'s expense and put up at a hotel to be on hand for the presentation and attendant ceremonies.

Like other *Post* readers caught up in the enthusiasm of the event, George Stallings, the manager of the Red Sox, offered the park free of charge to the *Post* for the occasion. The *Post* meanwhile was planning an extravaganza. The paper announced that the entire cast of a musical comedy that was performing at Mechanics Building would entertain. The Ancient and Honorable Artillery Company, the oldest military company in the country, would parade and would be joined by the Boston School Boy Cadets, whose parades were one of the major annual events in the city. The *Post* proudly proclaimed that anywhere from 10,000 to 20,000 persons would attend. No admission would be charged.

On the day of the event, Waitt was on hand at 7:00 A.M. The *Post* had announced that the gates would open at 9:00 A.M. and the fun would start at 10:00 A.M. Waitt, an old hand at promotions, had arranged for thirty police officers to be detailed to maintain order. At 7:15 A.M., he went to check the elephants to make sure that they were fed and ready for their last major performance. He was congratulating himself on the condition and appearance of the elephants, when a park custodian came running up to him.

"Mr. Waitt! Mr. Waitt! We can't hold them any longer."

"Hold what?"

"We can't hold those kids outside any longer."

Waitt said something about it being only 7:30 A.M. and that gate time was set for 9:00 A.M. With the custodian, he went to the roof of the park building. Down the street toward the gates of the park, children were streaming as if in the wake of the Pied Piper. On every street they could see from the roof, children and adults were on their way to the park. Downstairs they were surging against the gates. At 7:45 A.M. Waitt ordered the gates opened and then called the *Post* and police for reinforcements. When 10:00 A.M. came, there were 70,000 persons in the stands and in special seats on the grounds; that left barely enough room for the artillery company and the boy cadets to march. Three hundred police were hastily mustered to ensure the public safety.

Governor David I. Walsh, on behalf of the children, made the presentation to Mayor James Michael Curley, who accepted for the city. Howard Brock, the *Post*'s city editor, was on hand with Edward J. Dunn, who would succeed him as city editor and who had assigned half a dozen reporters to cover various aspects of the show. The Orfords put the elephants through their paces. The military marched, the children cheered, and soon the ceremony was over—but not the work of the *Post*. Forty children had been lost in the crowd. This, Waitt had anticipated. He had a fleet of automobiles ready to drive the children home as soon as they were found and identified, which in some cases took several hours. All, nevertheless, were in due time restored to their families. The field was a messy clutter; but *Post* janitors, reporters, and editors made a fifty-man line across the field and swept it clean.

The elephants were installed at Franklin Park and became in effect a special concern of the *Post*. When Molly died two years later, the paper bought another elephant to replace her and gave the new one the same name so the euphony of Molly, Waddy, and Tony would not be lost. Several years later, the *Post* arranged the purchase of a hippopotamus for the zoo, which brought crowds flocking to Franklin Park for the presentation ceremony. On that occasion, the indefatigable Waitt rode up from Philadelphia in a truck with the hippo, all the while playing a water hose on the unhappy animal, whom the children of Boston in a contest had named Happy.

The enthusiasm that *Post* readers had for the paper's enterprises, both large and small, should have forewarned the *Post* when a reader one day wrote in that she would like to have a photograph of Hindy, the *Post* cat. Hindy's celebrity came almost by accident. An alley cat, baleful and misbegotten, Hindy had wandered into the *Post*'s city room one day in the early 1920s. The room already possessed a cat, however, a handsome black cat named Victoria, after the late English queen. The name was misleading, for Victoria was actually a he, a massive tom grown soft through the indulgence of *Post* reporters. The newcomer was a giant tiger, street smart and mean spirited. The two did not get along; and one day in Pi Alley, before anyone could interfere, the newcomer killed Victoria.

The *Post* staff was outraged. The conquest won for the newcomer only kicks, threats, and abuse. It also won him the name von Hindenberg. A decade later he would have been called Hitler or Himmler. But he had a strange career before him because, in the space of two or three years, he was to become the most-famous newspaper cat in the world.

The *Post*'s daily circulation in the early 1920s had risen above 600,000 and rival papers were luring away *Post* stars. City editor Howard Brock and Paul V. Waitt, who had presided over so much of the *Post* hoopla, were hired by the *Boston Traveler* to see if some of the *Post* magic could be transferred to that paper. The *Post* had just won the Pulitzer Prize for public service for exposing Charles Ponzi, the notorious con man, and the reporter who had brought the key information from Montreal was something of a hero. He was Herb Baldwin, and he was idling away an afternoon in the *Post* city room, eager for some new enterprises, when he wrote a light-hearted story about von Hindenberg. The cat, despite the maltreatment accorded him, had adopted the city room as his home, sleeping on the stacks of copy paper, on window sills in summer, and near the radiators in winter. Charles Young, then assistant managing editor, was amused by Baldwin's story and asked for more. They had had nothing like it since Kenneth Roberts's codfish stories.

"I became the cat editor," Baldwin recounted years later. "My story made Hindy—the name had long since been shortened—a redoubtable hero. My subsequent stories were signed 'By Hindy,' who had taken to talking in the first person. In the stories, Hindy's nature changed." In the city room, Hindy remained the same ill-tempered animal that he was before. No cajolery or kindness from the *Post* staff softened Hindy's heart. Baldwin's stories took flight from fact to fiction. Hindy was rescued from a fire in the restaurant on the first floor of the *Post* building. Hindy challenged and defeated the pet cat of city hall on the city hall lawn while hundreds watched. Hindy expounded on his philosophy of life in a variety of stories. At length Hindy was entered in the cat show, a special class of "Alley Cat" being recognized for the occasion. The attendance at the show tripled that year because of *Post* readers' coming to see Hindy. He took first prize. The next year Hindy was displayed at the dog show and was given a prize as the "best cat at the dog show." Baldwin was assigned to display him. "I had to wear stout leather gloves all the time." Hindy bore his celebrity with equanimity, if not indifference.

When that woman wrote in asking for a picture of Hindy, Baldwin took the cue and wrote a story in which Hindy offered a picture of himself to *Post* readers. Clifton B. Carberry, managing editor, demurred at running the story as too ridiculous, arguing that no one would want a picture of an alley cat. City editor Edward J. Dunn contended that as many as 5,000 *Post* readers would write in for a picture. Carberry, who was deaf, wore a hearing aid that he turned off when he had heard enough of anyone's presentation. He turned it off on Dunn with, "Eddie, you're an ass." But at Dunn's insistence, he ran the story. The requests came in bulging canvas bags, letters by the hundreds and then by the thousands. The *Post*'s photographic staff was swamped trying to keep up with the demand. Eastman Kodak was appealed to, and a reporter was rushed to Chicago to arrange with a firm there to turn out copies of the Hindy photograph that had appeared in the paper with Baldwin's story. It showed the tiger lying in a wire letter basket with letters underneath him and a copy of the *Post* at his head. When the smoke cleared, the *Post* had delivered 112,000 photographs of Hindy.

At the height of Hindy's fame, in 1923, it was contended that a letter addressed simply to Hindy and dropped in any mailbox in the country would be delivered to the *Post*; some so addressed were delivered from great distances. In that same year, Hindy got an infection in the leg, the result of a scrap with another cat. He was rushed by taxi to the Angell Memorial Hospital, which was operated by the Massachusetts Society for the Prevention of Cruelty to Animals, popularly known as "the society with the long name." Reporters were assigned to a twenty-four-hour death watch, and progress reports on the cat's condition were sent out to the country by the Associated Press and other wire services. Hindy's death was duly reported, as was his burial in the animal cemetery in Methuen, Massachusetts, where a simple stone reads:

> Here Lies
> HINDY
> The Boston Post's
> Famous Cat

City editor Dunn, during the demand for the cat's picture, had ordered the staff to lay off Hindy stories. But the legend didn't die. During World War II, two decades later, he received a letter from a woman in Shanghai. She had lost her picture of Hindy in an air raid by the Japanese. Could the *Post* provide her with another? The paper obliged.

Although further stories on Hindy were squelched, the *Post*'s confidence in the pulling power of animal stories continued. At mid-century, when John Griffin took over as editor under publisher John Fox, he all but banned them, declaring, "Remember, for everyone who loves a dog, there is one who hates them."

CHAPTER EIGHTEEN

From Curley to Truman

Until the William Jennings Bryan–William McKinley presidential election of 1896, the *Globe* had been the leading Democratic paper in Boston, even to the extent of endorsing the "beast," Ben Butler, for governor. After declining to endorse Bryan, just as the *New York Times* and other papers had refused because of the free-silver issue (the free coinage of silver), the *Globe* would endorse no more candidates locally or nationally until the 1950s. Under the Greenes the *Post* had been the leading Democratic paper in Boston, but its collapse after they relinquished ownership following the great fire of 1872 left it a paper of little consequence. After 1900 and Bryan's second defeat, the *Post* under Grozier was left with an open field. Its circulation had risen above 100,000 and by 1903 would be 178,000. As an independent Democratic paper, it was ready to support worthy Democratic candidates for whatever office and was promptly wooed by every candidate who ran. By 1910, its circulation was over 250,000; in the next three years, it would add another 100,000. It became a political power and, with the genius of Grozier behind it, a responsible one. An honest man and an honest publisher, Grozier remained ruggedly independent and willing to back for office only those candidates he deemed deserving.

In the city at this time there was a man of matching genius who cast his first vote five years after Grozier took over the *Post*. He was James Michael Curley, and he would become a legendary figure in the city of Boston. He was a politician, a political buccaneer, and a statesman of vision. He would serve two terms on the Boston Common Council, two terms in the Massachusetts Legislature (known as the General Court), six terms on the Boston Board

of Aldermen, two terms on the Boston City Council, four terms in
the U.S. Congress, four terms as mayor of Boston, and one term
as governor of Massachusetts. He would also serve two brief
terms in jail. He was the first man in the history of the commonwealth to declare his sole profession to be politics. He was not a
political "boss," not in the sense that Frank Hague in Jersey City
or Thomas Pendergast in Kansas City or Richard Daley in Chicago were "bosses." He was part of no machine in the traditional
sense, nor did he seriously try to build one. To a great extent, he
was a loner marked by an ironic detachment.

He had charm, charisma, intelligence, great wit, and a golden
voice that made him the greatest orator in the state since Daniel
Webster, who, it should be noted, was no more honest a politician
than Curley. He was the model for Frank Skeffington in Edwin
O'Connor's celebrated novel *The Last Hurrah*. Joseph F. Dinneen,
one of the *Globe*'s ablest reporters, wrote a biography entitled
The Purple Shamrock and credits Curley with the most profound
social vision of any mayor in the city's history. Because of his
staunch support in his one term as governor, more progressive
social legislation was passed then than had been approved under
all his predecessors. As mayor he was energetic, visionary, exciting, amusing, and expensive.

He was in no way a political thief such as Tammany bosses
William Marcy Tweed and Richard Croker in New York. He lived
well all his life, modestly in his last years, and left no considerable
estate. He was unfortunate in his nine children. Some died in
infancy. The most brilliant died young, at the start of a promising
career. Others accomplished little. At this writing only one survives. There are no grandchildren.

His early career was built on personal service to thousands
and control of a small political club in Roxbury modeled after
Tammany Hall in New York. In his beginnings the *Post* smiled on
him; but in his first campaign for mayor, in 1914, all the newspapers opposed him and regarded him with alarm, as he promised
to raise the assessments on the real property of the business community. When elected, he did just that. Also he soon proved that
he was not above using intimidation to make sure that the city
got the loans it needed for the projects he planned. These projects
were numerous, calculated to appeal to the working class, from
which he sprang, and the submerged poor, for whom he had real
sympathy. His monuments still adorn the city and the state: the

Quabbin Reservoir (the largest body of water in the commonwealth), the bridges over the Cape Cod canal, Boston City Hospital, and the sweep of shore line and beach and accommodations
at Pleasure Bay in South Boston, to name a few. Early in his
career, the *Post* dubbed him "Sympathy Jim" because of his pro-
testations on behalf of the poor. The implied sarcasm didn't take
hold. The people saw it as an attempt to sneer at the charitable
work he had done in his own ward and elsewhere and to discredit
the genuineness of his championship of the underdog. Although
the charitable work was done with an eye on its political value, it
was genuine nonetheless.

In his first campaign for mayor, he defeated a distinguished
lawyer, Thomas J. Kenny of South Boston. The latter was president of the Boston City Council and had the backing of the Good
Government Association, composed for the most part of Republicans. Curley all but nullified the effect that this endorsement
might have had among his constituents by referring to the members of the association as "the Goo-goos." In his rich voice, the
term made them slightly ridiculous.

There were sound reasons for the *Post* to prefer Kenny over
Curley. In 1899, Curley had been elected to the Common Council,
a large body with little power and subservient to the more powerful Board of Aldermen. Curley so manipulated the council that he
appeared to be a troublemaker. In 1902-03, he served in the State
House of Representative on Beacon Hill and showed a radical
concern for the underdog. In 1904, he was jailed for impersonat-
ing a friend, Bartholomew Fahy of Cambridge, in a civil-service
test but managed to make political capital of the matter and was
elected to the Board of Aldermen in the same year he was jailed.
He went from there to serve two terms on the nine-man Boston
City Council elected at large, a new body created by the 1909
charter change. While serving his second term on the council, he
was elected to the U.S. Congress and was reelected in 1912.

Then he decided to run for mayor. To those who knew him, it
was obvious that he could not afford to be a congressman, which
paid too little to maintain homes in both Boston and Washington
and had small patronage. Thus Curley looked to the mayoralty (in
his eyes, a better job) to help his finances and to serve the city.
Because the office of mayor paid more than did the office of a
congressman, the *Post*, which saw him as a self-serving dema-
gogue, felt justified in sensing that he was looking for political

loot. The paper consequently endorsed Kenny. It was not as partisan as the *Boston American*, however, which, as a cutoff line under every story, printed, "Vote for Thomas J. Kenny."

Curley had also been opposed by just about every ward boss in the city. Yet he won and, resigning his seat in Congress, thus entered city hall owing little to anyone except the voters and determined to raise taxes and spend the money to improve the city. He did. When he ran for reelection in 1917, the *Post* opposed him again and may have had a hand in persuading Congressman James A. Gallivan of South Boston, who succeeded to the Congressional seat that Curley had vacated, to run against him, thus splitting the Irish Democratic vote and allowing Yankee Democrat and socialite Andrew J. Peters to win. The *Post* endorsed Gallivan. In his autobiography, Curley narrates how he sat in the mayoral office in city hall, around the corner from the *Post*, awaiting the returns. He was surrounded by his supporters, including John L. Sullivan, the Boston Strong Boy, then sixty, who had been heavyweight boxing champion of the world. As the returns came in, Curley said, "I'm taking the count." Sullivan, alluding to his defeat by "Gentleman Jim" Corbett, replied, "I know what it is to take the count."

Curley, however, in a way had his revenge. Andrew J. Peters, an honest but ineffectual man, was utterly unable to stop the larcenous depredations that took place around him as he tried to manage city hall. He was thoroughly inept, and it was obvious that he had to go. Curley never forgave Gallivan for his role in the 1917 mayoral campaign. He accused him of being a plant for Peters. Attempting to even the score, Curley ran against Gallivan for Congress in the fall of 1918, although he had moved out of the district to Jamaica Plain. He lost. On March 25, 1918, the Republican-controlled Massachusetts Legislature passed a special act, aimed at Curley (they knew he would be back), that made it impossible for an incumbent mayor to succeed himself. In 1921, the man who announced that his profession was politics was eligible to run again for mayor and did so. He knew that the *Post* would not endorse him but more than likely would endorse his opponent, whoever it might be. He also knew that the *Post* could be a deadly opponent. Before the campaign opened, Curley charged that the publisher of the *Post* was in effect in the pay of England to oppose Irish independence. He launched or, better, continued his attack—it had become an ongoing theme with him—before a large crowd on Boston Common at the St. Patrick's Day celebration in 1920. That March the first of the Black and Tans, British irregulars who were to become the most hated of British armed forces in Ireland, had arrived in that country, where the war for independence was on.

Grozier then published on page one of the *Post*—across two columns, in large type, and running more than half the length of the page—one of the more curious offers ever to appear in a major newspaper. The headline read:

A CORDIAL INVITATION TO
EX-MAYOR CURLEY
HERE IS AN OPPORTUNITY FOR HIM TO
PROVE HIS INTERESTING CHARGES
AGAINST THE *BOSTON POST* AND
EDWIN A. GROZIER, ITS EDITOR

At a public meeting on Boston Common, March 17th, ex-Mayor James M. Curley is reported to have made the interesting statement that in 1917 during his (Mr. Curley's) term as Mayor of Boston, Edwin A. Grozier, editor of the *Boston Post*, purchased $250,000 worth of City of Boston bonds; that he (Mayor Curley) wondered where Mr. Grozier obtained so much money at such a time; that he inquired of the city treasurer what form of payment was made for the bonds, and was told that the payment was made by a draft on a London, England, bank; and that the money was part of an immense propaganda campaign fund spent in this country by Lord Northcliffe to influence the American mind in favor of Great Britain; that, in brief, (summarizing the pleasant allegations of Mr. Curley) Edwin A. Grozier and the *Boston Post* were purchased to betray the cause of Ireland . . .

. . . If Mr. Curley has a scintilla of evidence to back up his charges of improper conduct, I hereby ask him to produce it for free and conspicuous publication in these columns.

If he or anyone else can produce proof to show that Edwin A. Grozier or the *Boston Post* as conducted by Edwin A. Grozier, ever received at any time, anywhere, anyhow, from Lord Northcliffe or his representative $250,000 or $1, or any sum or any other consideration, directly or indirectly, to influence its attitude on the question of the League of Nations or any other question, Edwin A. Grozier will take pleasure in presenting to James M. Curley his entire interest in the *Boston Post*.

Here is an opportunity for the genial Mr. Curley to secure the control of a newspaper of some little value by simply proving his repeated allegations.

(signed) Edwin A. Grozier

Editor and Publisher of the *Boston Post*
since March 19, 1891.

The letter has the ring of having been written by Grozier himself. In similar instances today, publishers will call upon one of the staff to prepare such a document and then submit it for approval. But in the first two decades of the twentieth century, most publishers thought of themselves as editor as well and had a hankering for writing. In the letter in question, Grozier undoubtedly took pleasure in hurling a challenge to the vituperative Curley, certain that the charges Curley had made were a lie and that his challenge would be ignored. It was. Curley would continue to make outrageous charges against Grozier, sometimes in Newspaper Row with the rear seat of a touring car serving as his platform. The Row was the place to be heard, and it was a place that any hour of the day or night would guarantee a crowd.

While Curley made no effort to produce any proof of his allegations, for it was clear enough that they were not true, he announced that he would debate the subject anytime, anywhere, on any platform with Mr. Grozier whenever the latter was ready to do so. Such a challenge was safe enough. Unlike General Charles H. Taylor, who was a rollicking after-dinner speaker, Grozier did not make speeches in public; and Curley knew that Grozier would never grace a platform beside him if he did. Curley would have welcomed such a contest, for it was a brave man indeed who would debate Curley at any time. Thomas H. Eliot, once a congressman from the Eleventh Massachusetts District and afterwards president of Washington University in St. Louis, recalled an occasion when he was running for reelection to Congress against Curley. Eliot got so carried away by Curley's oratory against him that he began to clap enthusiastically and had to be restrained by his wife.

Despite its challenge, the *Post* continued to be meticulous in its reporting on Curley, his activities, and his campaigning. Curley in turn was consistently gracious to *Post* reporters and political writers.

Clifton B. Carberry, managing editor of the *Post*, had by this time developed into Boston's foremost political commentator on local contests and wrote under the name of John Bantry. In the 1921 campaign for mayor, Curley was opposed by John R. Murphy, a man who had served the city with honor in several positions, including that of fire commissioner under Mayor Peters. Carberry, writing under his pen name, wrote of Curley:

> He is a Puritan at heart. No New England deacon can show a cleaner personal life than Jim Curley ... He is constantly taking the most reckless chances with his political future ... He antagonized Fitzgerald, Lomasney, Gallivan and others, when he knows they are mighty susceptible to a taste of sugar ... Who but James M. Curley seeking votes in a close district, would have the colossal nerve to address his audience as "milk bottle thieves" and then carry the ward?
>
> He was marked by fate for a high position in life. Just think of Curley's strong face for a moment and draw his black hair over his brow. Is he not the perfect double for those pictures of the stern old Caesar in the school books? Power is stamped undeniably upon him. Curley belongs to the imperial race ... Don't put Curley down as the average dull-witted product of machine politics like to so many Tammany mayors of New York. He is a cultured, well-educated man, with a fund of general high class knowledge that would do credit to a live college professor.

Carberry could and did go on from such laudatory comments to tell why Curley was not good for the city of Boston. In that particular campaign, despite the *Post's* opposition, Curley defeated John R. Murphy to begin his second term as mayor. His victory was astounding to his enemies. The *Herald*, which had also opposed him, wrote: "He was without the assistance of a single political leader of either party and with every machine of recognized standing against him."

The incident Carberry referred to in which Curley called his audience "milk bottle thieves" was a dramatic instance of the man's personal and platform power. The story became legendary, and there are several versions of it. Curley was speaking on behalf of a local candidate in Roxbury whose enemies had packed the hall and were howling to keep Curley from speaking. He was dressed, as he often was, in a cutaway coat, very formal attire for campaigning. While the crowd hooted and hollered, he removed his coat, draped it over a chair, and rolled up his sleeves. The deliberation with which he did this brought the crowd to silence. He then turned to them and said, "I intend to remain here and speak if I have to wait until every porch climber and milk thief in the audience has gone about his early morning work." He spoke to great applause, and his man carried the district. It was rough, tough campaigning in those days, a time in which bodyguards were needed and one set of toughs would throw another out of the hall. Curley recounts asking a vociferous, hired heckler in a derby to come to the platform at one rally to say what he had to say. As the heckler stopped at the bottom of the steps, Curley leaned forward and asked him to please remove his hat, as there were ladies present. When the heckler did so, someone hit him with a blackjack and carried him away.

Francis Hatch, an advertising executive and civic leader who was also a songwriter, caught much of Curley in a song beginning "Vote early and often for Curley " and containing the lines, "He'll talk with his fists in a South Boston brawl, and the very next evening, it's no trick at all, he'll lecture on Browning at Symphony Hall." While still mayor in 1924, Curley ran for governor against Republican Lieutenant Governor Alvin T. Fuller and was defeated, losing by 160,000 votes. The election turned the course of history in a way, for had he been elected, the chances are he would have commuted the death sentence imposed on Sacco and Vanzetti. He didn't share their anarchic views or think them innocent; but his antagonism to the Brahmin establishment in Boston and his ongoing sympathy for the underdog would have prompted him to mercy.

Grozier died in 1924, the year that Curley, while serving as mayor of Boston, ran against Fuller. Grozier's health had been failing; but in his last years, although pretty much immobilized in his office chair, he continued to direct the paper and to write editorials. His death in no way abated the paper's opposition to Curley.

In 1929, Curley announced his candidacy for mayor again. His opponent was Fredrick W. Mansfield, a labor lawyer, former treasurer of the Commonwealth and legal advisor to William Cardinal O'Connell, the archbishop of Boston. Mansfield had the support of the Good Government Association and the *Post*. The paper's opposition was now automatic; yet, because its columns were always fair, the paper remained the favorite of the Irish voters, and Curley remained their favorite candidate. He won the election. Ineligible to run for reelection as mayor, Curley turned his attention again to the governor's seat and in 1934 was elected, defeating Republican Lieutenant Governor Gaspar Griswold Bacon. In 1936, at the end of his lively two-year term on Beacon Hill, he ran for the U.S. Senate against Henry Cabot Lodge, Jr., who was thirty-four at the time. Curley kept referring to him as Little Boy Blue, but his sarcasm and oratory didn't save him. Lodge won.

Curley did not like being out of office too long and in 1937 decided to run for mayor again. It was said that one of his reasons for running for office was that, as a candidate, he made money from the contributions that poured into his coffers. In his statewide campaign against Lodge, Curley had still carried the city of Boston. When he announced his candidacy for mayor in 1937, therefore, the *Post* was fearful he would be elected.

Curley had served as governor in the first years of the New Deal, when progressive social legislation was stirring Washington and the nation. Curley's record as governor in that regard was impressive. He had supported Alfred E. Smith for president in 1928; but in 1932, with the political prescience that marked him, he threw his support to Franklin D. Roosevelt. The *Post* had instinctively backed Roosevelt for that first term. By that time, however, the genius of the elder Grozier was gone; and his son, Richard, who showed so much promise in the 1920s, had begun to show signs of the mental illness that would at last confine him. He had in great part already withdrawn from the operation of the newspaper. Carberry's editorial control was all but absolute, but he was aging and growing conservative and gloomy. The *Post* became alarmed at Roosevelt and the New Deal and would continue to snipe at him until World War II began. Curley's enthusiasm for the New Deal and its progressive legislation did nothing to alter the *Post*'s opposition to him. Carberry was determined to see Curley defeated in the 1937 campaign for mayor.

Early on the paper decided to back Maurice J. Tobin, an employee of the telephone company who was serving on the school committee. Tobin was in fact a political protegé of Curley but ready enough to break the apron strings and strike out on his own. The *Post* knew it would be a close fight.

If Curley had been unfair to Grozier in slandering him so rashly, the *Post* would be equally unfair to Curley in the Curley-Tobin campaign in an incident that is still talked about in Boston's political circles fifty years later. At the top of its front page each day, the *Post* carried a box running the full eight columns. In it was printed a one-line quotation, an adage, or a line of verse. It proved a popular feature and started the reader's day off with an optimistic or patriotic thought. On election day that box read:

VOTERS OF BOSTON!

Cardinal O'Connell, in speaking to the Catholic Alumni Association, said, "The walls are raised against honest men in civic life." You can break down those walls by voting for an honest, clean, competent young man, Maurice J. Tobin, today. He will redeem the city and take it out of the hands of those who have been responsible for graft and corruption.

A reader had to look closely to observe that the quotation marks stopped at ". . . civic life." The quotation paraphrased some remarks the cardinal had made a month before on a Sunday morning at a communion breakfast following Mass at the Immaculate Conception Church in the South End of Boston. It had no reference to any particular candidate, let alone to Maurice J. Tobin. The voters of Boston and certainly all the politicians were aware that the cardinal was very careful not to endorse one candidate or another. Indeed, he was a man of conservative views and was widely believed to vote Republican. This heightened the impact of his apparent endorsement of Tobin on the morning of the election.

Election day that year fell on All Souls' Day, when Catholics attended Mass in great numbers to pray for the dead. Hundreds of workers for Tobin were out in front of the churches as the faithful emerged from Mass. They had 30,000 copies of the *Post* printed in an overrun and were distributing them free to anyone who appeared to be of voting age. No doubt thousands of *Post* readers, seeing the box at the top of the front page, misread the quotation and the addition to it and made up their minds to vote for Tobin. Until that moment, some of them may have been vacillating, while others would have voted for anyone they thought the cardinal preferred.

The Curley forces, understanding all this, were frantic, realizing that the deception could be fatal to their candidate. One telephone call after another was made to the cardinal's residence in

Brighton, but he was unavailable for comment. Curley hoped to get him to repudiate the implication of the banner-box, as it was called, and then announce the repudiation over the radio while voters were still going to the polls. The Curley forces learned that a telephone call had gone from the *Post* to the cardinal's residence the night before, but what was said was never revealed. As the cardinal was known on occasion to refer to Curley as "the thug," Carberry could be fairly secure in his estimation that, even if he had not consulted with the prelate, any repudiation would come too late to matter, and the *Post* would suffer no rebuke. Tobin won the election by 25,000 votes, and it may well be that the *Post's* semantic trick turned the tide. Tobin even went on to win a second term as mayor in 1941 (defeating Curley a second time). He was also elected governor with the *Post's* support and ultimately served as President Harry Truman's secretary of labor.

Curley was nothing, however, if not resilient. He would again be elected to Congress (twice) and again to the mayor's office. He had the satisfaction of seeing most of his bitter enemies die before him, and he lived to see the *Post* go under but regretted its demise. In his later years, he remembered its opposition to him with amusement. He died in 1958.

The *Post's* influence in Tobin's eventual appointment to Truman's cabinet was significant. In Truman's campaign against Thomas E. Dewey, after all, the *Post* had been one of few major dailies in the country that endorsed the man from Missouri and only one of two on the East coast. That endorsement helped him to carry Massachusetts. In 1948, the *Post's* circulation was well over 300,000, the largest among the morning papers in the city. Although its circulation was just half of what it had been at its 1928 peak, when Alfred E. Smith was the Democratic standard bearer, the paper's appeal to the voters of Boston was as strong as ever. In New England Truman carried only Massachusetts and Rhode Island. Thus the editorial supporting Truman, in view of its unique role in the journalistic history of the United States, makes interesting reading today. It was written by Henry Gillen, a long-time assistant editor of the paper. Gillen was best known to the readers of the *Post* for his verses, which were published in the paper on page one. They appeared on all the major holidays, usually in bold face. Although he frequently wrote editorials, too, the public was unaware of it; all *Post* editorials were unsigned. Gillen's most famous editorial, which appeared on the eve of November elections in 1947, was headed:

Captain Courageous

Boston, Hub of New England, extends today to Harry S. [*sic*] Truman, President of the United States, a hearty and hospitable welcome. It is his first visit here since destiny made him the man to lead the nation to a surpassing victory in the final, furious hours of the greatest war that ever tortured mankind. In that welcome the *Post* not only joins. It espouses his cause. It urges votes for him next Tuesday.

The *Post* takes this stand after thoughtful consideration and not alone because it is New England's independent Democratic newspaper. It can find no outstanding reason to oppose him and a heartening one why it should support him. . . . When Franklin D. Roosevelt, zealous guardian of his prerogatives, sought a successor—knowing the end was near—he chose Mr. Truman, above all men, as the one to whom he could entrust his dreams and hopes for a better America and a finer world. . . . President Truman did not fail him. . . .

The man has courage—the courage to speak out—the courage to take a stand—the courage of the forthright citizen who, when faced with a problem, meets it head on, regardless of personal consequences. That courage to be President instead of a politician has been responsible for a nation prosperous, a world at peace and Communism halted at the crossroads of Europe . . . .

By that token he should win. America likes a fighter. In that respect and on the record, we urge votes for him, Harry S. Truman, captain courageous—unflinching warrior.

James Michael Curley remains a legend, a mythic figure, in Boston. He was never a machine politician. He was a lone, and in many ways a lonely, figure. Tall, handsome, impressive, his voice was a musical instrument that made him the greatest orator in the state since Daniel Webster. He had wit and style. He lived well during his professional life, but he had no Swiss bank accounts, no cache of loot to enable him to end his days in luxury. When he finally quit the political arena, he lived modestly in Jamaica Plain, content in the company of his second wife and his friends. He was also content to look around him in the city and the state at the monuments he had created. Whatever controversy his name still stirs, it can be said of his career and his accomplishments that the good outweighs the bad.

CHAPTER NINETEEN

★★★★

The *Boston Transcript*

The *Boston Evening Transcript* was founded in 1830 and died in 1941. For eighty of those years, it held down the south end of Newspaper Row. In that time, it made more of an impact on literary history than any other Boston paper, although it made less impact on journalism and on the people of New England than did either the *Post* or the *Globe*. It had the first woman editor of a major daily newspaper, and it had the first black literary editor in the country. It was not so much an institution as a myth and not so much a newspaper as a house organ for the gentry of greater Boston. In its early stages, it had its moments of vulgarity and of aggressive heroism. Even in its great days, it was never regarded by the other papers in Boston as a competitor, mostly because of its stuffy appeal; it was, however, looked upon with admiration (for its style) tempered by amusement. In 1930, its biographer made the boast that it was probably a "unique example of an American daily paper which has for one hundred years been under the controlling ownership of a single family."

Between 1830 and 1840, there were fifteen daily newspapers, twelve at one time, most of them hovering around Newspaper Row. They came and went. In the first half of the nineteenth century, it was not too difficult to start a daily paper. One needed only an imaginative literary man and the owner of a job-printing shop. Lynde Minshull Walter was one such literary man just out of Harvard College, and Henry W. Dutton and James Wentworth owned a job-printing shop. With them began the *Transcript*. By 1847, the Dutton family was the paper's sole owner. Not until 1860 did it move to Newspaper Row.

Before the Civil War it was less difficult to *get* a newspaper going. The trick was to *keep* it going once it had got started. Eleven were in the city when the *Transcript* started in 1830. When its first history was written fifty years later, only four of the fifteen that were published between 1830 and 1840 were still printing: the *Transcript*, the *Post*, the *Traveller*, and the *Advertiser*. By 1960, all those names had disappeared from the mastheads of the Boston papers. No sooner had the *Transcript* appeared but it seemed about to disappear. After its third paper, printed on July 27, 1830, it suspended publication. A month later, on August 28, it resumed and continued six days a week until its demise.

In pre–Civil War days, the phrase "yellow journalism" didn't exist. The phrase then for those newspapers that were less concerned with ethics than with income was "black journalism." The connotation may well have been not so close to that which we find in "black humor" as to that which we find in "blackmail." More than one such paper was known as a "shake-down sheet." After the Civil War there were no longer any instances of such coercion on the part of publishers, although individual reporters in sensitive positions may well have capitalized on the power than chance put into their hands and looked for bribes to turn the edge of a story. On a lesser scale in Boston, as elsewhere, newsmen sometimes bent the facts to lessen the impact on an individual for immediate or future friendship or favor. Time and again the newspapers were not entirely fair to candidates they had not endorsed or didn't care for. But generally speaking objectivity was the order of the day, and thousands of reporters turned down bribes and favors in order to be true to their craft. Not until 1952 would a major publisher so abuse the ethics of the newspaper business in Boston as to descend to selling the political support of a major metropolitan Boston daily for cash (see the section of Chapter 22 regarding John Fox).

The *Transcript*, for all its tone of quality and its disdain for the "yellow" journalism of its fellows, had not been above such tactics in its early days and, in its heyday, was not above twisting the facts to favor its conservative point of view. When mill workers in Lawrence, Massachusetts, struck in 1912 for better working conditions and higher wages, Lucien Price, one of the great names in Boston journalism, was sent by the *Transcript* to cover the strike. He telegraphed stories daily but didn't see the paper because few managed to get into the strike-bound city. He returned to find that the essence of all his stories had been altered to present an antilabor point of view. Lucien walked out the door of the *Transcript* and went to work for the *Globe*. There he remained until his death in 1966 following a brilliant career writing as one of the major literati who composed the editorials in the *Globe* over the signature Uncle Dudley, editorials that were distinguished for their lofty literary style but that rarely took sides in the meat-and-potatoes issues of the day.

The strike incident was not the only time that the *Transcript* would doubt the reports of its employees because of preconceived notions. While editors cannot, however, be held responsible for the delinquencies of their staff, they are certainly responsible when a reporter's facts are altered back at the office.

When the *Boston Post* was building circulation with its intensive coverage of such cases as that of Reverend Clarence V. T. Richeson and his electrocution for the murder of Avis Linnell, the *Transcript* was being excessively genteel. All headlines on all stories on the news pages of the *Transcript* in those years, 1911 and 1912, were one column; and pictures were just being permitted in the paper and were for the most part confined to the feature pages. For a long while after they had become available, they had not been run.

About the time when Richeson was in the death house awaiting execution and trying to emasculate himself, and the psychiatrists were debating whether or not he was sane, the *Transcript* gave a discreet two paragraphs to Richeson's case but managed a full page of poems, evidently commissioned by the paper to celebrate the centenary of Robert Browning. Seventeen poets contributed. Henry Van Dyke, very popular at the time, wrote an introductory essay, and William Stanley Braithwaite, the paper's literary editor, "collated" the texts. Braithwaite, the only black literary editor up to that time in Boston and perhaps the first on any major metropolitan newspaper in the country, was distinguished by his annual anthologies of magazine verse. Joshua Jones, a black writer, had gone from the staff of the *Boston Post* to edit Boston's *City Record*, the city's official bulletin.

Braithwaite was far from the only *Transcript* critic to publish in book form. H. T. Parker, the most famous critic in the city, whose initials H.T.P. at the end of an article had Biblical authority for *Transcript* readers, as well as William Hovey and Epes

Sargent, editors of the paper, published in book form frequently while still on the staff. Literary figures were the paper's strong suit, and scores of aspiring writers went to work for the paper, seeing it as the right place to start a literary career. (Lucius Beebe, however, began his on the less reputable *Telegram*.) Any number of men and women went from the *Transcript* to literary careers. Lucien Price, mentioned above, was one; Brooks Atkinson, the famous *New York Times* critic, another. John K. Hutchins became book editor of the *Herald Tribune* in New York and then a judge for the Book-of-the-Month Club, while Charles W. Morton became the assistant editor of the *Atlantic Monthly* and wrote more humor for that magazine than has appeared in it since.

Morton loved to tell anecdotes about the easy indolence that seemed to pervade the editorial rooms of the *Transcript* in the 1920s, when he was there as an office boy running copy. He observed one staff member who never seemed to move from his chair or take his feet down from his desk. Morton finally got up courage to say to one of the reporters, "What does that fellow do?" The reporter looked, then turned to Morton and said, "If it isn't banks, he doesn't touch it." Henry Cabot Lodge, Jr., who would become a U.S. senator and serve as one of the most exciting ambassadors to the United Nations, began his career as a reporter on the *Transcript*.

The *Transcript's* offices were first on Exchange Street and then on Congress Street, a stone's throw from Newspaper Row. In 1860, when it moved to Newspaper Row at Washington Street on the corner of Milk Street, on the site of the birthplace of Benjamin Franklin, it was a very successful business. In 1871, it built its own plant, which in the next year was partly destroyed in the great fire. The owners promptly rebuilt bigger than before. The age was one of confidence.

Epes Sargent, a celebrated author of the day, had succeeded Cornelia Walter as editor of the paper and continued more or less the liberal policies of its founding editor, Lynde M. Walter. Besides being a pungent critic if the occasion arose, the latter Walter was a stalwart defender of the Irish immigrants in a city whose degenerate mobs were sacking Irish homes, stoning Irish units in patriotic parades, burning a convent and all religious articles in it to the ground, and finally becoming so riotous in their destruction that it was necessary to declare martial law. Walter, like most responsible Bostonians, felt a sense of shame at such outrages and put his outrage into the columns of his paper. He didn't lack courage. Bostonians of today have forgotten, if they were ever taught, how riotous the city was in the two decades preceding the Civil War, what with the anti-Irish riots mingling with those caused by people who detested the "immediate" abolitionists. (William Lloyd Garrison was almost lynched in 1835; and the anti-Irish-Broad Street riots occurred in 1837.) Throughout those turbulent times, the *Transcript* under Walter was heroic.

His sister was less concerned with politics. Her successor, the poet Epes Sargent, set the literary tone that would dominate the paper until the end; under him, however, the paper lost interest in the Irish immigrants and, indeed, leaned toward the Know-Nothings, a party of bigots that had a brief success. In 1849, a murder case shocked the city because of the eminence of the persons involved. Doctor George Parkman, a physician of an old Boston family, was murdered. John White Webster, a professor at Harvard Medical School, was accused, tried, found guilty, and hanged. The *Transcript* covered the story in great detail and included a gruesome description of Doctor Webster's hanging, giving it three columns—its last fling with sensational journalism.

Twenty years later when it moved to Newspaper Row, the *Transcript* was the foremost newspaper in New England, although not in circulation. That never reached the 50,000 mark. It was Pulitzer's transformation of newspaper publishing and the rise of mass circulation that would bring the paper down. In *The Boston Transcript*, a history of the paper published in 1930, Joseph Edgar Chamberlain writes:

> In a marked sense, the eighties represented the best achievement of the journalism of the 19th century. That achievement was less strenuous, less voluminous, but rather more intellectual than the current production of the 20th century. There was then surely no lack of newspapers to represent prevalent interest and opinions. In 1886 eight dailies and forty-four weeklies were published in Boston. The daily papers were the *Transcript*, the *Daily Advertiser*, the *Post*, the *Herald*, the *Traveller*, the *Journal*, the *Globe* and the *Evening Record*. Every one of them, no doubt, was trying to fill its niche honestly, though three or four of them were moribund, and had begun to know it. The *Daily Advertiser*, which had stood at the head of morning papers in the general estimation, and of which, in 1884, the chief editor was

Professor Charles F. Dunbar of Harvard and the managing editor, Edwin M. Bacon, had ceased to be profitable, and had entered a somewhat long period of deliquescence. The *Transcript* was taking over the *Advertiser*'s estimation, its readers, and the important people who wrote letters to the editor when they wanted to reach the public. The *Journal* was beginning to "yellow" with scare-heads, matter in "boxes" and in other sensational ways which spoiled it with its old supporters. The *Herald* was gaining ground under the editorship of a very sagacious man, once a school-master, John H. Holmes. The *Globe*, started as an ultra-highbrowed and literary paper, had languished along that line—the public did not want a paper that was absolutely too bright and good for human nature's daily food—and was on the material upgrade again under the more popular management of Colonel Charles H. Taylor. The *Post*, very Democratic and also very readable, was in a period of decline, from which it was afterward lifted by the enterprise of E. A. Grozier who had been trained under Joseph Pulitzer on [the] *New York World*. That sort of conservative Boston preference that keeps its quality while accepting and welcoming the real gifts of progress was rapidly centering its patronage on the *Transcript*.

The picture is an exact one of the Boston journalism scene when Grozier arrived five years later to capture the city.

In the days when the public still watched the hangings of criminals, the *Transcript* had not hesitated to publish such a lurid description of a hanging (Doctor Webster's in 1849) that it was criticized even by its peers. On another occasion, in 1848, it gave over almost all the paper (not very large at the time) to a murder case. Conservativism came in only later, and the *Boston Evening Transcript*, having found its audience and the advertisers who wanted to reach that audience, disdained "yellow journalism" and left it for the other papers. If crime doesn't pay for criminals, however, it does for newspapers. Thus the public interest in hangings and the like continued long after the *Transcript* described a murderer swinging in the wind.

Not long after Henry Turner Claus was named editor of the *Transcript* in 1925, he declared:

> Our readers are entitled to know what is going on in the world, whether it be an international event, a local election or a crime. We do not believe those who subscribe to the

Transcript want the lurid or sordid emphasized. In other words, they prefer that we keep a true sense of values. We publish crime news, for one reason, to help society protect itself . . . . When a paper devotes two pages to a sensational murder case, much other matter must be omitted. We simply prefer the other matter. . . .

The statement was made shortly after the *Post* had battered the other newspapers in the city into the ground with its scoops on the Ponzi (see next chapter) and Garrett cases. Included in the "other matter" the *Transcript* preferred to print were regular pages of genealogies of Boston's first families. It seems obvious that one of the *Transcript's* advertisers had suggested to the editors that, if they perked up the paper, they might sell a few more. The statement by Claus has a very defensive ring to it.

The *Transcript* was content with the circulation it had so long as its advertising held up. It had a hammerlock on the financial advertising of the city and much from the wool business. In 1912 it was able to boast that in the month of April, it carried 38,501 lines of financial advertising, which was 77 percent more than the next Boston paper. At that time that would have been the *Herald*, with three times the circulation of the *Transcript*. The *Herald* would in time get most of that financial lineage. The *Transcript* had a sturdy hold on its Back Bay readers. The editors presumed that those pages of genealogies would keep the first families reading their paper. They did, but they bored Boston's new families to death.

The *Transcript's* historian, Joseph G. Chamberlin, wrote about Claus's statement that, "The principle laid down in this utterance by the present editor of the *Transcript* shows how far the tone or governing sentiment of the paper has advanced since it was started in 1830, when the 'little Transcript' made its first start in real life by devoting its entire sheet to the Knapp murder case, to the exclusion not only of all other reading matter but of advertisements as well. The first editors were wiser than the last. They changed with the times."

Louis M. Lyons, in his *Newspaper Story: One Hundred Years of the Boston Globe*, writes eloquently of the *Transcript*:

Much the most distinctive of the Boston newspapers was the *Transcript*. Archaic but intensely individualistic, its special character, like the purple windowpanes of Beacon Street, reflected the atmosphere of old Boston. The *Transcript* comforted the Brahmin old stock with its editorials and with a cultural menu that dealt authoritatively with genealogy, grandfather clocks, the departed chestnut tree and the Constitution which it printed in full for a full page every Wednesday.

> *Transcript* make-up was as changeless as Bulfinch architecture . . . .

The man who ruled the *Transcript* in the days when it displayed itself in the idiosyncrasy that characterized it thereafter was George S. Mandell, the last of the line founded by Henry W. Dutton. In 1914, after graduation from Harvard, he succeeded his father, Samuel Mandell, in the publisher's chair. His death in 1934 was more grievous for the *Transcript* than the death of Grozier had been for the *Post* ten years earlier. Mandell had ruled with a loose rein, and the various departments of the paper were described as more of a federated republic than a monarchy. For Mandell, it worked, and if strange contradictions appeared at times, he shrugged them off as necessary flukes in a system that worked too well to change. Four years after he died, the ownership changed. Richard N. Johnson, a New England textile executive, got some old Boston families to join him in refinancing the paper and tried to change its image, even to the extent of backing the New Deal. As a result the paper lost many of its old readers without winning any new ones. In the spring of 1941, it died.

Some *Post* executives tried to get Richard Grozier to buy the *Transcript* and so to offer to advertisers morning and afternoon papers, which both the *Globe* and the *Herald Traveler* then had. Grozier was either disinclined to do anything or could not be reached, and the *Transcript* went abegging. Marshall Field, who had just launched the *Chicago Sun*, bought the *Transcript* library; and Hugh Boyd, an enterprising advertising executive, bought the name. He started a magazine entitled the *Boston Transcript*, but a shortsighted board of trade would not approve it as an advertising medium for its members, and the magazine soon followed the newspaper whose name it had borrowed.

If it failed in the twentieth century as a newspaper, it succeeded to immortality in the world of literature. T. S. Eliot wrote a poem entitled "The Boston Evening Transcript," the first two lines of which read:

> The readers of the Boston Evening Transcript
> Sway in the wind like a field of ripe corn.

The poem catches the ennui that brought about the paper's demise.

A catchy limerick with variations is often quoted:

> A young girl in Boston's Back Bay
> Had manners that were quite outré
> While still in her teens
> She refused to eat beans
> And once threw her Transcript away.

Cleveland Amory, whose book *The Proper Bostonians* was almost a social history of the *Transcript's* audience, has a verse the tenor of which is that proper Bostonians prayed daily that when their time came to die, it might be a Friday so that the obituary would appear in the Saturday *Transcript*.

Surely it is a tribute in the history of journalism to be remembered as the *Boston Transcript* is remembered, to have created a myth of having been a great newspaper despite its having been a unique paper that not many people wanted to buy. The pattern of the myth when imposed on reality does not quite fit, however; and for the vast majority of newspaper readers in New England, the *Transcript* was too unreal. Their mundane concerns were reflected in the *Globe*, the *Post*, the *Herald*, and the Hearst papers, and those were the papers they bought and read.

CHAPTER TWENTY

The Ponzi Case

While the newspapers and the newspapermen usually provided or created the nuttiness in Newspaper Row, there were many times when the sanity was on their side and the insanity lay elsewhere. There is no better instance of this than the celebrated Get-Rich-Quick Ponzi case, which had everyone in Boston talking about it and tens of thousands investing their money for a period of eight months in 1919–20, during the Era of Wonderful Nonsense. The case was one of the great swindles of all time, incredible in certain aspects.

Carlo Ponzi was born in Parma, Italy, on March 3, 1882, and claimed to have attended the University of Rome for three years. He came to the United States aboard the S.S. *Vancouver* in 1903 when he was twenty-one years old, Americanized his name to Charles Ponzi, and went to work.

His own recitation of his beginnings, taken here from a July 1920 interview by the *Boston Post*, went thus:

> I had $200 when I started with a ticket for New York by way of Boston. A cardsharp took away all but $2.50 of my money in a card game. That was my first foolish move and so I took care to guard against foolishness ever since. Landing in Boston with such a small sum of money I was downcast. I didn't have a friend in the city nor a relative in the country. So I went on to where my ticket carried me, to New York. There I did manual labor. Then I moved to Pittsburgh in search of some friends whom I believed were there. I didn't find them so I went on working from place to place, working now as a clerk in a business office, next as a grocery clerk and often at menial tasks.

Caricatures such as this one abounded as the *Post* chronicled the meteoric rise and fall of Charles Ponzi, one of the most celebrated swindlers of the century. William Norman Ritchie, the *Post*'s celebrated political cartoonist, signed all his drawings with his middle name.

Three years after I landed in Boston I was back there again. But I didn't remain long. I went to Vermont and then I "floated" through nearly every state and large community in the Eastern part of the country. I was not satisfied with small wages. I had come to America to make a fortune, intending to return to Italy after I had done so. I could have written home for money and it would have been sent to me and I might have gone back. Although I was lonesome I was also ashamed to admit failure, so I hung on. Make money in big amounts was my motto. Back to Boston I came in 1917. Somehow, there was an attraction about this city. Now I knew that I loved this old city better than any other place in the world, and I intended to show my gratitude by doing what I can to make this little spot the brightest and most prosperous on the whole earth.

Well, in January of 1917 I went to work for the J. B. Poole Co., merchant brokers on South Market Street. My salary was $16 a week. In February 1918 I was married to Rose Gnecco, a young Boston woman. We have no children. I had planned early to go to Italy to visit my mother, the only member of my immediate family now living. I bought my tickets. Then my business began to grow in such a colossal scale that I decided to have my mother come here. I cancelled my sailing and she arrived and is now in my house.

Such was the account he gave to a *Boston Post* reporter early in July 1920. The brief biography omitted, among other things, that he had served time in two jails in America. When he granted the interview he was known as the Wizard of Finance. The month before that story had appeared, 7,824 investors had poured $2,546,944.89 into his coffers. In return he gave each investor a promissory note that he would pay 50 percent on their investment in forty-five days or 100 percent in ninety days. A few days after the *Post* story, the number of investors and the amount of their investment had all but trebled, reaching a total of $6,415,675. Ponzi stood five feet, three-and-one-half inches tall, dressed impeccably and with style, and was plausible, ingratiating, and courteous. He was most articulate, and his accent was slight, although he knew no English when he left Italy. He had hours of solitude to perfect it, however, in the few years he had spent in jail before returning to Boston in 1917. One of the jails was in Montréal and one in Alabama. In his brief account of his wanderings—"floating" about—failure to mention those two prison terms was the major omission.

When he went to work for J. R. Poole Co. (which he later bought up with investors' money), he was dapper and smiling but bored by his small income. He learned quickly and, after getting a grasp on the export-import business, determined to publish a trade journal for that sort of enterprise. He did for a while, calling it *The Trader's Guide*. It was a good idea and might even have succeeded had he been able to get financing for it. But even his wife's relatives declined to put more than a few dollars in it. The venture was losing money when chance put the basis of his get-rich-quick scheme into his hands.

A customer sent him some International Reply Coupons from Spain. Such coupons are still available in some countries (including the United States). Their purpose is most simple. If an author wishes a publishing house in a foreign country to examine his manuscript for possible publication and is asked to enclose return postage, he cannot enclose stamps of his country, nor are stamps from the foreign countries available in his country. He then purchases International Reply Coupons, which could be cashed by the publishing house in the local post office. Ponzi went to the Boston post office with the International Reply Coupons from Spain in order to mail a copy of the *Trader's Guide* to that country and found that the Boston post office gave him five cents for a stamp that in Spain has cost one cent. The difference was in part governed by the fluctuations in international monetary exchange.

One New York financier later explained it for the readers of the *New York Sun*: "Take $100 in New York and cable it to a Bucharest bank. In accordance with the exchange rate between dollars and leys, that would give the sender a credit of $100 in the Bucharest bank or 5,000 leys. Now the bank in Bucharest or an agent would take the 5,000 leys at the rate of about four coupons to the ley and would receive 20,000 coupons. The Bucharest bank or an agent would send those 20,000 coupons to a bank or agent in Paris who would then present them to a post office in Paris. He would then receive 20,000 postage stamps at the value of 25 centimes each or altogether 5,000 francs in stamps.

"But as the stamps in France are legal tender he may go into a French bank with these 5,000 francs in stamps and buy with them a cable transfer to a New York bank for the equivalent of 12 francs to the dollar which amounts to about $400 or thereabouts. The exchange rates vary from day to day but the above may be taken for a fair illustration. The man would receive $400 on his original $100."

Ponzi, having found out that this could be done and having made one or two tests of the system through a merchant seaman he knew and by friends in Italy, didn't bother to pursue the actual exchange any further. He simply promised any investor 50 percent on his money in forty-five days or 100 percent in ninety days.

He promptly formed the Securities Exchange Company at 27 School Street, Boston, on the edge of Newspaper Row, halfway between city hall and the doors of the *Boston Post*. He then opened for business and wondered how best to get customers. He was not so generous at first. When he met Ettore Giberti he was offering 50 percent in ninety days. Giberti, a 22-year-old North End workman, became Ponzi's first salesman, or customer's man, as the phrase went in the brokerage business.

In December 1919, Giberti brought him $870 from a dozen investors, all men who worked in the same factory as Giberti. They were promised 50 percent on their money in ninety days. There was a tedious period of waiting but when the Securities Exchange Company paid off its first notes, the rush began. In January, he had only three investors. In February he had 17, with a total investment of $5,290. In March, the number grew to 110 investors, who had given him $28,724.83. In April, he had 471 investors and a total of $141,671. He was now living well, had paid off his domestic debts, and had hired the office staff needed for the clerical work involved in the receipt of cash and the disbursing of payments to those investors wise enough to take their 50 percent and run. The scheme worked with the public like a chain letter. A very few made some money; before it all ground to a halt, an estimated 40,000 investors got stuck for something in excess of $9 million, and $15 million had passed through Ponzi's hands.

Ponzi made no secret of the manner in which he purportedly invested the public's money, explaining the International Reply Coupon Exchange carefully but never revealing how or where he cashed the coupons that finally brought him his profit. Postal authorities got wind of the scheme before it was publicized in the newspapers and went to investigate. He was most open with them but explained patiently that, if he told them how he managed to cash so large a number of reply coupons, then anyone else could get in the business and compete with him. As a matter of fact, two groups did, one of them in his own building, but they were dealing with nickels and dimes while Ponzi juggled millions.

The fact was that Ponzi never bought any coupons to speak of. Indeed, as was observed by Clarence W. Barron, distinguished Boston financial publisher of the *Boston News Bureau* (forerunner of the *Wall Street Journal*) and *Barron's Weekly*, there weren't enough reply coupons in print to take care of the volume of business that Ponzi was doing. This was in June 1920, when the law was closing in on Ponzi, who then declared that the stamp exchange was a blind to keep financiers from finding out his secret. Then Barron asked the key question. If Ponzi could make 100 percent by dealing in International Reply Coupons, why did he have several million dollars in Boston banks at 4 and 5 percent interest? By the time that question was asked, Ponzi had become not merely a director of the Hanover Trust Company, which had been run by Henry H. Chmielinski, an honored Polish-American publisher, but its dominating figure. Ponzi's manipulations ruined that bank and also ruined the Tremont Trust Company, which was run by Simon Swig, a highly respected Russian immigrant who had risen from junk peddler to banker.

The Ponzi claim, his plausibility, and the gossip of the few investors who were walking away from his School Street office with their money doubled was too much for the postal inspectors and police. Some who came to investigate invested their own money. The bankers, of course, were furious. Men and women were withdrawing their life savings or a good part of them to invest with Ponzi. Why indeed leave money in a bank at 5 percent per year when you could get 50 percent in a month and a half?

Complain as the bankers might to Massachusetts Attorney General J. Weston Allen, that officer replied that there was nothing illegal in promising to pay 50 percent interest on a loan and then paying it. He had had no complaints from investors who claimed to have been bilked. When one complaint was made, Ponzi paid off promptly.

Throughout the month of May, when he was quietly taking over control of the Hanover Trust Company and putting large amounts of money in the Tremont Trust Company, which its controller and vice president Swig would live to regret, Ponzi was the talk of State Street. Although he had 1,529 investors that month alone, however, the general public had not really heard of him. They were beginning to. He had branch offices in a couple of cities, which was a mistake. Worse still for his peace of mind, one of his former cellmates from the Montréal prison came around to see him, and Ponzi had to pay what amounted to blackmail.

Ponzi had bought an expensive home in Lexington (Massachusetts) and furnished it richly. His wife had given up her job, which had helped support them for part of 1918 and most of 1919, when he was struggling; and he had brought his mother from Italy. If one were totting up the virtues of Charles Ponzi, one would have to enter in the book of merits, beside his courtesy and affability, his fondness for his wife. He was a devoted husband, intent not merely on living the good life, but also seeing that Rose Gnecco did as well. She in turn, innocent of all the nefariousness of his scheme, was as loyal a wife as ever emerged from a story-book. She had servants and furs; he had cigars, a chauffeur for his limousine, and the magnificent inspiration that comes from wielding power. Bankers and other dignitaries jumped when Ponzi spoke. He felt it was necessary to hire guards for his home and a public-relations expert. The man he hired was William McMasters, a familiar figure in the Boston political scene and later twice an unsuccessful candidate for governor on a third-party ticket. The climax for Ponzi came in the month of July 1920 and the dénouement in August, when the *Post* finally began to expose Ponzi for what he was.

That July was the month that McMasters recommended to Ponzi that he grant an interview to the *Post*. He did. The story appeared with a headline that read "Double the Money Within Three Months." There were also two subheads: "50 percent *Interest Paid* in 45 Days by Ponzi—Has Thousands of Investors" and "Deals in International Coupons—Taking Advantage of the Rate of Exchange."

The story, with a picture of Ponzi dressed like a fashionable banker—boutonniere in his lapel, handkerchief peaked from his breast pocket, and cigar in his hand—not only brought the matter to the attention of more than two million readers, it broke the dam of reserve in many persons who knew of his operation but had hesitated to invest. The *Post* story seemed to some almost like a recommendation.

When the month of June closed, the number of Ponzi's investors had risen from 1,525 to 7,924 and the amount of money invested with him from $442,515.22 to $2,546,944.89. By July, 20,230 men and women gave him $6,415,675.88, and more was coming in.

The *Post*'s city editor dubbed the line of investors in Ponzi's get-rich-quick scheme "pigs being led to the slaughter." Here, the hopeful crowd extends from the door of Ponzi's office alongside city hall and into Pi Alley, a distance of about one hundred yards.

The line of investors ran from the door of his office, alongside city hall, and into Pi Alley, a distance of about one hundred yards. Newspaper Row had not seen such excitement since Joe Knowles appeared in his noxious bearskin.

The *Post* story read as follows:

> A proposition fathered by Charles Ponzi as head of the Securities Exchange Co. at 27 School Street, where one may get 50 percent in 45 days, 100 percent in 90 days, on any amount is causing interest throughout Boston.
>
> The proposition has been in operation for nine or 10 months, rolling up great wealth for the man behind it and rolling up much money for the thousands of men and women who are tumbling over themselves to entrust him with their money on no other security than his personal note, and the authorities have not been able to discover a single illegal thing about it.
>
> Ponzi, starting last October or November, with hardly a "shoestring," so to speak, is today rated as worth $8,500,000,

a purchaser of business blocks, trust companies, estates and motor cars.

His investors—and they run the gamut of society, richmen, and women, unknown and prominent—have seen their money doubled, trebled and quadrupled. The originator will talk of his successes, of everything—did last night to a Post reporter. [Not quite everything, as he omitted, among other details, the prison terms.]

The people are trusting Ponzi—the most of them. There are some of them among his investors who give him their money and at the same time call on the federal, state and city authorities to advise them.

"Is it sound?" they ask. "Can it be real?" they ask. The federal, state and city authorities are able only to tell those questioning ones that they have been unable to find that he is doing anything illegal.

So meantime the people are falling over themselves—this almost literally—to loan him their money. They flock to his office, some of them with the savings of a life-time, others with a "bit" of their fortune.

Even government officials sent to investigate him have wound up by investing with him. At least that is so in the case of two inspectors from Police Headquarters.

There's no secret about how Ponzi conducts his business, according to him. He says he makes the money for himself and his investors, makes every one dollar grow to four dollars by buying International Reply Coupons exchangeable into stamps, buying where the rates of exchange are such that one dollar of American currency is really worth four. His only secret, he says, lies in his connections, in the names of the agents who buy and sell the international coupons for him.

Ponzi was boasting that his company had offices in Portland and Bangor, Maine; Manchester and Portsmouth, New Hampshire; Burlington, Vermont; Pawtucket, Providence, Woonsocket, and Central Falls, Rhode Island; Hartford, Meriden, Bridgeport, and New Haven, Connecticut; and Bayonne and Clifton, New Jersey. He also had offices in Massachusetts, he said, at Plymouth, Barre, Fall River, Taunton, Framingham, and Milford, and he was planning offices in Worcester, Springfield, and Holyoke. He was also planning a New York City office. Obviously there was a touch of madness in Ponzi, a hubris driving him to destruction.

He was paying the men in his out-of-town offices—and it is questionable how many offices he had—10 percent of all the money they sent in. On top of that, he was promising 50 percent interest in forty days on the total. One wonders how he thought he would ever escape from the monstrous web he was weaving for himself. What is certain is that he was putting no money into International Reply Coupons and displayed no alarm when Italy, France, and a couple of other countries withdrew from the Universal Postal Union, under which the International Reply Coupon agreement operated. He was simply using yesterday's receipts to pay today's demands.

The *Boston Post*, in publishing the original story on Ponzi, had shown less than top-flight journalistic talent. Richard Grozier, the only son of Edwin A. Grozier, was directing coverage of the Ponzi case in view of his father's failing health. Indeed, he had sent reporters out to trace Ponzi's background, but the story carried no hint that financiers thought the scheme ridiculous or that the post office had knowledgeable men who kept insisting that there were not enough International Reply Coupons in the world to take care of one hundredth of Ponzi's pyramid.

By this time he was under intense investigation. The offices of Massachusetts Attorney General J. Weston Allen and U.S. Attorney Daniel J. Gallagher, along with postal inspectors and the office of District Attorney Joseph Pelletier of Suffolk County, were beginning to scrutinize the Ponzi operation. Whether it was the greed that was in the air in those years or merely a coincidental outbreak of political and legal corruption, it is of interest to note that Adams, Gallagher, Pelletier, and Daniel H. Coakley, whom Ponzi hired to defend him, were all later disbarred. Their derelictions of duty, however, had no connection with the Ponzi case.

The ruination of the Hanover Trust Company and the Tremont Trust Company were, on the contrary, directly related to the Ponzi swindle. Ponzi had such large deposits in both banks that he controlled the first and, by demanding an enormous cash withdrawal from the latter, put it in a position that made it unsalvageable. In the case of the Tremont Trust Company, a number of its depositors had taken their savings to lend to Ponzi, who returned the money to the bank in his account. The whole was a piece of financial madness, a result of the lunacy that possesses people who want to make easy money. No person gets flimflammed who is not motivated by greed. As W. C. Fields said often, 'You can't cheat an honest man.'

The story of Ponzi's operation had appeared in the *Post* on Saturday, July 24, 1920. That morning School Street, City Hall Avenue, and Pi Alley were jammed with eager investors. The people in Ponzi's office called him in hysterics. He was unperturbed and seemed delighted. His theory was simple: As long as the money kept pouring in, he could continue to pay off; and as long as he continued to pay off, the authorities could do nothing to him. True, he was being sued by one early creditor who was asking that he be given a percentage of Ponzi's profits. Another person of unsavory reputation was asking to purchase the entire Ponzi operation. Yet he posed calmly for both the Fox-newsreel cameramen who came to his Lexington house to photograph him and the cameramen of newspapers demanding interviews, irate at having been scooped by the *Post*.

Investigators were asking questions all over Europe. McMasters, whom Ponzi had hired as press agent, was getting frightened, even though Ponzi waved in front of him a certified check for a million dollars that he always carried in his vest pocket to show his solvency.

Only with difficulty was his staff able to close his office Saturday afternoon, having taken in more than $3 million. Ponzi knew that on Monday the crowd would be even larger.

The following day was Sunday and the *Boston Post*, now hot on Ponzi's trail, was interviewing Clarence W. Barron. On Monday, when Ponzi rode to work in his limousine, he read a story that outraged him. An enormous headline read, "Questions the Motive Behind Ponzi's Scheme." Barron pointed out that the Ponzi scheme was on the face of it, ridiculous. He declared that even if John D. Rockefeller promised to pay 50-percent interest on his note and then was putting money in the bank at 5-percent interest, no sensible investor would continue with him. Despite the *Post* interview with Barron, thousands of persons were on School Street Monday morning, money in their hands ready to invest. Some of them had the *Post* story in one hand and their money in the other. Some who had read the Barron story and whose notes were due took their interest. Others cashed their notes at face value. The vast majority left money with Ponzi.

That was the day McMasters convinced Ponzi that he should go to the district attorney's office and agree to an investigation. Ponzi told Pelletier that he didn't mind an auditor going over his books, but he insisted that only one auditor should do the job for all investigating authorities. He also agreed to stop taking money after noon on Tuesday. That morning the *Post* carried a headline that Ponzi was closing his operation and was not likely to resume. It caused a run on his holdings and he probably paid off more than $3 million, most of it to persons whose notes were not yet due, which inclined many others to still give him money or leave with him whatever money they had lent him.

The *Post* was after blood now. Richard Grozier, the paper's assistant publisher who was acting in his father's stead, knew he was in a dangerous game. Ponzi had been convicted of nothing, nor had he been indicted. Neither state, city, nor county officials, nor federal law-enforcement agencies had charged him with any illegality. If the paper made a mistake in its accusations against Ponzi (who obviously had sufficient money on hand to hire lawyers), it might well find itself sued for libel.

Ponzi had warned city editor Edward J. Dunn that the story that the former might not reopen had hurt him badly and that, before he was through with the *Post*, he would "own its presses." It was at this moment in the affair that McMasters, certain that Ponzi was paying today's bills with yesterday's receipts, as Barron had suggested in his article, came to Richard Grozier and offered to sell him a story exposing Ponzi as doing just that. Grozier agreed to pay McMasters $6,000 for the story and, when he read it, gave him another $1,000 as a bonus. McMasters always maintained that he had taken no money from Ponzi for his services, but he may have received money for expenses. The *Post* carried the story on August 2, 1920, with headlines that ran eight columns across page one reading, "Declares Ponzi is Hopelessly Insolvent" and several subheads that continued, "Publicity Expert Employed by Wizard Says He Has Not Sufficient Funds to Meet His Notes, States He has Sent no Money to Europe, Nor Received Money from Europe Recently." Another subhead added that Ponzi's money in banks was taken from investors. The story was a crusher for Ponzi. It started an incredible run on his money, but he paid another $3 million to investors, most of whom cashed in their notes before the expiration date of forty-five days and got only their original investment.

"What bank in Boston could stand a run like that?" Ponzi boasted. But perhaps he knew by this time that the jig was up.

On one occasion, when the *Post* had printed that Allen, Gallagher, and Pelletier were all investigating him, Ponzi had been received with cheers by the crowd queuing up to invest their money with him.

"Three cheers for Ponzi!" someone called out, and the crowd responded. Ponzi waited until the thunder of the cheers had died out and then shouted, "And three groans for the *Post*." The crowd responded with laughter and more cheers. City editor Edward J. Dunn, whom Ponzi enjoyed threatening, had walked from the *Post*'s office on Washington Street to observe the crowd of would-be investors queuing at Ponzi's office. He remarked, "Pigs being led to the slaughter." The McMasters story was to play a significant part in winning the Pulitzer Prize for public service for the *Post*. Nicholas Murray Butler, the president of Columbia University, which presided over the awarding of the Pulitzer Prizes, called it the best newspaper story he had ever read.

But Ponzi was still a free man. No law-enforcement agency had moved against him, and he was threatening to sue Barron, the *Post*, and McMasters. Grozier knew that there was some information somewhere that, if printed, would administer the coup de grâce to the diminutive, cocky wizard of finance.

The clue to finding that information came from P. A. Santosuosso, the *Post* reporter assigned by the paper to the day-to-day coverage of the Ponzi case. Santosuosso was as fluent in Italian as Ponzi was in English and, while digging up information in the North End, Boston's "Little Italy," heard from a woman he knew that Ponzi had spent time in jail in Montréal.

He informed Grozier, who dispatched Herbert L. Baldwin, one of his leading reporters, to see what he could find. The task proved difficult, as Ponzi's police record in Canada was buried under the name Bianchi, alias Ponsi, with no cross-reference under his own name. Baldwin was armed with several photographs of Ponzi and a cunning sense that he would have been engaged in a swindle probably involving an Italian bank.

After exhausting all leads at police headquarters, Baldwin began showing the pictures to a number of Italian-Canadians who remembered a bank failure involving a Louis Zarossi, a banker who, to his regret, had once hired a Carlo Bianchi, who had gone to jail. At length, Baldwin found a woman who had worked for the bank and recognized a photo of Ponzi. "Yes," she said, "it is Bianchi. But he has no mustache." That name was enough for Baldwin. Back in Montréal police headquarters, he found the rogues'-gallery pictures of Charles Bianchi, alias Ponsi, with the information that he had served time for forgery. It filled in one of the omissions that the financier had left in the rather romantic life story he had given to a *Post* reporter. Baldwin wired the information to the *Post*.

Grozier wired back: "Are you sure?"

Baldwin, who was never shy, replied: "Do you think I am making it up?"

The *Post* story the following day led the paper with the headline, "Canadian 'Ponsi' Served Jail Term." The subhead declared boldly, "Montréal Police, Jail Warden and Others Declare that Charles Ponzi of Boston and Charles Ponsi of Montréal Who was Sentenced to Two and Half Years in Jail for Forgery on Italian Bank are One and the Same Man." It also added that he had been jailed for a get-rich-quick scheme at the bank where he worked.

The story read:

By Herbert L. Baldwin

Montréal, Aug.10—Charles Ponzi, Boston's financial wizard and Charles Ponsi, alias Charles Bianchi, a convicted forger who spent two-and-a-half years behind the bars of one of Canada's jails, were pronounced one and the same man today.

A rogue's gallery expert, a police inspector who arrested Charles Ponsi (Bianchi) at St. Vincent de Paul, a clerk who worked in the same office where the forgeries took place and an Italian banker, one of the best known in this city, were among those who saw photographs of Charles Ponzi of Lexington, Mass., and with one accord told a *Post* reporter:

"Why, that's Bianchi," or "That's Ponsi," as happened to be the name they knew him by.

"But where's the mustache?" they all wanted to know.

The story was devastating for Ponzi and could have been for the *Post* if there had been any mistake.

Before printing the story, Richard Grozier sent two reporters to Ponzi's Lexington home to confront him with it. He laughed, denied every line of it, and swore that he had never been in Montréal, had never been arrested there, and had never been known as Bianchi. He then threatened to sue the paper for libel if the story appeared.

Grozier ran the story. It was the end for Ponzi. The *Post* carried the pictures from the rogues' gallery in Montréal. They printed a similar picture of Ponzi as Boston knew him and painted a mustache on it to bring out the resemblance. The prosecutors waited no longer. The whole nation knew Ponzi for what he was. Within a few days, it was revealed he had also spent some time in a jail in Alabama.

Two days later he was arrested. He continued to protest his innocence and said, if the authorities would leave him alone, he would pay 50 percent in ninety days on all money invested with him. The crowd does not relinquish a dream readily. The first two weeks in August found School Street and the agora filled with excitement. Handbills were distributed defending Ponzi and denouncing the attacks on him as the work of unscrupulous bankers. Rumors circulated that he was worth billions and could pay off for ever. He had discovered a gold mine. He had beaten the financiers at their own game. Even when Bank Commissioner Joseph C. Allen closed the Hanover Trust Company, friends of Ponzi denounced the action. Officers of the bank insisted they were solvent. The Hanover Trust dragged down with it the Polish Industrial Association, a credit union. Ponzi's friends insisted all would be well. It was not until the next year that the Tremont Trust Company went down as a result of Ponzi's malfeasance, despite Simon Swig's valiant efforts to save it.

In August, Ponzi continued to pay off. There seemed to be no bottom to his barrel. Norman Ritchie, the *Post*'s celebrated cartoonist, produced a cartoon depicting the mad scramble. Handbills supporting Ponzi were distributed in the streets, especially to those standing in line to get their money back. One handbill, signed James Francis Morelli, burst into verse on behalf of the Wizard of Finance.

> What is all the excitement folks?
> Why these speculators?
> Ponzi's notes are good as gold.
> So why these black-hearted raiders?
> If they should ask you to sell your notes
> Just step forward and exclaim
> No, indeed, I'm sorry, lad
> 'Cause my notes bear Ponzi's name.
> Just step in line and wait with ease
> and avoid all sorts of commotion

For Ponzi has as many dollars
As there are ripples in the ocean
He will pay you all, and thank you, too,
And solicit your funds once more
And instead of serving doughnuts and coffee
He'll serve turkeys by the score.

The reference was to Ponzi's habit of serving doughnuts and coffee occasionally to people waiting in line. He was courtesy itself and courtly to women. If the summer heat was intense, he opened a side door and brought elderly women into his office out of turn. Time and again he warned his investors as they stood in line against selling their notes to speculators.

Mrs. Ponzi said later that Ponzi was a "born aristocrat." Indeed, his manner was such. His dress was impeccable. When he alighted from his chauffeur-driven limousine each morning, with his cane and a long cigarette holder, his manner was majestic and exuded confidence, which reassured his investors. At no time did his good manners fail him.

On one occasion he brought a number of New York bankers to Boston and wined and dined them and outlined a plan for setting up a $200 million corporation that would establish profit-sharing banks. His manner then was the same as it was on August 13, 1920, when United States Marshal Patrick J. Duane arrested him without ceremony. Duane himself was wearing a tall silk hat, striped trousers, and a Prince Albert coat, but not for the occasion. It was his customary dress, a charming eccentricity that added another touch of glamour to the whole crazy episode.

The arrest precipitated one of the most complicated legal situations in the history of the commonwealth of Massachusetts. There were innumerable civil and criminal trials, bankruptcy hearings, hearings before bank examiners, parole and pardon hearings, suits by Ponzi against former employees and suits by employees against Ponzi and appeals that went in time before the Supreme Judicial Court of Massachusetts. Some of the legalities dragged on for fifteen years. On November 30, 1920, in federal court, on the advice of Daniel H. Coakley, to whom Ponzi reputedly paid $300,000 for his legal expertise, Ponzi pleaded guilty to using the mails to defraud and was sentenced to five years in the Plymouth House of Correction, which the federal government used because it had no jail of its own in Massachusetts. His cell is still pointed out to visitors. In the jail, he immediately began the study of law. He spent three-and-a-half years there, a time interrupted by visits to Massachusetts General Hospital and Suffolk Superior court, where he pleaded not guilty to twenty-two counts of conspiracy and larceny. At Christmas, he sent out cards to many of his investors.

Meanwhile, his house in Lexington was confiscated and auctioned off, as was a house in Winthrop (Massachusetts) that he had bought about the same time and a summer cottage in Plymouth, not far from the jail where he served his time. Massachusetts would try him three times before the authorities were able to jail him. In his first trial, he defended himself and won acquittal on four counts. In the second trial, he made an emotional appeal to the jury, which disagreed among themselves as to his guilt or innocence and let him walk out of the courthouse a free man. The argument he presented had a touch of genius.

"Remember," he told the jury, "that four years ago I had $9 million. Today I am so impoverished that I cannot hire a lawyer. This fact of my circumstance should be sufficient evidence that I did not intend to steal.

"If you were able to lay your hands on $9 million, what would you do with the money? I think it is very important to establish what became of the money in order to establish intent. If a man takes a watch and returns it, it is not a theft; it may be a joke. I do not mean to imply that my business was a joke. Intent to steal and misrepresentation must be shown to establish intent to commit a crime. You have heard some witnesses here say that I dealt in International Reply Coupons. Many persons who had the money and wished to invest took a chance because they heard of the large profits. But the promise of a profit is not larceny; it is merely a promise, and a promise may or may not be kept, according to circumstances. If I took the money and the investors thought I was going to invest it in coupons and did not do so, that is not larceny. There may have been circumstances making it impossible for me to give the returns promised. There is no question that I dealt in foreign exchange. Therefore you have only to judge my good faith in attempting to obtain a large number of coupons. You have heard witnesses say that they knew of no laws or rules to limit the amount of coupons to be bought."

The jury bought the argument, or enough of them did to have a hung jury. It was no wonder that his friends contended he had a touch of genius about him.

But the authorities were not going to let him off the hook. At his third trial, he was defended by William H. Lewis, a most distinguished member of the bar, the first black chosen for an all-American football team, the first black captain of a college football team, and the first black named an assistant attorney general of the United States. Despite Lewis's wizardry in the courtroom, Ponzi was found guilty of grand larceny and sentenced to seven-to-nine years in state prison. Dramatic appeals by him and his wife on the grounds that he had already paid for his crimes in Plymouth were to no avail. He was released on bail and promptly disappeared. Incredibly, when the authorities found him two months later, he was already in business in Florida, selling real estate as the Charpon Real Estate Company (Charpon being a contraction of his two names). The state of Florida had already indicted him for fraud. His lots were under water. While Florida was trying to jail him and Massachusetts was trying to extradite him, Ponzi again jumped bail, was spotted in Texas, and escaped again, this time to Louisiana, where at last he was collared trying to ship out of the country as an able-bodied seaman. He was returned to Boston on February 16, 1927, to begin serving his sentence.

Seven years later, he was released. One of his first visits was to the *Boston Post* to chat with city editor Dunn. He walked past the bronze plaque awarded to the *Post* in 1921 for bringing him to justice. He was as dapper as ever, if corpulent; his manners had not deserted him. He shook hands with Dunn and sat down with him to talk over old times. He had threatened Dunn many times, but that was all forgotten. Ponzi, however, faced deportation now. He had never become a citizen.

The rest of his career had little to do with Newspaper Row. Governor Joseph B. Ely refused to save him from deportation just as Governor Alvin T. Fuller had declined to commute his sentence. On October 7, 1934, Inspector James K. Kealey, an immigration officer, escorted Ponzi to the steamship *Vulcania*. Benito Mussolini was in power in Italy, and when Ponzi looked back from the gangplank to some of his old friends who had come to see him off, he gave the Fascist salute. He managed to use his charm on Il Duce, who gave him a job in Brazil as manager there of the

On October 7, 1934, the Ponzi affair came to its inevitable conclusion as immigration officers escorted Ponzi onto the steamship *Vulcania* for his deportation. Ponzi had never taken the trouble to be naturalized.

office of Italy's growing airline. He served for three years and was fired, he claimed, because of his protest against "widespread departures from the organization's original, strictly honest commercial operations." The airline had been trafficking in foreign exchange, a subject on which Ponzi had a good deal of knowledge. He tipped off the Brazilian government and hoped to get a percentage of the fines. He must have missed out, for he died in a charity hospital in Brazil on June 8, 1949.

CHAPTER TWENTY-ONE

The Garrett Case:
Another *Post* Scoop

At the tail end of the Ponzi case, with the Pulitzer Prize for public service on its walls, the *Post* brought off one of the greatest scoops in the history of the city. On November 30, 1930, with Ponzi all but forgotten by newspaper readers, the *Post* announced that Patrolman Oliver B. Garrett, who had been sought nation-wide for five months, was about to give himself up to authorities voluntarily to face a charge of extortion. The case is the epitome of the Prohibition era.

From 1923 to 1929, Garrett had been the czar of the Boston Police Department, although he had never risen above the rank of patrolman. He had amassed a fortune—a quarter of a million dollars—and many hinted that it was two or three times that. His case won the attention of the entire nation during the lunatic period of the 1920s. The scoop on his return—his "capture"—was the work of Lawrence R. Goldberg, the *Post's* top crime reporter, who had worked on the *New York World* for a short time and attended the Columbia University School of Journalism.

The Garrett case was unparalleled because of the widespread public interest in all aspects of Prohibition and because of the notorious corruption that seemed to exist everywhere in New England as bootleggers provided liquor to their customers and gangsters organized and battled to take over and control the liquor trade. Police here and there, if not everywhere, were paid to look the other way.

The age was one of post-war decadence, hootch and jazz, the Charleston and the Black Bottom, flappers, wild stock-market speculation, the bucket shop (where untrustworthy brokers sold untrustworthy stocks), and the speakeasy. Newspaper editors estimated that there were 10,000 speakeasies in the Greater Boston area. They ranged from "blind pigs," where booze was sold in the kitchen of a home, to elaborate hotels, where membership cards were required, to night clubs with steel doors and peepholes, where introductions were required and the phrase "Joe sent me" had a gag significance. Rum running was big business on land and sea, so hijacking became commonplace, and piracy returned to the high seas. Doctors' liquor prescriptions were at a premium, private stills were not uncommon, and home brew was a specialty. Bootleggers and the gangsters who protected or controlled them were suddenly welcomed in social circles, where previously they would have been abhorred. If you wanted to drink, you couldn't be too choosy about your company.

In 1909, Oliver B. Garrett came to Boston to look for work after an unhappy childhood in Maine, where, like the dynamic magazine publisher Frank Munsey, he had worked for the Western Union Telegraph Company. He worked first as a bakery-wagon driver and then foreman of a milk company, an experience that would help him later. He entered the Naval Aviation Corps in World War I, after which he returned to the milk company. He was still working there when, following the police strike of 1919, he donned a police uniform. He was a forty-dollar-a-week patrolman in the Boston Police Department when he was selected to head the vice-and-liquor squad. Why a Maine Protestant with only four years' experience was chosen for the job on a police department whose majority were Boston Irish Catholics was never made clear, although it was suggested that Police Superintendent Michael Crowley made the appointment to preserve peace between two Irish factions on the force. There were at the time 2,421 men in the department, but Garrett became the czar because of a link he quickly established with the police commissioner. It is no exaggeration to say that Garrett became one of the most-influential men in New England. Among the citizens who live by terror, he became the most feared. His position as head of the vice-and-liquor squad in the age that was dawning gave him incredible clout.

Jimmy Walker was mayor of New York at this time, and the two men resembled one another. Both were personable, dapper, and flippant to the point of insolence. Both liked parties and luxury and spent money like water. Both were corrupt. The years in which Garrett reigned were days of fabulous prosperity. The stock market had no ceiling, and everyone in it was making money. Fortunes were burgeoning on every side, and it was hard to tell if a man had made his fortune in the stock exchange or by exchanging stocks of liquor for illicit cash. Not too many people cared if both stocks were watered.

By 1929, Garrett had been head of the liquor squad for six years. He lived in luxury with the air of an English lord—one of youth, vigor, and exuberance. He had a stable of race horses and drove a sulky himelf at various New England fairs, where trotting horses had always been fancied. He owned a dairy farm in Hingham, south of Boston, that was listed in the name of a bootlegger friend and some relatives of Mrs. Garrett.

She was Florence Redden Woodside, a divorcee, and, at thirty-nine years of age, she was eleven years older than Garrett. She had nursed the first Mrs. Garrett during her last illness. They were married in 1923, shortly after she divorced her first husband. At the time of their wedding, she had $28.76 in the bank and he had $28.16. They withdrew it to enjoy a two-day honeymoon at the home of a friend in the town of Rockland. They set up housekeeping in a modest apartment in Boston. He was made head of the liquor squad shortly after their marriage, and four years later, she told friends, they were "sitting pretty." Two years after that, investigators traced $225,000 in bank deposits to them.

The position Garrett was given was unique, and he handled it uniquely. Rhode Island and Connecticut were the only two states to refuse to ratify the Eighteenth Amendment, which was proposed by Congress on December 18, 1917, and ratified on January 16, 1919, to take effect a year from that date. Thirteen years later it would be repealed. With what many pepole deemed ultimate good sense, Rhode Island simply tried to ignore the whole matter. The New England coastline was designed by nature for rum running, and so the area was somewhat insulated and suffered Prohibition differently from the rest of the nation.

One contention has been made that the Boston police organized the liquor trade before it got out of hand. The final touches of that organizaion were applied by Garrett, who displayed not only the insolence of genius but something of its ability. He was credited with conducting 25,000 raids in six years. Some put the figure at a more modest 15,000. Without question, Garrett was a busy man. The raids and the attendant publicity left the public with the impression that the police were indeed holding bootlegging in check. The public didn't see too much of Garrett's race horses, his dairy farm, his various homes, and his lavish entertainment at the Hotel Ritz in the South End (not to be confused with Boston's stylish Ritz Carlton).

The Ritz was a modest if modish establishment. It was positively shabby beside the Hotel Woodcock, said to have been run by Charles "King" Solomon, who was a partner of Al Capone and kingpin of the rackets in Boston. The Woodcock was extremely fashionable. The customers had to wear evening clothes and were admitted only by card. Inside were five horseshoe bars of polished mahogany, each seemingly cut from one piece of wood. The waiters wore tuxedos; the liquor stewards, white coats. You were assured of good service, good food, and good liquor, and reasonably fair prices. There were many hotels like it in the city but none so lavish. Each gang had its own place. In the North End was the Cosmo Club, and in South Boston was a similar oasis. In Charlestown was the Stork Club, and the newspaper men had the Pen and Pencil Club. In Roxbury there was the Brunswick Civic Club, and other parts of the city enjoyed similar places of refreshment. It was all quite orderly and not without purpose. While Garrett was in charge, it was said, no one ever died or went blind in Boston from bad booze. If anyone did, it was the result of sheer carelessness.

Such organization was due to the energy and acumen of Ollie Garrett. He persistently raided those places that sold inferior products. He also raided many places that sold good liquor until some arrangement was made. But even the places that were paying him off did not escape. He raided them also. If someone charged that such and such a club was paying off Garrett, the doors of the club were knocked down the next day, and great quantities of liquor were poured down the sinks. Superintendent Michael H. Crowley, who came through the subsequent scandal untouched, would send frequent complaints to Garrett; and whenever he did, they were acted upon immediately. The police commissioner at the time was Herbert A. Wilson, and there is an amusing irony in his dismissal, which occurred because he was deemed responsible for the scandal. James Michael Curley was mayor of Boston from 1922 to 1926. To prevent him from having any control over the police department, the Republican-dominated General Court (the state legislature) passed a law stipulating that the police commissioner of the city of Boston be appointed by the governor and not by the mayor. Curley was well aware that Wilson was hand in glove with Garrett and took great pleasure in denouncing Wilson's administration, which, Curley claimed, had made the city as "corrupt as a mining town."

In the days after Prohibition, bootleggers reminiscing with misty eyes about the good old days used to describe what they called the Garrett System. Each speakeasy that had been "certi-fied" had a series of special sinks installed. When Garrett's men raided such an establishment, they poured rye down one sink, gin down another, and beer down a third. Underneath the sinks in the basement would be the employees of the speakeasy, with barrels ready to receive the liquor being dumped. The Garrett sink system insured minimal loss during any "show" raid. If fed-eral agents joined with the Boston police on a raid, however, the liquor would be dumped in the sewers, with photographs being duly taken. Such tragic losses the hostelers endured as among the risks of a risky but profitable business.

Complaints against Garrett began almost as soon as he took his post. They were constantly being lodged. Vengeful bootleg-gers were the worst complainants, but they in turn were fearful of "King" Solomon and other racketeers who did not want the smooth functioning of the Garrett System to be disturbed. The system of payment—extortion—was also smooth. Bootleggers did not pass Garrett any money. They deposited money in his wife's bank accounts and mailed him a copy of the deposit slip. Tremen-dous deposits were made to her account, and the state would later contend that they were the result of extortionate demands.

Garrett was a man with vision. He had occasion to visit the Cohasset, Massachusetts, estate of Clarence W. Barron, father of American financial journalism and publisher of the *Wall Street Journal* and its predecessor, the *Boston News Bureau*. Barron ran a model dairy, internationally famous for its Guernsey cattle. Gar-rett had learned something about that sort of thing while foreman of a milk company in Charlestown. Barron's setup impressed Gar-rett. Consequently, he started the Pine Grove Dairy in Hingham, with his wife as one of the incorporators and the wife of a friend, a Dorchester druggist, Dudley J. C. Mulrenin as another. Mulrenin was later described as a "well-known bootlegger."

The Pine Grove Dairy almost immediately did a bang-up busi-ness in Boston. Every speakeasy and house of ill fame in the city bought milk from the Pine Grove Dairy, some of them paying twenty dollars a quart. The dairy, it was also later charged, developed a home-delivery liquor service. Governor Frank G. Allen wrote Police Commissioner Herbert A. Wilson about the dairy and Garrett's quality of life. Wilson replied that there was nothing illegal in a woman owning property under her maiden name.

The complaints now became a torrent, and Wilson finally had to order Garrett back into uniform. "After all I've done for him," Garrett said to a friend. He promptly went on vacation. A brief respite from all the charges came for Garrett in a curious way. An enterprising confidence man, posing as him, had been going to any number of small speakeasys and shaking them down for fifty or one hundred dollars. They arrested the impostor, and Wilson tried to make more of it than it deserved, but ultimately there wasn't enough there to save Garrett. He might have saved himself by actions other than those he took. He seemed driven by a hubris, like some protagonist in a Greek tragedy.

What must be remembered is that he had his defenders. He was very smart in the handling of complaints and very fair in all his illegal dealings. His word was his bond. His "clients" were rarely angry with him. He was also tremendously loyal to the men on his squad. He stepped forward more than once and took the rap for their inadequacies, and he faked reports to cover their derelictions, a practice that, when discovered, helped to precipitate his downfall. Superintendent Michael Crowley, however, had no patience with him or affection for him. When a gambling raid led by Garrett trapped a number of police officers at the tables, Garrett let them slip away. Crowley felt Garrett's report was not honest. He refused to accept it and asked for another. The second report went over his head to the commissioner, who both accepted and buried it.

A chain of events that began in 1927 now developed that would lead to the czar's downfall. On June 25, 1927, while leading a raid, he was assaulted and his nose broken and teeth chipped. On August 2, 1927, he was riding in a police car that collided with another automobile, and he was treated at Massachusetts General Hospital. On September 2 of that year, he was X-rayed at the hospital; the X-ray disclosed a linear fracture of the skull on the right-hand side of his forehead. Two years later, shortly after being ordered back into uniform, he was riding a sulky at the Marshfield (Massachusetts) Fair, was thrown, and suffered a brain concussion. Having sworn he would never serve when he was ordered back into uniform, Garrett now applied for a pension on a disability arising from the August automobile accident. Superintendent Crowley sent Captain James J. McDevitt to interview Garrett about his injuries. Garrett tried to threaten McDevitt; but as a man whose reputation was above reproach, McDevitt didn't scare. He and Crowley refused to approve the pension. Wilson tried to evade the issue at first by charging Garrett with refusing to provide McDevitt with sufficient information. But when Garrett engaged one of the leading criminal lawyers in the city to press his case, Wilson quailed. He sent Garrett's papers to Doctor Frederick J. Bailey, the city physician. Bailey examined Garrett and turned in his report on October 18. Garrett didn't bother to tell Bailey that, a month earlier, he had passed a physical examination for life insurance and disclaimed any injury or sickness in the previous five years. On October 19, Wilson approved the pension. Garrett was given $1,050 a year. Wilson dismissed the charges that Garrett had not been candid with McDevitt. Wilson even had Bailey insinuate in the report that the skull fracture "was quite sufficient to cause this officer to be irresponsible." It was a stupid attempt to anticipate and defuse future charges. Garrett and Wilson had simply duped Bailey, an amiable and easygoing man.

The granting of disability pensions to police in Boston had always been a lax procedure. Garrett's pension was the spark that caused the explosion that would lead to his indictment. A Hearst newspaper, the *Boston American*, published a story quoting Garrett as saying that he would "blow the top off the department." He denied that he had ever said any such thing, and William E. Brennan, a *Post* reporter who had been present when McDevitt interviewed Garrett, also denied that Garrett had said it. But Garrett's insolent application and insistence on a pension did "blow the top off" of his own house of cards. The state legislature voted Attorney General Joseph E. Warner special powers to investigate the granting of the "Garrett pension" and "other matters" relating to his work as head of the vice-and-liquor squad. The federal government moved in and attached Garrett's property and on November 14, 1929, he paid a $5,000 tax penalty to the Bureau of Internal Revenue.

Meanwhile, a grand jury was summoned and Damon E. Hall named as special investigator. The initial disclosures were so lurid that the scope of the investigation was promptly broadened. Testimony showed that John F. Sullivan, the proprietor of the Hotel Ritz, Garrett's favorite hangout, had paid graft to Garrett. In all more than eighty witnesses testified. The attorney general submitted his report on May 1, 1930, and branded Garrett as a "grafting police officer," charged that his pension was obtained fraudulently, and excoriated Commissioner Wilson for his work. The report declared that there was no evidence that Wilson, Crowley, or Garrett's immediate superior, Captain George Patterson, had received any money illegally. The governor removed Wilson from office. He died four years later, a disgraced man.

In the same month, the grand jury returned bills of indictment against Garrett, his wife, and Lillian V. Hatch, a friend of Garrett, who operated the hat-check room at the Hotel Ritz and through whom Sullivan made payments to Garrett. In return for these payments, Mrs. Garrett tipped off Sullivan whenever it was deemed prudent to raid the Hotel Ritz. The case was set for a June 23 trial, but Garrett had flown the coop. For the next five months, he was the most-wanted figure in the United States. His name was on everyone's tongue. Witnesses reported seeing him everywhere, except where he was. His raiding squad was dissolved. His dairy was sold. His wife moved to a cottage in Franklin to await trial whenever he was finally found.

A poster was sent out, headed "Wanted For Larceny, Oliver B. Garrett" and signed by Superintendent Michael H. Crowley. The poster described Garrett as follows: "Age, 35 years; height, five feet 10 inches; weight, 160 pounds; complexion, medium; eyes, chestnut; hair, chestnut; slightly bald in front; usually wears a Leghorn or Panama straw hat, double-breasted suit, with coat open; neat dresser; walks jauntily. He frequents fights and race tracks." The picture showed him wearing a felt hat.

"We hold an indictment warrant," the poster read, "charging Garrett with larceny of $107.92 in U. S. currency in this city, Nov. 30, 1929; larceny of $87.50 in U. S. currency in this city, Dec. 31, 1929; larceny of $87.50 in U. S. currency in this city Jan. 31, 1930; larceny of $87.50 in U. S. currency in this city, Feb. 28, 1930; larceny of $87.50 in U. S. currency in this city, March 31, 1930; larceny of $87.50 in U. S. currency in this city, April 30, 1930, all of the above moneys being the property of the city of Boston, a municipal corporation legally established and existing. Arrest, hold and wire at my expense. Signed, Michael H. Crowley, superintendent." It was dated June 26, 1930. It is amusing that, with all his depredations, Garrett's poster should list only his illegal pension payments, the last one being received by him on the eve of Attorney General Warner's sensational report.

The *Post*, in the midst of the uproar, assigned Lawrence R. Goldberg to follow the Garrett case. Goldberg knew Garrett, as did most newspapermen in the city, not merely from covering his raids, but from having a drink or two at the Hotel Ritz. In the interval between Garrett's application for a pension and the indictments against him, the stock market had crashed and the Era of Wonderful Nonsense had come to an end. During this period, newspapermen, Goldberg among them, were interviewing Garrett and other figures every day.

From the legislature, where the persistent voice of State Senator Joseph J. Mulhern had served to goad Republican Governor Frank G. Allen into action against the Republican commissioner, new voices flung more charges. There was a clamor for more indictments. The charge was made that the police didn't dare find Garrett. Some, including many police officers, believed he was dead. Others said he was alive and in Boston. To some it seemed logical that he must have been murdered. Murders were common in the game he had been playing. Many asked how anyone so well known could disappear so completely.

A lot of people certainly wished he were dead. There were a number of police officers who could have been hurt if Garrett talked. There would have been any number of bootleggers who could have been jailed if he talked. There were a lot of thugs who might have wanted to get even with him. He was more feared than hated and more envied than feared. He was not without his defenders, and there were many who remembered him as a staunch friend. Even his enemies acknowledged that when "Garrett was your friend, he was your friend." Captain James J. McDevitt, one of the police officers who had nothing to fear from any confession by Garrett, believed Garrett had been murdered. McDevitt was eager to find Garrett, dead or alive, because of the trouble Garrett gave him on the pension.

District Attorney William J. Foley remained steadfast in the belief that Garrett was alive. The police dragged Boston harbor for Garrett's body. Foley issued new circulars for his arrest. The summer slipped away. A new twist was given the case when Frank A. Rhodes, a Boston marine photographer, found a bottle bobbing in Boston Bay off Castle Island. In it was a note from a sailor on a rum-running ship, saying that a man named Garrett had been shanghaied and was aboard. It was a very plausible story but as phoney as a succession of others. A number of notes were received from impostors claiming to be Garrett, many of them making absurd and not-so-absurd charges against various authorities.

Letters were received, allegedly signed by Garrett, reading, "You'll never get me." People reported seeing him in all sort of places: Boston, New York, Providence, and even Mexico. He was reported seen in Franklin, and his wife's cottage there was searched. He wasn't found. In November, he decided to surrender and wrote to Goldberg to make arrangements. On November 30, 1930, the *Boston Post* splashed its front page with an eight-column headline and the sensational story.

GARRETT RETURNS HOME;
ALL READY TO SURRENDER

The subheads read:

Famous Fugitive Will Give Self Up Today or Tomorrow—Has Been Hiding in Wife's Cottage in Franklin for Past Five Weeks, Used Recess in Wall as Refuge When Visitors Came—Wandered Far After Flight—But Never Was North of Boston as Often Rumored—Traveled South as Far as Mexico—Only $30 Left. Close to Capture Once While in North Attleboro but Managed to Escape. Often Talked With People Whom He Knew—Wrote Letter to Reporter from Texas.

The story carried the byline of Lawrence R. Goldberg and a copyright line for the *Post* Publishing Company. The later prevented the opposition papers from lifting the story for an extra edition for a twenty-four-hour period. The lead read:

Oliver B. Garrett, fugitive from justice, for whom a nation-wide search has been in progress since his disappearence from the city on the eve of his trial on charges of extortion, conspiracy to extort and larceny, is on his way to Boston to surrender.
He will arrive in Boston sometime today or tomorrow barring some unforeseen delay or some unexpected contingency. He will give himself up to Superintendent Michael H.

Crowley and District Attorney William J. Foley and ask for an immediate trial. Unless this is granted he will seek temporary freedom on bail.

A two-column picture of Garrett ran beside the story, displaying the very jaunty appearance for which he was famous and showing his lips curled in the very slightest of smiles.

Besides the lead story with its copyright line, the *Post* ran a second story two-columns wide in bold-face type, headed:

GARRETT'S OWN STORY TO POST
Fled in Fear of Insanity Verdict or of
Being Used as Political Football
During Sensational Trial

Inside the paper, this story was accompanied by a picture of Garrett dictating to Goldberg, who was seated at a portable typewriter, an uncharacteristic pipe clenched between his teeth. The picture was also copyrighted.

The other papers were without a line. The *Globe* replated the front page of its Sunday paper with a two-column picture of Garrett and four paragraphs of type that quoted District Attorney William J. Foley as acknowledging that he expected Garrett to surrender, as the *Post* had stated. The other papers didn't even do that well. The next day, Monday, December 1, they were struggling to come abreast of the story, using much of the *Post's* material. The *Post*, however, had the jump on them. Only it knew when Garrett would surrender. Goldberg and a photographer brought him to the Charles Street Jail at 12:30 A.M. on December 1. Before the surrender was made, the *Post* had the story in type. The other papers had to turn themselves upside down after their first editions and recover as best they could.

The *Post* headline read:

GARRETT GIVES SELF UP
NOW BEHIND BARS AGAIN
Fugitive Walks into Charles Street Jail at 12:30 This Morning—Nonchalantly Greets Attendants and Lieutenant Daley of District Attorney's Office—Formalities Soon Over— Intended to Surrender Sunday but Overslept—Drives Through Business District in Taxi with Attorney on Way to Jail—Spends Day in Boston Hotel —Not Recognized—Leaves

Home in Franklin with Wife—Not Molested on Journey to
Boston—Made Refuge in Wall Himself—Noticed Similar
Ones in his Days as Raider

Besides the story, the *Post* presented an exclusive picture of
Garrett looking out through the bars of the jail. This picture was
copyrighted to prevent use by the other papers. Underneath the
lead story was once again a first-person story by Garrett as told to
Goldberg. The other papers were sick with envy. The *Boston
American* gave its story the headline, "Sanity Test for Garrett."
The emphasis in the headline was seen as an attempt to demean
the *Post*'s story.

Early in 1929, after he had left office, former President Calvin
Coolidge had begun writing a column that was syndicated to various major newspapers. In Boston, the *Post* carried his column,
customarily on the front page; but this week, Coolidge was rele-
gated to the inside pages. The Garrett story smothered all others;
if you hadn't read the *Post*, you were out of the conversation.

There was a bit of frosting to the cake on that particular
December 1, too. The *Post* had the most popular sports columnist
in the city, a big Texan by the name of Bill Cunningham; he had
starred on the Dartmouth football team before entering the newspaper business. Each year, sports fans in the city waited eagerly
for Cunningham to pick and publish his all-American football
team. Like all such honors, it always provoked conversation, discussion, and argument. His 1930 team made national news and,
in a way, minor journalistic history. He provoked more conversation, discussion, and argument than ever before and incredible
applause for the insight and audacity of his choice. For his first-
team choice, he simply picked the first string of Notre Dame University, which had had an undefeated season and one of its
greatest. His second and third teams were composed of athletes
from all over the country. On his second team, he managed to
pick one Dartmouth man and one Harvard man. That, too,
heightened local attention. The election of the entire Notre Dame
eleven to those sacred niches on the *Post*'s all-American team,
however, was a journalistic stroke of genius, as Cunningham was
able in the story to justify the choices. With that and the Garrett
exclusive, the *Post* reached a momentary apotheosis.

The aftermath of the Garrett scandal has an amusing side
marked by memorable irony. Garrett underwent two trials for ex-

tortion, and in both instances the jury disagreed. It was difficult to empanel a jury that did not have on it one or two men who had taken a drink in one of the speakeasies that Garrett had protected or one who felt that a man who was lucky enough to shake down some bootleggers and protect the public against bad booze couldn't be all bad.

District Attorney Foley was preparing doggedly for a third trial when Garrett, who was as weary of it all as was the district attorney, agreed to plead guilty and accept a two-year sentence in the house of correction, a much nicer place to serve time than the old Charlestown State Prison, which had been built in part before the Battle of Waterloo. Garrett served twenty-one months, earning three months off because of good behavior.

He made news even while confined. Rumors circulated that he was living like a prince in the house of correction, then on Deer Island off the shore of the town of Winthrop. Newsmen were allowed to interview him as he took care of the cows at the prison, a chore he rather liked, he explained, as he had once run a dairy in Hingham. The remark was made with the little smile curling the ends of his lips. He came out of prison in 1933 and tried his hand as a master of ceremonies in a Boston nightclub. He was familiar with the routines; he had watched them in many a speakeasy. But it wasn't his gift. The jaunty air was there, but he was more used to giving orders than making people laugh. He dropped from sight but in 1949 came back to make headlines. It was then the irony of his case surfaced.

If he had not insisted on a pension at the time of his reduction from head of the liquor squad to a street beat, he might never have been subjected to an investigation and indicted. The wanted poster that went out for him when he disappeared, after all, had charged him with theft of the pension money from the city of Boston. Yet he was tried, not for theft, but for extortion from the proprietor of the Ritz Hotel. The irony is that, in 1949, he sued the city for his back pension, charging that it had been unlawfully withheld from him. He had a case. He had been in a police car when his skull was fractured, and the fracture might well have induced a neurotic state in him. The city settled and paid him $19,000. He then moved to California to live more or less happily ever after and, incidentally, to survive the demise of the *Post*.

CHAPTER TWENTY-TWO

☆☆☆☆

The Death of Newspaper Row

The death of the *Boston Post* came in 1956; its demise, along with the relocation of the *Boston Globe* from the heart of the city to the Dorchester section in 1958, meant the death of Newspaper Row, a social phenomenon that lasted for more than half a century. This book has been an attempt to tell the story of Newspaper Row with the emphasis on Edwin A. Grozier and the *Post*, although it might well have been told with the emphasis on the *Globe*, the last newspaper to leave the Row. Two reasons can be advanced for emphasizing the *Post:* One was its tremendous hold on the Democratic population of New England, which gave it, for a short while, the largest circulation among standard-sized (as opposed to tabloid) newspapers in the country. Second, it was the only paper in Boston until after the mid-century mark to win the Pulitzer Prize for public service (for its efforts in the Charles Ponzi case).

That was the high point of the Grozier influence. The paper at that moment appeared indestructible. Richard Grozier, the only son, had taken over and was in charge during the Ponzi case. It was he who had to make the decision to put the newspaper on the line when a miscalculation would have ruined it. But four years later, the elder Grozier was dead and his son's mental health was soon to show signs of failing. By the 1930s he had withdrawn from the paper, and closeted himself in the family home in Cambridge. A recluse, he sent memos to the paper, not unlike Joseph Pulitzer in his last days, excepting that Richard Grozier was no Pulitzer. He died in 1946.

The Depression hurt the newspaper business everywhere, and the *Post* and the *New Orleans Times-Picayune* were, it was said, the only two major papers in the country that did not cut the salaries of their employees. The *Post* emerged from the Depression with the largest morning circulation in New England, but its sources of revenue were being diminished by the inroads of radio and, later, televison. Because of its large circulation, a good part of which reached northern New England, the *Post* had been the recipient of that sort of advertising which turned most quickly to radio. The first of these were those items for which people shop almost daily: cigarettes, toilet articles, candy, and the like. The second were such institutional advertising as involved famous brand names: Ford, Coca-Cola, Longines watches, gasoline brands, and so forth. Such advertisers became the patrons of hour-long radio programs and reduced their newspaper budgets.

The *Post* had no afternoon paper, but the *Herald-Traveler* was pressing the argument that women read afternoon newspapers and also spend eighty-five cents out of every purchasing dollar. The *Herald-Traveler* was also quick to point out that, although its circulation was less than the *Post*'s, it was concentrated in the Greater Boston shopping area, whereas much of the *Post*'s was in Maine, New Hampshire, and Vermont. One might have expected that the *Herald-Traveler*, as the virtual mouthpiece of the Republican Party, would have done well in Maine. The *Post* outsold it there by far, however, and wielded great influence. Indeed, in 1932 it was responsible for helping elect Louis J. Brann, the first Democratic governor in Maine in twenty years. The department-store advertisers turned more and more to the *Herald-Traveler*, although three major stores that withdrew their advertising from the *Post* went out of business. The *Record-American* also made inroads on the *Post*'s lineage by luring away several of the cheaper furniture stores, known, heaven knows why, as borax shops and heavily dependent on newspaper advertising.

While this battle for department-store lineage in the Depression years was going on, the *Globe* stolidly built up a classified-advertising section, giving it a hidden strength that would save it in the future. The *Post* had neglected classified advertising for the curious reason that setting any considerable amount of such type was a problem in the cramped quarters of the jury-rigged buildings where the paper was produced. Still another factor that hurt the *Post*'s standing: The paper lowered its advertising rates on the eve of World War II and was stuck with those rates for the duration because of wartime regulations. Although circulation suffered under Fox, it still remained the highest in the city among morning papers. That preeminence, however, was threatened. More and more papers were turning to home delivery and away from street and store sales. Home delivery was seen as the wave of the future. It was expensive but would prove worthwhile. The *Post* did not have the financial resources to hire the help and mount a home-delivery system. An ingenious attempt was made in 1954 to counteract its weakness in this regard. In one section north of Boston, it arranged to enclose the local weekly paper with its Sunday paper. For a while in that area, that offered stiff competition to the opposition.

In 1941 the *Transcript* went out of business, the Depression having dealt it a mortal blow. Financial and wool-trade advertising had kept it alive. These now failed it, and the Mandell family, which had run it so well for so long, sold it. Many of the *Post* executives thought it was natural for the *Post* to buy the *Transcript;* the combination would present to the advertisers a morning and an afternoon paper to rival the *Globe*, the *Herald-Traveler*, and the *Record-American* and to capitalize on their strong argument for the value of afternoon papers. Unfortunately, the ailing Richard Grozier could either not be reached or energized to enter the battle, and the *Transcript* vanished into the slipstream of history.

When Richard Grozier died, Henry Gillen, an assistant editor who had won Grozier's confidence because of his success managing the *Post* Santa over the years, and Henry Gallagher, the plant electrician, were named executors of the will. Gallagher was evidently chosen because Grozier had met him when he was called to the Grozier home to repair fixtures. The Post Publishing Company trust was to be managed by co-trustees: Walter Carley, the company's auditor and a man utterly without imagination, and Chester Steadman, a small-time lawyer running a one-man firm. The trustees were to choose the future publisher from among Richard's teen-age children. It was immediately evident that the two men were unequal to the task of saving the *Post*.

Steadman advised Grozier's widow to sell the paper. Although it had long been referred to as the "Sleeping Giant of Newspaper Row" (even by Robert G. Choate, the publisher of the *Herald-Traveler*, who feared its awakening), there were no immediate buyers. Steadman tried to sell it to the *Globe*. In his history of the

Globe, Louis M. Lyons recounts the lawyer's meeting with William O. Taylor, a son of Charles and at the time the publisher of the *Globe*. Steadman was a man out of his depth.

He invited the *Globe* publisher to meet with him and the trustees at the Parker House. He opened the conversation.

> "We want the *Globe* to buy the *Post* for $7,500,000, which we think is a fair figure."
> "Chester," W. O. Taylor replied, "I want you to know that I don't want on my conscience putting Boston newspapermen out of their jobs when I think that there is a chance for their paper. How much did you make last year?"
> "We lost half a million dollars," Steadman replied.

"This disclosed extraordinary weakness in management in a period of small tight papers," Lyons wrote.

> "You aren't going to like what I'm about to say, Chester," W. O. Taylor replied, "But if you really want to sell the *Post*, go out and raise about $3,000,000 on the securities I understand the *Post* has, for a new building."

"Steadman reddened at this rebuff and didn't speak to his old friend for six months," comments Lyons.

Taylor knew that the inefficiency of the *Post* plant was part of the reason it was in the doldrums. He was well aware that the fast-developing trends in newspapering were going to drive the *Globe* into building a new plant somewhere that would enable it to extricate its delivery trucks from the ever-constricting traffic tangle in downtown Boston. The guardians of the Sleeping Giant did not see the value of Taylor's advice. They had had similar advice from a recent employee whose ambition was to be a newspaper publisher in Boston and had served an apprenticeship in Chicago. He was Philip S. Weld, who later became the successful publisher of four papers on the North Shore and a director of the *Boston Globe*. After his service in World War II, he was hired by Steadman to find new sources of white paper for the *Post*, a commodity in great demand at the time. Weld was stunned at the antiquated business methods prevailing in the auditor's office and in the advertising department, but his advice fell on deaf ears. He left to buy two daily papers of his own and launch his own publishing career.

During the early 1950s, Joseph P. Kennedy, the financier-father of the late President John F. Kennedy, tried to buy the *Post* and the *Globe*, refusing either unless he could have both. The *Globe*, the Taylors assured him, was not for sale; thus, the *Post* had to go abegging.

Steadman turned to John Fox, then regarded as a wizard of finance. His meteoric financial career had won him control of the Western Union Telegraph Company, among other massive holdings. He became the mystery man of finance for a short while and then the publisher of the *Boston Post*. Steadman had read about him in *Fortune* magazine and saw that the man had the financial ability to absorb the *Post*. His fortune was reputed to amount to $54 million. Steadman also discovered that Fox had a colossal ego and a fear of communism. The *Post* offered an opportunity to attack such an enemy.

The price was said to be $4 million. Fox never paid. He had a technique of not paying, permitting himself to be sued and then settling out of court for less than he owed. He was unfortunately a drunken genius touched by megalomania.

He had been a bright boy of Irish-Catholic background from South Boston; his father, Michael, had worked at different times in humble positions for the United Fruit Company and for the Boston Edison Company. Although Fox said at one time that his father had worked for the *Post*, it does not seem to have been so. Fox distinguished himself at Boston Latin School with his scholarship and at Harvard University with his drinking. He boasted that he consumed a fifth of whiskey a day while he was there. He certainly seemed to do at least as well as that while in command of the *Post*. Employees kept out of his way when his secretary would report that he had a "toothache."

After graduation from Harvard, he enlisted in the Marine Corps but was honorably discharged because of ulcers. He turned to real estate in New York, where large properties were going for little and dilapidated buildings for practically nothing. Fox restored a few and made a fortune. He had worked in a brokerage office for a while in Boston, knew the market rather well, and was proud of his knowledge. In the midst of these endeavors he entered Harvard Law School, never attended class, bought notes from his classmates, and passed the Massachusetts bar six months before graduation. When he emerged as the man who controlled Western Union, *Fortune* carried an article on him. It gave him a good deal of publicity, but he came to the notice of the man in the street in Boston only after he purchased the *Post*. He was then not only the major stock holder in Western Union, he also had impressive gas holdings in Pennsylvania. Within three decades, he would be found dying, a drunken bum in the streets of Boston.

His term as publisher of the *Post* was marked by a ridiculous anticommunism campaign, by his continual wheeling and dealing in a variety of enterprises, by his editorials, and by his stock-market column written under the byline of Washington Waters, a pen name that coupled the names of the two streets outside the *Post*'s windows. Fox was greatly impressed by his own literary style, which was marked by his insistence on using, English style, a plural verb with a common noun—"the government are"—a habit of which he was never cured.

Although he provided mostly embarrassment for the editorial staff, he also provided excitement. The night city editor always had on his desk a number of stories, all marked *Hold for Release from Mr. Fox*. One told of the proposed construction of a new *Post* building with an atomic-bomb proof cellar, another of the purchase of a Boston radio station, another of the discovery of oil in Newfoundland, another of the purchase of a bank in Perth Amboy, New Jersey, and others of gas and oil companies in Pennsylvania and Texas.

Some of these came to be printed. He ordered publication of the *Post*'s constructing a new building on property it owned on Pearl Street, nearer the waterfront, the place where the farsighted Grozier had installed extra presses. The structure was never built.

Although Fox maintained an office on State Street, he spent a good deal of time at the *Post* and, on one occasion, stayed there forty-eight hours straight negotiating the purchase of a radio station that then had the call letters WCOP. That story was published. The story on the discovery of oil in Newfoundland was still on the desk when the *Post* folded. He did buy the bank in Perth Amboy, and that was duly announced to *Post* readers. He was drawn to U.S. Senator Joseph McCarthy, who was by then making an unhappy name for himself; but Fox found that the senator was getting in his hair and began to avoid him. He was striving to get a television channel in Boston for the *Post* and used a lot of influence in Washington to no avail. To further the *Post*'s position as an applicant for a television channel, in 1953 Fox launched a television guide, the first such weekly supplement in the country. He was not successful. The license went to an opposition paper, the *Boston Herald-Traveler*, which managed to get it by means so tainted that it ultimately had to surrender it, a loss that doomed that paper.

This struggle for a television channel involved Fox in a fight with Sherman Adams. A former governor of New Hampshire, Adams was President Dwight D. Eisenhower's chief of staff. He also had an ongoing acquaintance with Bernard Goldfine, a New England manufacturer who wheeled and dealed better than Fox but who ended up in jail, a fate that Fox escaped. Fox always claimed that Adams and Goldfine ruined him by having the Internal Revenue Service investigate him. Whether it was true or not, the IRS did bring Fox's empire, shattered as it was, crumbling into dust.

While these maneuvers were extraneous to the *Post*, the paper suffered a devastating effect from Fox's nonsense. Almost immediately on acquiring the paper, he promoted John Griffin, a distinguished reporter and editorial writer, from Sunday editor to editor-in-chief, with other changes along the line that raised the hopes of the staff. Griffin was an extremely able newspaperman who undoubtedly saved Fox from many excesses. In the end, however, he was unable to control Fox, and the staff believed that Griffin's death from ulcers was precipitated by Fox's arrogance. Then Fox's waning economic strength necessitated dismissals, which lowered the morale of the remaining workers.

His anticommunist campaign also proved embarrassing. On one occasion he ordered a story indicting the Boston Public Library because it made available to the general public copies of *Pravda* and *Isvestia*, the two leading Russian newspapers. The point was that their presence would contaminate the school children of Boston. The story was written and ready to appear on the front page, without it being noted that the papers were in Russian, which reduced the number of school children who might possibly read them to about five. When the night city editor called this to the attention of the editors, and they called it to the attention of Fox, he still ran the story. Such antics became laughing matters in the city room.

Although the *Post* was often referred to as a staunchly Democratic, Irish, and Irish-Catholic newspaper, it never was quite that. While the Boston Irish were giving overwhelming support to Franklin Delano Roosevelt, the *Post* was trying to nibble him to death. James Michael Curley remained, off and on, the hero of the average Irish-Catholic voter until his final days, but we have seen how the *Post* spent its strength subverting him. It endorsed all Democratic candidates in the city contests, but there never were any serious Republican ones. Edwin A. Grozier endorsed Calvin Coolidge for president but never any other Republican. It was a wise policy; they weren't going to win.

The paper sought out what its managing editor, Clifton B. Carberry, believed to be the lesser of two evils. While of Irish background, Carberry was not a Catholic but, like Grozier, a journalistic pragmatist. This is not to detract for the honest concern of Grozier for the welfare of the Irish-Americans or other immigrant groups in Boston. He was an idealistic man. The irony is that, when the paper was at last controlled by Fox, a man of Irish-Catholic background (he had long since abandoned the faith of his fathers and delighted in arguing the case for atheism), it supported Dwight D. Eisenhower, its first nonlocal Republican candidate, in the 1952 presidential election. Grozier's support in the twenties of the candidacy of Calvin Coolidge, who had been governor of Massachusetts, appealed to the local pride of the Bay State Democrats. The Eisenhower candidacy was something utterly different, and the public response was bitter. The Democrats of Boston were well aware that the *Post* had abandoned its tradition, and for days afterwards, the telephone lines into the *Post's* offices were hot with all sorts of vituperative, abusive, denunciatory messages.

Circulation suffered but remained the highest in the city among the morning papers—well over 300,000—surpassing that of the *Globe*, the *Herald*, and the *Record*. But for the *Post*, worse was to follow. To support Eisenhower for president might have been a tactical mistake for the independent Democratic *Post*, but it was not dishonorable. Dishonor came when John F. Kennedy was running for the Senate, also in 1952. Fox demanded and got from Joseph P. Kennedy $500,000 in order to ensure the *Post's* support of the one man who, above all others, it should have automatically supported. The $500,000 was disguised as a loan, but it was nothing but payment to a blackmailer. Kennedy's election might have been a boon for the *Post*, but Fox's duplicity only served to give him another enemy in a high place. Fox contended that he paid the money back, but that was never substantiated.

The beginning of the end came in 1956, when the *Post* closed its doors for the first time. It would reopen for a few months under different, court-approved masters, but they could not save

The end for the *Post* came in 1956, when it closed its doors, reopened them for a few months, and then closed for good on the fourth of October. Here, the paper reflects premature optimism.

it. That fall it closed for good; its final edition was published on October 4.

In his downfall, Fox took with him Sherman Adams, the advisor to President Eisenhower, and Bernard Goldfine, the manufacturer-financier whose gifts Adams should never have received. Appearing before the House Subcommittee on Legislative Oversight, Fox hurled innumerable wild charges against Goldfine and Adams, claiming Goldfine had bribed Adams in return for White House influence.

The *New York Times*, the *Herald-Tribune*, the *Boston Herald-Traveler*, and the *Washington Post*, among other papers, denounced the procedure of the subcommittee in permitting Fox's testimony—almost all hearsay—to be given in public. One of them, the *Herald-Traveler*, said it was obvious Fox was pursuing a vendetta against the two men. That was true enough, and it worked. Adams had to resign, having admitted that he accepted a vicuña coat and other minor gifts from Goldfine but denying, as Goldfine did, that the latter had bought him a house. Not long after, as a result of the hearings, Goldfine went to jail.

This all happened a year after the auctioneer's hammer fell on the *Post*. The *Globe* bought the *Post* library and its good name. The new owners of the property on Washington Street tore down the buildings and built a garage and some stores. By that time, Fox had finished his testimony in Washington, D.C., the *Globe* had left Newspaper Row and set up shop in its present plant in Dorchester, and no newspaper was left in Newspaper Row.

The advice W. O. Taylor had given Steadman in 1951 was sound: Build a new plant. It was honest, too: He was planning the same thing himself. The quarters of both papers on Newspaper Row were highly inefficient as production plants, not merely with regard to typesetting but also with regard to getting the papers out of the city for delivery to distribution points. Technology was rapidly reordering the manner in which newspapers were put together. Heightened competition, which was putting newspapers out of business across the country, demanded efficient production.

Looking back on the *Post's* heyday, when it was producing and delivering 400,000 to 600,000 papers a day from Newspaper Row, an observer can only be astonished. Besides burrowing six stories underground to accommodate additional presses, Grozier had had to have special trucks manufactured in order to bring newsprint into Pi Alley for delivery to the pressroom. His prescience might well have saved the paper had he lived through the Depression, for he had long before had the alternate plant in another part of the city.

Not long after the *Globe* had moved from Newspaper Row to Dorchester, the *Herald-Traveler* left its quarters on Mason Street and built a plant in the South End. It was the fourth site for the *Herald*, the third since it had left Newspaper Row in the early 1900s and gone to Tremont Street. By moving from downtown Boston to the roomier fringes of the city, the papers were able to build more efficient plants and arrange for more rapid and less expensive delivery of newspapers; but something was sacrificed, something exciting, stimulating, and energizing.

Something more than nostalgia recognizes that when Newspaper Row was vacated, the city was the loser. The core of the community was lost; the daily intellectual exchange among editors and reporters and the city's movers and shakers was gone. The happy chance meeting between *newsmaker* and *newswriter* became infinitely rarer. The wash of gossip that always surged through the Row—and could become front page news, in a minute—dried up. The eyes of editors were turned more and more toward Washington or to international events; and, while the educational level of the news staffs rose remarkably, the intimate knowledge of the city and its problems, which had previously been shared by almost every reporter and editor, had dissipated. In those years between the two world wars, the average reporter was assigned to a variety of stories, regardless of his expertise. It was assumed that, if he could bring himself to understand the matter, he could communicate it to the average newspaper reader. For better or worse, we have moved from that into an age of specialists.

Whatever the city lost by the death of Newspaper Row, the average newspaperman has lost half the fun of the game. He has gained a good deal more dignity and a great deal more money. One hopes that he delights in his work, in the thrill of a scoop, in the excitement of the chase, in the satisfaction of a story well written. It may well be difficult to delight in beating the opposition when there is no opposition. In the years of yellow journalism and those immediately following, when there was real competition in the matter of news gathering, every day was a win-or-lose battle for every newspaper and for every man on every story. Granted, each age has its own pleasures, and, as memory controls the past, it can always be made to appear more attractive. Yet one fact stands out: Newspaper Row, whatever it was, is no more.

Bibliography

Baedeker, Karl, ed. *The United States with an Excursion into Mexico: A Handbook for Travellers.* New York: Da Capo Press, 1971.

Berger, Meyer. *The Story of the New York Times.* New York: Simon & Schuster, 1951.

Bird, George L., and Frederick E. Merwin. *The Newspaper and Society.* New York: Prentice-Hall, 1942.

Bridgham, Percy A. *Law by the People's Lawyer of the Globe.* Boston: Percy A. Bridgham, Publisher, 1891.

Burke, Clifford. *Printing It.* New York: Ballantine Books, 1972.

Canham, Erwin D. *Commitment to Freedom: The Story of the Christian Science Monitor.* Boston: Houghton Mifflin, 1958.

Casey, Robert J. *Such Interesting People.* New York: Bobbs-Merrill, 1943.

Chamberlain, Joseph Edgar. *The Boston Transcript.* Boston: Houghton Mifflin, 1930.

Churchill, Allen. *Park Row: A Vivid Re-creation of Turn of the Century Newspaper Days.* New York: Rinehart & Co., 1958.

Dinneen, Joseph F. *The Purple Shamrock.* New York: W. W. Norton, 1949.

———. *Underworld U.S.A.* New York: Farrar, Straus & Cudahy, 1955.

Editor & Publisher.

Finch, Florence. *The Flowing Stream.* New York: E. P. Dutton, 1937.

Fowler, Gene. *Timberline.* New York: Covici, Friede, 1934.

Goodwin, Doris Kearns. *The Fitzgeralds and the Kennedys: An American Saga.* New York: Simon & Schuster, 1987.

Gross, Gerald, ed. *The Responsibility of the Press.* New York: Simon & Schuster, 1971.

Harris, Neil, ed. *The American Culture.* 6 vols. New York: George Braziller, 1970.

Hohenberg, John. *The Pulitzer Prizes.* New York: Columbia University Press, 1971.

Ickes, Harold, ed. *Freedom of the Press Today.* New York: Vanguard, 1941.

Johnson, Gerald W. *An Honorable Titan: A Biographical Study of Adolph S. Ochs.* New York: Harper Bros., 1946.

Kaplan, Justin. *Lincoln Steffens: A Biography.* New York: Simon & Schuster, 1974

Kluger, Richard. *The Paper: The Life and Death of the New York Herald Tribune.* New York: Alfred A. Knopf, 1986.

Karolevitz, Robert F. *Newspapering in the Old West.* Seattle, Wash.: Superior Publishing Company, 1965.

King, Moses. *King's Handbook of Boston.* Boston: Moses King, Publisher, 1885.

Lindstrom, Carl E. *The Fading American Newspaper.* Gloucester, Mass.: Peter Smith Company, 1964.

Lee, James Melvin. *History of American Journalism.* New York: Garden City Publishing Company, 1923.

Lyons, Louis M. *Newspaper Story: One Hundred Years of the Boston Globe.* Cambridge, Mass.: Harvard University Press, 1971.

Morgan, James. *Charles H. Taylor: Builder of the Boston Globe.* Boston: James Morgan, Publisher, 1923.

Mott, Frank Luther. *American Journalism: A History of Newspapers in the United States Through 270 Years, 1690-1960.* New York: Macmillan, 1959.

Nash, Roderick, ed., *The Call of the Wild, 1900-1916.* Vol. 6, *The American Culture.* Neil Harris, General Editor. New York: George Braziller, 1970.

Newspaperman: A Monthly Journal of Fact, Fiction, Humor and Opinion Written by Working Newspapermen. Boston: Tribune Publications, 1944-46.

Roberts, Kenneth. *I Wanted To Write.* New York: Doubleday, 1953.

Rowsome, Frank, Jr. *They Laughed When I Sat Down.* New York: Bonanza Books, 1959.

Schlesinger, Arthur M., Jr. *A Thousand Days: John F. Kennedy in the White House.* Boston: Houghton Mifflin, 1965.

Schudson, Michael. *Discovering the News: A Social History of*

American Newspapers. New York: Basic Books, 1978.

Sullivan, Robert. *Goodbye, Lizzie Borden*. Brattleboro, Vt.: Stephen Greene Press, 1974.

Swanberg, W. A. *Citizen Hearst: a Biography of William Randolph Hearst*. New York: Scribners, 1961.

Tebbel, John. *Open Letter to Newspaper Readers*. New York: Heineman Paperback, 1968.

Villard, Oswald Garrison. *The Disappearing Daily*. New York: Alfred A. Knopf, 1944.

Index